Woolf Nietzsche Wilde

Butor André Gide Marinetti Woolf Lor

E. M. Forster Derek Walcott Augustine

Kavafy Charles Baudelaire Michael Aflaq Jol

Aragon Edgar Allan Poe Malraux Baroja

Mc Almon

netti Butor Kafka Woolf Joyce

John Dewey T. S. Eliot

Lorca Nietzsche

Kafka Benjamin Kavafy Woolf Beckett

Proust

Malraux John Dos Passos Proust Ezr

William Carlos Williams E. M. Forster Koeppen Thomas Mann

ayce Benjamin Baroja John Dos Passos Kafka

Ezra Pound Koeppen Michael Aflaq Beckett

alcott R.

ett Nietzsche Robert Mc Almon Butor

Marinetti Aragon Joy

arinetti Proust Edg

Jol

Baroja
Joyce
Marinetti
Proust Kavafy T.S. Eliot
Beckett E.M. Forster Ezra Pound Edgar Allan Poe
Koeppen Charles Baudelaire Robert Mc Almon
William Carlos William Woolf Proust Joyce
Gide Marinetti Nietzsche Derek Walcott Baroja
John Dos Passos Charles Baudelaire Marinetti
Walcott Joyce Michael Aflaq Koeppen
Wilde Nietzsche
Kavafy Aragon Edgar Allan Poe Benjamin
Marinetti Koeppen Proust
Charles Baudelaire Augustine
Woolf John Dos Passos Derek Walcott Kafka
John Dewey Augustine
Malraux Beckett
Kavafy William Carlos William Robert Mc Almon
Lorca André Gide Butor
Mc Almon T.S. Eliot
Wilde Butor Woolf Kafka
Thomas Mann Derek Walcott Joyce
Augustine netti

INTERTEXTUALITY AND MODERNISM IN COMPARATIVE LITERATURE

ACKNOWLEDGEMENTS

This volume is made up of revised papers from a day conference held at Middlesex University on 'Modernism and Intertextuality' in April 1999 and of additional invited papers. We would like to thank Middlesex University and, more particularly, Prof. Gabrielle Parker, the Dean of the School of Arts, for their support of Comparative Literature. We both benefited from periods of research leave which helped us complete this project and again we would like to thank Middlesex University for this. We also wish to thank our colleague Dr David Berry for his help and advice regarding our manuscripts. Dr Jan Udris deserves special thanks for his help in all the stages leading to the final manuscript. Our special thanks too to Paul S. Vlachos for the artwork of this volume and Christos Georgiou for the book cover illustration. The book cover illustration belongs to the Philomel private collection. It is taken from a series of pictures by Christos Georgiou designed to illustrate a text entitled *Philomel, The Forest's Nightingale: A Modern Greek Fable*, by Ange S. Vlachos. Our grateful thanks for permission to use the illustration.

INTERTEXTUALITY AND MODERNISM
IN COMPARATIVE LITERATURE

Edited by
Emily Salines and **Raynalle Udris**

First edition 2002

Published by **Philomel Productions Ltd,** Dublin, Rep. of Ireland.
UK contact address:
No 1 Queen's Gate Place Mews, London SW7 5BG, UK
Tel.: ++44 (0) 20 7581 2303   Fax: ++44 (0) 20 7589 2264
E-mail: philomelbooks@hotmail.com

ISBN 1 898685 42 8

British Library Cataloguing in Publication Data
A catalogue record for this book is available from the British Library

All rights reserved. ® © Philomel Productions Ltd, Dublin, Ireland
No part of this publication may be reproduced in any material form (including photocopying or storing it in any medium by electronic means and whether or not transiently or incidentally to some other use of this publication) without the written permission of the copyright owner except in accordance with the provisions of the Copyright, Designs and Patents Act 1988 **or under the terms of a licence issued by the Copyright Licensing Agency, 90 Tottenham Court Road, London, England, W1P 9HE.**
Applications for the copyright owner's permission to reproduce any part of this publication should be addressed to the publisher.

PHILOMEL

INTERTEXTUALITY AND MODERNISM IN COMPARATIVE LITERATURE

EDITED BY

Emily Salines, Raynalle Udris

PHILOMEL

TABLE OF CONTENTS

INTRODUCTION   13
NOTES TO INTRODUCTION   35

CHAPTER I by *Leon Burnett*
Cultural Continuities?   39
NOTES TO CHAPTER I   59

PART I: MODERNISM AND LITERARY INFLUENCES

CHAPTER II by *Emily Salines*
Intertextual modernity: Baudelaire and Poe's
'Man of the Crowd'   69
NOTES TO CHAPTER II   89

CHAPTER III by *Carol Diethe*
Intertextual Sun-worshippers: Marinetti's *Mafarka* and
Nietzsche' *Zarathustra*   95
NOTES TO CHAPTER III   113

CHAPTER IV by *Edward Neill*
The Waste Land and The Death of the Author:
Intertextuality and the Politics of Modernism   121
NOTES TO CHAPTER IV   139

CHAPTER V by *David Houston Jones*
'If One Word Did not Cease to Exist When it has
Sounded…': Some Augustinian Presences in Beckett   147
NOTES TO CHAPTER V   163

CHAPTER VI by *Eric Robertson*
Rites of Passage: Intertextuality and the Metaphysics
of Space in Aragon, Benjamin, Butor and Koeppen   167
NOTES TO CHAPTER VI   185

PART II: MODERNISM AND THE ENCOUNTER WITH THE FOREIGN OR EXOTIC OTHER

CHAPTER VII by *Fiona Richards*
Staging Sinbad's Return
The 'Ithaca' chapter of *Ulysses* and 'The Death of Sindbad:
A Narrative in One Act', by Michael Aflaq   195
NOTES TO CHAPTER VII   215

CHAPTER VIII by *Alberto Mira*
Closets with a View: Sodom, Hellas and Homosexual Myth
in Modernist Writing   221
NOTES TO CHAPTER VIII   241

CHAPTER IX by *Katharine Murphy*
The Processed Landscape: Italy in Pío Baroja's
El laberinto de las sirenas and E. M. Forster's
Where Angels Fear to Tread   245
NOTES TO CHAPTER IX   265

CHAPTER X by *Maria Cristina Fumagalli*
Derek Walcott's *Epitaph for the Young: A Poem in xii Cantos*:
Modernist Texts and the Caribbean Experience   271
NOTES TO CHAPTER X   285

PART III: INTERACTIONS WITH
OTHER MODERNIST ART FORMS

CHAPTER XI by *Raynalle Udris*
Modernity and 'Cinematographic Writing' in
André Malraux's *Days of Hope* and John Dos Passos'
The Big Money   293
NOTES TO CHAPTER XI   313

CHAPTER XII by *Eric White*
Contact and the Deweyan Local: The Evolution of
William Carlos Williams' 'American Critical Attitude'   317
NOTES TO CHAPTER XII   331

CHAPTER XIII by *Garin V. Dowd*
'Connect-I-Cut': Hanging on the Telephone with Kafka,
Woolf, Proust and Joyce   335
NOTES TO CHAPTER XIII   351

INTRODUCTION
Emily Salines, Raynalle Udris

Despite the very large number of books and articles written to date on the separate subjects of Modernism and Intertextuality, the question of the links between the two concepts has been little studied as a whole. The existing studies of individual modernist authors' intertextuality need to be complemented with a more global view in order to enhance the importance of intertextuality in modernism. This may indeed provide a new insight into modernism – the paradoxical coexistence of the search for the new and the *avant-garde* and of the intertextual dimensions of literary and artistic creations proves, as the chapters in this collection suggest, a fruitful area of study. To bring together the notions of modernist text and intertextuality in the context of comparative literature may be seen as a daunting task: indeed this avenue of research links together three concepts which themselves are at best ambiguous and/or heterogeneous and which may, at 'worst', seem almost impossible to define.

Modernism has been seen as 'the major achievement [of] and the central influence' on the literature of the 20th century,[1] but to define its nature has proved a difficult task, as outlined by Malcolm Bradbury and James McFarlane in their invaluable anthology on modernism:

> The name is clear; the nature of the movement or movements – the where, when, why and what of it – is much less so. And equally unclear is the status of the stylistic claim we are making. We have noted that few ages have been more multiple, more promiscuous in artistic style; to distil from the multiplicity an overall style or mannerism is a difficult, perhaps even an impossible task.[2]

Modernism has now been widely researched and documented, and as a result variously defined throughout the 20th century, since 'the problem of establishing valid criteria by which to identify modernism is, as various commentators have pointed out, a function of the ambivalence and plurality of modernism itself'.[3] And to elaborate on the implications of Raymond Williams' 1983 claim that 'the period of conscious modernism is ending', one could declare with Tony Pinkney that

> [n]o doubt all aesthetic innovations are felt as startlingly modern in their own historical moment [...] Yet when such unavoidable novelty, mere formal by-product of stylistic innovation whose substance derives from other (religious, social) sources, is at last abstracted as a content in its own right – a form become a substance, a matrix now paradoxically serving as its own material – we have indeed entered the epoch of 'conscious modernism'.[4]

One may however argue that form cannot so easily be divorced from its ideological context and that rather than talking about Modernism in the singular, one should perhaps use the term as does Peter Nicholls,[5] in its plural form and, in so doing, avoid the too common one-dimensional (postmodernist?) view of modernism whereby it 'came to be presented as a sort of monolithic ideological formation' seen (in England at least) 'through the reactionary politics of canonical modernists such as Ezra Pound, T.S. Eliot, Wyndham Lewis and D.H. Lawrence'.[6] And indeed we would agree with Nicholls that modernism should be viewed as a 'more complex inscription of ideologies in the modernist styles which frequently became their most powerful and ambiguous vehicle'.[7]

Beyond the problem of its definition, the ambiguity of modernism also resides in the fuzziness of its chronological boundaries, '[t]he beginnings of modernism, like its endings, [being] largely indeterminate, a matter of traces rather than of clearly defined historical moments'.[8] Richard Sheppard notes that

> [a]lthough the broad consensus agrees on 1885-1935, some critics set its starting-date as early as 1870 (so as to include Nietzsche and Rimbaud), while others, notably North American critics, set its ending in the 1950s (so as to include the early novels of Vladimir Nabokov, the late poetry of William Carlos Williams, the Abstract Expressionists, and work produced under the impact of 'émigré' European modernists).[9]

Indeed 'the boundaries of this epoch prove troublingly elastic' in so far as 'the chronological spectrum' could include, as Tony Pinkney suggests, aspects of romanticism, especially 'Romanticism's exploration of the perils and possibilities of cultural deracination ('Liberty') and its infinitized subject' as well as 'much of what we might otherwise regard as *post*-modernism'.[10]

While it is worth noting that modernism 'is more a transitional phenomenon than a period or movement', it should also be seen, as indicated earlier (and certainly in Europe), 'not as a single, unified response, but a range of responses to a perceived crisis' in so far that modernism 'developed out of a complex of socio-historical experiences, of which the shocks caused by the modern megalopolis and the Great War were simply the most violent'.[11] As a result, modernist characteristics varied from culture to culture, and Sheppard stresses for instance that it was easier for British intellectuals 'to find more common ground with their societies' than for German modernists and other European counterparts. As a result, the British situation 'generated much smaller, less radical and less threatening avant-gardes (i.e. the Georgians, Imagists and Vorticists) than was the case on the continent'.[12]

The aim of this book is thus to look at modernism across national and disciplinary borders in the hope that an intertextual, comparative approach will help illuminate the specificity of individual trends. We hope to contribute to a comparative study of literary Modernism in a way which would move away from individual author studies or analyses of modernism as a national movement, and attempt to look at the movement across frontiers. As already suggested, it is clear that 'modernism' in the English, French or Spanish traditions does not refer to the same reality. This is noted by many critics, amongst whom is Antoine Compagnon in *Five Paradoxes of Modernity*.[13] This openness of the concept noted by Compagnon in words such as *modern, modernity* and *modernism* in French, English and German means that a comparative approach aware of the different trends of modernism is the only way to gain a global idea of this movement.[14] In fact, not only are these trends different in nature depending on the cultural system to which they belong, they also appear and develop in different manners depending on the media and arts involved, as Alexis Nouss emphasises. And yet, it seems necessary to overcome the difficulties posed by those national and media differences in order to form a more accurate and complete picture of modernism, where 'national as well as disciplinary borders' mean very little.[15] Clearly, an intertextual, comparative approach is the best basis on which to proceed in this respect.

But what do we mean by 'intertextuality'? This term, ubiquitous in contemporary criticism, runs the risk of becoming over-diluted and vague. It would be unnecessary to repeat the history of intertextuality theories, already excellently outlined in Michael Worton and Judith Still's introduction to *Intertextuality: Theories and Practices*,[16] and, more recently, by Graham Allen's *Intertextuality*.[17] To sum up briefly, the present book looks at intertextuality in its two strands, as highlighted by Worton and Still. First, the concept is based on the idea that 'a text [...] cannot exist as a hermetic or self-sufficient whole, and so does not function as a closed system'.[18] This openness of the text may be realised through the fact that its writer, himself/herself a reader, consciously or unconsciously calls upon his/her readings as part of the writing act. The second strand of intertextuality approaches the text from the point of view of reader-response theory: the reader establishes links between the text s/he is reading and other texts s/he has already read. Such links enrich the text and open it. Within the context of interdisciplinary studies, it is important to stress that texts are to be understood to include not only literary, verbal texts, but also other media, such as music, cinema and the visual arts.

The concept of comparative literature which here provides the context for the linking of modernism and intertextuality is itself not easy to delimit. Since the 1950s, it has been the object of much debate concerning the identity of what is seen by some as a discipline and by others as just a field of study. During the second half of the 20th century such a concept has lost its perceived radicality in the West, to be replaced by other objects of investigation such as Literary Theory, Women's Studies, Semiotics, Post-colonial Studies, Cultural Studies etc., which appeared more in tune with the specific preoccupations of their time. While Susan Basnett in her critical introduction to comparative literature rightly stresses that '[i]t could almost be argued that anyone who has an interest in books embarks on the road towards what might be termed comparative literature',[19] we would nonetheless argue in favour of the specificity of comparative literary studies, if only to bring to the fore the point Basnett recalls:

> Everywhere there is connection, everywhere there is illustration. No single event, no single literature is adequately comprehended except in relation to other events, other literatures.[20]

Indeed to place the emphasis from the outset on the interconnectedness of texts,[21] on the transgression of cultural and artistic boundaries through the deliberate activity of comparing and contrasting texts and genres, is notably to open the door to the full impact of intertextuality in textual construction and reading. The applications of the double definition of intertextuality noted above to comparative literature studies are clear: on the one hand we have studies of which the aim is to unearth the authors' conscious or unconscious, explicit or implicit use of other texts, and the co-presence and status of different previous texts within one. In the present collection, articles by Diethe, Dowd, Fumagalli, Jones, Neill, Robertson, Salines and White fall under this category. On the other hand, we have studies which aim, through the comparison and contrast of two or more texts, at uncovering common or distinct characteristics. The selection of the objects of comparison is the effect of the reader's response to these texts, rather than the result of conscious authorial decisions. The articles by Mira, Murphy, Richards, Robertson and Udris exemplify such an approach.

As suggested earlier, Modernism and Intertextuality do not entertain an easy relationship. At the risk of being charged with reductionism, we would like to posit that the concepts of modernism, with its avant-garde, and intertextuality function significantly as mutually *antithetical* notions and that this paradoxical relationship can contribute to a reassessment of modernism itself.

As Steve Giles points out, Bradbury and McFarlane identify five key modernist tendencies in the introduction to their anthology:

1. away from representational realism and towards abstract and autotelic art forms;
2. towards a high degree of aesthetic self-consciousness;
3. towards an aesthetic of radical innovation, fragmentation and shock;
4. towards the breaking of familiar formal and linguistic conventions;
5. towards paradox.[22]

The limitations of such an approach are undeniable since, as Giles signals, 'it brackets together ostensibly disparate textual strategies and incompatible aesthetic ideologies'; yet this way of looking at things nevertheless helps 'to identify the deep-structural factors which make it possible to establish the social and ideological problematic informing movements as diverse as Symbolism, Constructivism or Expressionism'.[23] Furthermore, for our purposes here, the five aesthetic shifts identified can help to emphasise certain key aspects of modernist writing, such as what Tom Gibbons has called an 'anti-democratic cast of mind',[24] best exemplified in a refusal of straightforward imitation of form and/or content and in a concern for individuality; modernist fiction can then be defined, albeit restrictively, on grounds of its rejection of techniques and conventions judged as no longer appropriate and an enlightened concern with individual/subjective consciousness. This strong sense of subjectivity in modernist authors may be seen as an extension of Baudelaire's precursive modernist period, of the artist's wish to withdraw into an ivory tower, as Gérard de Nerval and Gustave Flaubert respectively made clear:

> The only refuge left to us was the poet's ivory tower, which we climbed, ever higher, to isolate ourselves from the mob.[25]

> I have always tried to live in an ivory tower, but a tide of shit is beating at its walls to undermine it.[26]

Such and other reactions were arguably grounded in a comparable response to the cultural modernity of the authors' respective times. Perhaps as part of this reaction, modernist authors tended to view the identification of their works with others as something to be denied, avoided or strongly resisted. Thus the Futurist Filippo Tommaso Marinetti's refusal to acknowledge the influence of Nietzsche:

> I feel I really have to demonstrate here that the critics have been completely wrong in considering us as new Nietzscheans.[27]

Writers of the High Modernist period in England, apart from sharing the 'modern experience', also saw themselves as having little in common. Indeed Randall Stevenson stresses that 'instances of admiration or influence among modernist writers are significantly rare; expressions of antipathy or at best indifference are more regularly in evidence'.[28]

Concomitant to this urge for individuality and independence, the work of the modernist authors, as already stated, varies tremendously in terms of form and content as well as ideology. Common features can nevertheless be discerned, such as the place given in the texts to subjectivity, perhaps best epitomised by Woolf's stream of consciousness, the need as in Joyce to find a new means of expression, the emphasis given to dynamism, evident in Marinetti's avant-garde writing, the focus on the local as opposed to the universal, as well as the urge to invent new forms and contents particularly evident with the modernist avant-garde since 'what marks out this emphasis in both Modernism and the avant-garde is a defiance and finally violent rejection of tradition: the insistence on a clean break with the past'.[29] All these features allude to a strong desire to avoid imitation and, ultimately, repetition.

And it is this modernist move to create new forms and contents, to dispel the influence of other texts, which appears largely at odds with the notion of intertextuality: the concept of intertextuality is based on the idea that complete originality is impossible since everything derives from a previous text, no matter how transformative the relationship to that other text may be. Thus what Barbara Johnson calls the 'convergence paradoxale du nouveau et du répété',[30] or, in other words more specifically applicable to our present project, the balance between repetition (through intertextuality) and difference (through transformation and the search for the new), is central to any study of modernism and intertextuality.

This is not to say, however, that intertextuality and modernism should be seen as mutually exclusive. The example of futurism, as studied by Peter Nicholls, is a case in point: 'the content of Futurism [...] was hardly original, but its extremism – formal and conceptual – certainly was'.[31] The fantasies of self-generation we can note in many Futurist texts, and particularly in Marinetti's *Mafarka the Futurist*, should thus be seen in the context of the belonging to a clear tradition (see Carol Diethe's article) and the presence of strong intertextual links with other movements and authors. Thus Marinetti can be shown to be heavily reliant on Apollinaire, as Diethe has shown, or Nietzsche as Diethe demonstrates in this book. Similarly, the Dada movement established itself by drawing from futurism, expressionism and cubism. This importance of intertextuality in the development of modernism is all the clearer if we turn to early forms of the movement. The second half of the 19th century in general and the *fin de siècle* in particular was for instance characterised by a 'richness of international contact', as Nicholls stresses.[32] The advent of modernity, heralded by poets such as Baudelaire, was accompanied by a change in textual practices and an increased importance given to memory (Baudelaire's poems 'Le Cygne',

'Spleen - J'ai plus de souvenirs…' are particularly telling examples of this fact). Translation also became central to the literary production of the period, thus erasing the most tangible barriers to international communication and cosmopolitanism, both of which are central to the development of modernism, as the present volume will confirm.

The centrality of intertextuality to modernism is not only historical. It is also ingrained in its textual strategies. As Allen has shown, Barthes' theory of the text, defined as 'woven entirely with citations, references, echoes, cultural languages (what language is not?) antecedent or contemporary, which cut across it through and through in a vast stereophony',[33] particularly applies to modernism. As will be seen in this volume, modernist texts are engaged in complex transformations of their intertexts, transformations made all the more necessary by their desire for novelty of form and content. As a result, they foreground the productive role of the reader, in a way that earlier texts do not.

That repetition and difference are not necessarily engaged in an inescapable conflict has been demonstrated in studies such as Antoine Compagnon's seminal work on quotation.[34] Exact repetition, or exact copy, is impossible because of the change in context, voice and circumstances involved in the act of quoting. Borges' well-known story 'Pierre Menard, Author of the *Quixote*'[35] playfully stresses the very same point: despite all his efforts, Pierre Menard cannot become Cervantes, nor can he recreate *Don Quixote* or repeat it exactly as in the very act of repetition he brings difference.

As Worton and Still stress, the very distortion at work in any quotation, and more so in consciously transformative intertextual links, enables modernist writers to demarcate and proclaim their own creative space'.[36] Thus it is our aim to demonstrate the centrality of intertextuality to modernist experiments through the study of specific examples, as a summary of the chapters in this book will confirm.

Leon Burnett, in the first chapter of the present volume entitled 'Cultural Continuities', lucidly explores the significant extent to which modernist texts depend on intertextual influences and borrowings. 'Modernism's sense of its own 'radical otherness' (Octavio Paz) manifested itself in two polarised standpoints', stresses Burnett. 'There were those who saw fit to reject the humanist values of the late nineteenth century and called for a new critical method and those who sought to build a bridge across the epistemological chasm that separated the present from the past. Critics and theorists, when they have had to address the crisis in literature of the period, reflect this dichotomy in representing intertextuality either as a site of conflict (Bloom's 'anxiety of influence') or as a source of recognition (Shklovsky's 'resurrection of the word')'.[37]

In his essay, Burnett evokes the nature of influence apprehended by the Nobel prize poet Joseph Brodsky as a challenge to Harold Bloom's proposition. Influence is viewed no longer as a source of anxiety but rather as 'an anchor to secure a poet against the current'. The latter position is directly opposed to Pierre Menard's attempt to rewrite Don Quixote as a fictional embodiment of rupture with the past. Burnett shows that in many writers of the modernist period 'a sense of divorce between the past and the present gave rise to an image of spatial fissure' counteracted by a concessory attitude, with notably the literary motive of 'anamnesis' standing as a possible remedy for a number of modernist poets.

Burnett then turns to the work of the most frequently quoted Anglo-American modernist poet, T.S. Eliot, and to Russian poetry, in particular to Osip Mandelstam's writing, in which 'the interplay between continuity and discontinuity is most finely balanced'. Burnett later shows that for Mandelstam the answer to the question of continuity lies in the 'love of the word' which unifies literature. Poetry for instance becomes a matter of continuity and echo and Burnett concludes that 'influence is not affliction but abundance' before examining Taranovsky's intertextual critical approach based on a new definition of context and subtext. The latter's research method, asserts Burnett, 'owed much to the poetic alliance that Mandelstam had acknowledged through his association with the modernist movement known as Akmeism', which attempted 'if not to deny the existence of the chasm that others had discerned between the present and the past, at least to bridge the gap by establishing new lifelines, new continuities'.

In the ensuing essays of this volume, which broadly follow within each sub-section the chronology of the modernist works studied, the link between literature and intertextuality is further explored. Literary and other influences such as the encounter with the foreign or exotic Other are comparatively studied, as then are the various intertextual interactions between modernist literature and other art forms. In the final chapter, the impact of the telephone, one of the major new developments of the modernist period, is investigated as a central generative matrix in the works of key modernist authors.

Emily Salines focuses in chapter II on Charles Baudelaire's pioneering modernist input, and more particularly on the complex relationship between intertextuality and modernism, through an analysis of Baudelaire's versions of Edgar Allan Poe's 'Man of the Crowd' and the issues these versions raise. In her essay, Salines shows that Poe's story is the object of multiple rewritings on the part of Baudelaire: a direct translation 'L'Homme des foules', a passage in *Le Peintre de la vie moderne*, the prose poem 'Les Foules', and finally passages in *Un mangeur d'opium*. Salines demonstrates that Baudelaire's successive versions of 'The Man of the Crowd' are interesting from several points of view. First, the thematics of Poe's text, and more importantly Baudelaire's readings and rewritings of it, inaugurate a new aesthetics of the city which is both central to Baudelaire's concerns and very influential for later modernists. Second, Baudelaire's versions illustrate the complexity of intertextual writing, and of related issues of authority, originality and transformation, which are also at the core of modernist texts which they thus prefigure. Finally, the recurrence of the references to Poe's text in works central to the formulation of a modernist aesthetics (such as *Le Peintre de la vie moderne* and the *Spleen de Paris*) enable us to directly relate Baudelaire's variations on Poe to modernism.

Carol Diethe discusses a number of influences on Filippo Tommaso Marinetti manifested in his outrageous and haunting novel *Mafarka the Futurist* (1909), and that of Nietzsche is singled out for special discussion. Passages in which Zarathustra in *Thus Spoke Zarathustra* apostrophises the sun are compared with passages in Marinetti's novel which likewise show a reverence for the sun and for its power to irradiate particles (here the influence of Bergson is as strong as that of Nietzsche). Diethe shows that most important of all is the significance Zarathustra had for Nietzsche and compares it with that of Mafarka for Marinetti. Zarathustra, Nietzsche's brainchild, announces the coming of the man of the future (the *Übermensch*), but Marinetti does something even more extreme: his Mafarka gives birth to a machine with a will of its own. Diethe argues that the audacity of vision in both cases is marred by an underlying misogyny, downplayed in *Thus Spoke Zarathustra* but trumpeted in *Mafarka the Futurist*, a novel informed by the sexual anxieties handed down to Europe by a generation of Expressionists (themselves fervent Nietzscheans for the most part). Nietzsche's consummate style, asserts Diethe, is not matched by Marinetti, who compensates for his shortcomings with a dynamism as rare in literature as it is exhilarating.

Diethe also shows that the Eastern flavour of Zoroastrianism in *Thus Spoke Zarathustra* provides a scenario in which the past is evoked at the very moment when the future is invoked – and the same thing happens in *Mafarka the Futurist*. Not just the ruins of Carthage are suggested by the North African setting, but also the star-worshipping inhabitants of the desert. The casual reader takes some time to realise that the novel is not set in a bygone age, but in the 'here and now' which, Marinetti intends, will very soon be catapulted into an explosive future. Diethe further demonstrates that neither he nor Nietzsche can, however, live up to the hardness and misogyny which they lay down as first principles of behaviour. Intertextual comparisons show that this is actually one of the more interesting aspects of their authorial stance. Though Marinetti's declaration that childbirth is passé is ostensibly confirmed when Mafarka creates Gazourmah, the latter's destructive capacity is such that woman's maternal function is ultimately endorsed – an aspect of the novel strengthened by Mafarka's respect for his dead mother. While asserting that Marinetti and Nietzsche in real life showed civility and respect towards their mothers, Diethe discusses the hidden tensions in these relationships and makes a further comparison with Tereza in Kundera's *The Unbearable Lightness of Being* – another text deeply indebted to Nietzsche.

Edward Neill's examination of T.S. Eliot's *The Waste Land* concentrates on the 'Death of the Author and Intertextuality'. Neill argues that many of the most startling postulates and preoccupations of theory, such as the celebrated 'death of the author' and intertextuality, are broached or rehearsed by 'modernism'. *The Waste Land* is seen as an essential 'port of call' in Neill's essay, and indeed to call it Eliot's is immediately to slalom round his own emphasis on poetic impersonality and the massive intervention by Ezra Pound which at last turned the poem into itself. The poem as a particularly exhibitionistic piece of literary kleptomania seems unclear as to whether it plays 'host' or 'parasite' to the materials it collages, and this too, Neill asserts, resumes a theme of theory as it reflects or refracts the 'undecidable' relationship of modern 'America' to its European 'origins'.

In Chapter V, dealing with 'Disabling Sources in Beckett and Augustine', David Houston Jones sees Beckett's fiction as exemplary of the distressed intertextual relations frequently seen to be at work in modernist texts. While intertextual references or echoes abound, their sources are frequently obscured by fragmentary quotation, and Biblical references in particular are twisted out of context to apparently parodic effect. Houston Jones shows that Beckett's allusions to Augustine seem representative of a teleological exploitation of sources: the famous quotation of Augustine's reference to the thieves of the Crucifixion ('do not despair – one of the thieves was saved; do not presume – one of the thieves was damned') seems to put an unacceptable loading on the Christian doctrinal framework within which Augustine intended his work to be read. Houston Jones' contribution craftily investigates both the complex predicament of the versions of Augustine which appear in Beckett and the deeper formal or stylistic affinity which may be traced between their works; both, he asserts, have important consequences for contemporary critical notions of textual authority and intertextual referentiality.

While in his *Retractiones* Augustine attacked 'loquaciousness', the singular style of the *Confessions* paradoxically remains the key to the text's impact. Augustine came to disown the subordination of matter to formal concerns which he saw himself as promoting as a teacher of rhetoric and literature; Beckett, however, apparently embraces the move, claiming of his fascination with the Augustine reference that 'it is the form that matters'. Houston Jones argues that both standpoints may nevertheless be seen as representative of a deeply-rooted and analogous formal paradox which shows reflexive narratorial pronouncement to be peculiarly subversive of the larger narrative projects of which it is part. Houston Jones shows that the above quotation, from the *Confessions*, is the source of a remarkable echo in Beckett's *Molloy*; both formulations, envisaging the alteration of a voiced sound by another preceding one, provide a certain model of the process of intertextual reference itself. In other words, Houston Jones concludes, *intratextual* reference in both Beckett and Augustine is shown to be deeply problematic precisely by the *intertextual* relationship of Beckett and Augustine.

Such textual relationships between Beckett and Augustine, Houston Jones argues, prove uniquely provocative of current debates in critical theory concerning intertextuality. They push to the limit the modernist assumption of the ultimate possibility of referentiality, and constantly threaten the prospect of reference to anything other than *text*. The self-cancelling rhetoric of Beckett and Augustine appears to engage, in advance, with the critical debate as to whether intertextuality is to be considered a strategy in reading and criticism or a narrative mode.

In 'Rites of Passage: Intertextuality and the Metaphysics of Space in Butor's *La Modification* and Koeppen's *Der Tod in Rom*', Eric Robertson explores the multi-layered intertextuality of the two novels. He asserts that not only are they related to one another by what Gérard Genette terms hypertextuality, but both works also form part of a broader intertextual network operating on several levels. Most overtly, Wolfgang Koeppen's novel *Der Tod in Rom* (*Death in Rome*) compels the reader to take into account, explicitly or otherwise, Thomas Mann's novella *Der Tod in Venedig* (*Death in Venice*), which the conception and the title of Koeppen's work consciously recall. This tripartite relationship, shows Robertson, is extended further by the fact that *Der Tod in Venedig* generates what one critic has termed 'an intertextual dialogue with earlier discursivities, such as those by Socrates and Nietzsche', while some of the dream sequences in Butor's nouveau roman *La Modification* explicitly recall tales from classical mythology. Moreover, continues Robertson, while the novels of Butor and Koeppen are landmarks of post-1945 fiction, their foregrounding of urban space as a metaphor both of the psyche and of history shows them to be indebted to two iconic works of inter-war modernism, namely Walter Benjamin's monumental study *Das Passagen-Werk* and Aragon's surrealist narrative *Le Paysan de Paris*, which are themselves connected intertextually. In charting these routes, Robertson's essay places particular emphasis on the ways in which the notion of passage, both as physical locus and as action, not only informs the structure and narrative technique of Koeppen's and Butor's texts, but also serves as a connecting vessel linking them to the discourses of Aragon and Benjamin.

Chapters VII to X primarily examine the hypertextual encounter. First, Fiona Richards shows that James Joyce's ambiguous use of Orientalist trappings can be illuminatingly considered by contrasting the staging of the return of Sinbad in the 'Ithaca' chapter of *Ulysses* with Aflaq's 'The Death of Sinbad: A Narrative in One Act'. She recalls Ireland's ambiguous position within the British Empire, as both a colony and a part of the British Isles themselves, which has recently been considered by several commentators of Joyce including Vincent Cheng and Declan Kiberd. The use of a fantasised Orient in Joyce's writing demonstrates this ambiguity, Richards argues, figuring the contradictions of dreaming an exotic 'other' in complicity with an alien power that has already located 'otherness' in the Irish themselves.

Richards shows that in 'Ithaca', Bloom contemplates his failure to write a song for a stage version of *Sinbad the Sailor* (a pantomime of this name was performed in the Gaiety Theatre in 1903). The proposed verses would have dramatised local people and events, staging Dublin actuality within the Orientalised fantasy world of *The Arabian Nights*. His failure is due primarily to the problem of 'oscillation between events of imperial and of local interest'. As a contrast, Aflaq's 'The Death of Sinbad', written in 1936, the year of King Fuad I's death, also stages the drama of Sinbad's return, but not to the domestic comfort of the original (and *Ulysses*). The Sinbad of the Egyptian writer, ragged, emaciated and blind, is mocked and misunderstood. His refusal to communicate the secret his voyages have revealed is metaphorised into a black snake which issues from his mouth at the moment of his death, in striking contrast to the affirmation of Molly's 'Yes' following the return of Sinbad/Bloom.

In his essay 'Closets with a View', Alberto Mira deals with some issues of homosexual writing and representation in (male) authors associated with literary modernism. He starts by contextualising delimitations of homosexuality at the beginning of the twentieth century, pointing towards a tension between the expression of homoerotic desire on the one hand and new legal/medical definitions of same-sex desire. This tension is reflected in the work of a number of canonical authors such as André Gide, Marcel Proust and Thomas Mann. One way of resolving this tension was to resort to a common narrative motive: a trip to the Mediterranean countries is used as a metaphor for soul-searching and achieving a new (sexual) identity. In this case, biographical experience becomes reflected in writing. Another strategy for including homosexual expression in writing was to use intertextual references to powerful homosexual myths. Most notably, Mira's essay deals with the ways Sodom and Hellas were used in the work of authors such as those mentioned above and others like Lorca, Cavafy and Wilde.

In the following chapter, Katharine Murphy shows that in *El laberinto de las sirenas* (1923) and *Where Angels Fear to Tread* (1905), Pío Baroja and E.M. Forster develop an idea often present in the turn-of-the-century novel, transplanting Basque and English characters to southern Europe and observing their reactions to a foreign culture. Murphy argues that this transplantation provides the basis of the 'internalised' landscape created by Forster and Baroja in their Italian novels. Although Forster's Italy may appear to be portrayed in a more naturalistic fashion, the location is carefully manipulated by both authors to reveal a close relationship between mental and physical landscapes.

Murphy also shows that the sensuous depiction of the south in *El laberinto de las sirenas* suggests the presence of intertextual relationships with romantic and impressionist artists, in particular the Swiss painter Arnold Böcklin. Moreover, the *conversación preliminar* indicates that this unusual novel is written in the style of a fantasy or a 'melody'. A link between the arts is suggested in both *El laberinto de las sirenas* and *Where Angels Fear to Tread*. In *Aspects of the Novel* Forster calls for the novel to aspire to the 'expansion' attained by music, referring to the overall effect that music has on the listener. The link between the novel, the visual arts and music reveals a strong intertextual dimension in the comparison of Baroja's and Forster's novels. Moreover, by transplanting their characters to southern Europe, Baroja and Forster, Murphy argues, are able to suggest an encounter with the foreign, or the Other, central to the concept of intertextuality.

Forster's novels display a curious amalgamation of modernist and Victorian characteristics; the author retains the omniscient voice, while identifying art as an 'orderly' and autonomous product. Baroja stopped work on his series of historical novels, *Memorias de un hombre de acción* (written between 1912 and 1935) to write *El laberinto de las sirenas*. Although the author's change in direction from his early period (which reveals many of the concerns developed by the authors of European Modernism) to the production of historical novels theoretically suggests a transition towards a more objective and realistic type of novel-writing, Murphy asserts that it seems reasonable to suggest that some of the aesthetic preoccupations which pervade his early period still concerned him in the later years of his career.

In a chapter on 'Modernist Texts and the Caribbean Experience', Maria Cristina Fumagalli recalls that in 1948 Derek Walcott (then only eighteen) published *Epitaph for the Young: A Poem in xii Cantos*, a long poem written between 1946 and 1948. *Epitaph for the Young* depicts the voyage of a life from birth to manhood, the protagonist a youth/boat sailing through an archipelago of experiences. Fumagalli explains that the poem has been seen as a pastiche, as a conscious and deliberate exercise in imitation, since upon reading the text we can hear very distinctly the modernist voices of T.S. Eliot, Ezra Pound, James Joyce and of course of Dante, an important source of inspiration for all of them. It is however noteworthy, she goes on, that in his own voyage of discovery and in his attempt to draw a map of his inner self inclusive of both European literature and Caribbean experience, Walcott not only counteracts the epigraph to canto iv of the *Epitaph* stating 'There is not a West Indian Literature', but also provides some indications concerning the lines along which West Indian literature is/was actually developing. *The Epitaph for the Young*, Fumagalli therefore concludes, is not simply an apprentice's poem blatantly 'in the style of' various masters (although it is *also* this): her essay also shows how, within the poem, the young Walcott seems to have developed a narrative capable of questioning colonising cultural structures (ironically, in the *Epitaph* the 'colonised' becomes the 'discoverer') and conventional modes of representation of the Caribbean (i.e. Baudelaire's exoticism), dismissing history and the Eurocentric notion of tradition in order to give expression to a highly revisionist form of modernism, Caribbean Modernism.

Chapter XI addresses the intertextuality of cinema in examples of writing of the modernist period, and Chapter XII considers to what extent the American artist-run, avant-garde magazine *Contact* allowed for an intertextual exchange of ideas between the arts.

In 'Modernity and 'Cinematographic Writing' in Malraux's *L'Espoir* and Dos Passos' *Big Money*', Raynalle Udris contrasts two novels which were shaped by the growing importance of the cinematic medium in the 1930s, and explores the extent to which these two novels rely primarily on narrative techniques which metaphorically recall cinematographic writing, such as fragmented narrative structures and other cinematic devices: ellipses, cross-cutting, close ups. Udris finally considers to what degree the use of cinematographic style in the two novels constitutes, as Michel Zéraffa suggests about *Big Money*, an attempt 'to adapt the filmic techniques in order to reinforce and emphasise the specificity of the novel', or if it rather corresponds to a relation to the cinematic medium specific to modernist writing.

In '*Contact* and the Deweyan Local' Eric White explains that early in the twentieth century, a profusion of 'little magazines' began to appear in American literary circles. The emergence of these artist-run journals allowed challenging work to be presented on the artists' terms, and provided a vital means of communication between avant-garde communities. The comparative discourse encouraged by the 'little magazines' embraced many influential modernist movements (such as Cubism, Dadaism, Imagism and Vorticism) and created a lively exchange of ideas between the arts. In his study White examines the life of *Contact*, a unique (yet in some ways representative) example of such publications. Edited by American poets William Carlos Williams and Robert McAlmon, *Contact* explicitly foregrounded the intertextuality of the avant-garde climate using a localist context. The magazine's agenda attracted contributions from leading American modernists such as Stevens, Moore and Burke, but compared to Pound-dominated publications such as *Poetry*, *The Egoist* and *The Little Review*, White remarks, *Contact* has received little critical attention.

Williams and McAlmon, White goes on, created their periodical to cultivate an American aesthetic firmly grounded in its locality, an aesthetic that could respond to and compete with 'imported' thought. The essay discusses the importance of John Dewey's article 'Americanism and Localism' to Williams' (and thereby *Contact*'s) evolving literary model. By tracing the growth of this critical vector from Williams' first interaction with Dewey's work, this piece reveals the complexities and nuances of *Contact*'s directive. Primarily, White establishes that *Contact*'s localist paradigm does not, as has often been assumed, imply a rejection of or hostility to international artistic advances. Rather, the editors proposed that it was possible to apply a technical vigour to the American artist's own locality and achieve a more authentic work of art than that of the expatriate who rejected (or ignored) his or her place of origin. In this study, *Contact*'s intertextuality is presented as a function of that assumption.

By incorporating Deweyan doctrine and an interdisciplinary format, Williams and his magazine advocated the foundation of a cognisant centre from which 'the universal' might be understood. *Contact*, concludes White, thus allowed its editors to contribute a distinctive, and often dissenting, vision of American modernism to the publishing environment of the day.

As a concluding piece to the present volume, Chapter XIII explores 'Intertextuality as telephonics?'. With 'Connect-I-Cut: Hanging on the Telephone with Kafka, Woolf, Proust and Joyce', Garin V. Dowd conducts an original investigation of Intertextuality as hearsay? Or *ouï-dire* according to Jacques Derrida. To speak is already to have said yes, explains Dowd, to have heard the injunction to speak; it is to have acceded to the imperative and, specifically, to the telephonic imperative. To the extent that it features in modernist literature, the telephone is not merely metaphorical, Dowd argues, and is not always merely a decorative index of modernity. The telephonic, as this study shows, is constitutive. The context is one of programming and being programmed from afar: by another voice or site of enunciation, by other texts, by the great skein of voices that is the intertext. It is not the contention of this piece, Dowd specifies, that the four authors named in its title draw upon a common intertextual network; rather it is his aim to argue that in 'telephoning' themselves each author sets up a kind of feedback loop to a common matrix. That matrix, generative and central, but by the same token always outside, is the telephonic, the great switchboard, the skein of voices. It would seem, Dowd argues, that Kafka's fascination with the telephone is part of a larger concern with inscription – in particular with parasitic inscription at a distance and with the multiplicative interactions of networks of communication. Woolf's *To the Lighthouse* is a remarkable concatenation of lines forming a dense network. At the still centre of the novel lies her bizarre and mesmeric parenthetical telephony, the answering machine which cannot answer back, a little bit of dead in the living. The revenant also comes to haunt Proust's *Recherche*, Dowd continues, and once more in the form of a telephoned voice emptying the present, injecting, interrupting with alterity. In a chapter of *Ulysses* which explicitly gestures us towards some (telephone) call, namely that which in *The Odyssey* would lure the sailors to their deaths, the voice is ultimately that which must be graphed (as in Bloom's letter), the written word 'phoned', concludes Dowd.

NOTES TO INTRODUCTION

Notes to Introduction

1. Randall Stevenson, *Modernist Fiction* (London: Prentice-Hall, 1998).
2. Malcolm Bradbury & James McFarlane (eds), *Modernism 1890-1930* (London: Harmondsworth: Penguin, 1976), pp.22-23.
3. Steve Giles (ed.), *Theorising Modernism* (London: Routledge, 1993), p.172.
4. Raymond Williams, *The Politics of Modernism* (edited and introduced by Tony Pinkney) (London: Verso, 1999), p.3.
5. Peter Nicholls, *Modernism/s* (London: Macmillan, 1995).
6. ibid., p.vii.
7. ibid., p.vii.
8. ibid., p.1.
9. Richard Sheppard, 'The Problematics of European Modernism' in Giles, op.cit. p.1.
10. Williams, op.cit. p.4. 'When Deleuze and Guattari declare in *Anti-Oedipus* that 'a schizophrenic out for a walk is a better model than a neurotic lying on the analyst couch' (Gilles Deleuze and Félix Guattari, *Anti-Oedipus: Capitalism and Schizophrenia* (London: Viking Penguin, 1977, p.2), continues Pinkney, 'they clearly remain within the modernist problematic of Baudelaire's *flâneur* or Woolf's Mrs Dalloway ambling decentredly through central London. 'Flows' and 'deterritorializations' are here another jargon for Marinetti's 'beauty of speed' or 'multicoloured, polyphonic tides of revolution'; and the immobilising enemy is no longer the Italian art establishment but the Freudian Oedipus. Modernism, in short, has on this showing become a perennialism, encompassing virtually the entire span of post-feudal modernity'. pp.4-5.
11. Sheppard, op.cit. p.4.
12. ibid., p.7.
13. Antoine Compagnon, *Five Paradoxes of Modernity*, trans. Franklin Philip (New York: Columbia University Press, 1994).
14. In some languages there is no apparent distinction between modernism and modernity; for example in French, the same word, *modernité*, is used for both phenomena (with the additional help of *avant-garde* to denote the search for novelty normally associated with modernism).
15. Alexis Nouss, *La Modernité* (Paris: PUF, 1995), p.23 (the editors' translation).
16. Michael Worton and Judith Still (eds), *Intertextuality: Theories and Practices* (Manchester and New York: Manchester University Press, 1990).
17. Graham Allen, *Intertextuality* (London and New York: Routledge, 2000).
18. Worton and Still, op.cit. p.1.
19. Susan Basnett, *Comparative Literature* (London: Blackwell, 1993), p.1.
20. Matthew Arnold, *On the Modern Element in Literature*, Inaugural Lecture delivered at the University of Oxford, 14 November 1857, quoted in Basnett, op.cit. p.1.

21. The definition of 'text' is here both precise and broad. '[T]ext' is also used in a more general sense to mean anything perceived as a signifying system – therefore the reader is anyone who (consciously or unconsciously) receives something of the message, and the writer has to be understood in an abstract sense'. (Worton and Still, op.cit. p.33 note 2).

22. Quoted in Giles, op.cit. p.172. He specifies that his own schema is based on Bradbury and McFarlane (op.cit. pp.25-30, 49-50), and also on Eugène Lunn, *Marxism and Modernism: An Historical Study of Lukacs, Brecht, Benjamin and Adorno* (London: Verso, 1985), pp.34-37 *et seq.*

23. ibid., p.172.

24. Tom Gibbons, 'Modernism and Reactionary Politics', in *Journal of Modern Literature*, vol.3, no.5, pp.1140-157, p.1150.

25. Gérard de Nerval, *Selected Writings*, trans. Geoffrey Wagner (London: Panther Books, 1968), p.54, quoted in Nicholls, op.cit. p.13.

26. Gustave Flaubert, *Letters* (ed. Francis Steegmuller) (Cambridge, Mass.: Belknap Press, 1980, 1982), Vol.2 p.200, quoted in Nicholls, op.cit. p.13.

27. Filippo Marinetti, 'Contro i professori' and 'Guerra sola igiene del mondo' in *Teoria e invenzione futurista*, ed. Luciano de Mario (Milan: Mandadori, 1968), vol.II p.262, quoted in this volume in Carol Diethe's 'The Influence of Nietzsche on Marinetti's *Mafarka the Futurist*'.

28. Stevenson, op.cit. p.7.

29. Williams, op.cit. p.52.

30. Barbara Johnson, 'Quelques conséquences de la différence anatomique des textes', in *Poétique* 27, 1976: 450-465, p.452.

31. Nicholls, op.cit. p.85.

32. Nicholls, op.cit. pp.69-83.

33. Roland Barthes, *Image, Music, Text* (Fontana: London, 1977), quoted by Allen, op.cit. p.69.

34. Antoine Compagnon, *La Seconde main, ou le travail de la citation* (Paris: Seuil, 1979).

35. Jorge Luis Borges, 'Pierre Menard, Author of the *Quixote*', trans. by James E. Irby, in *Labyrinths: Selected Stories and Other Writings* (Harmondsworth: Penguin, 1970), pp.62-71.

36. Worton and Still, op.cit. p.13.

37. This citation is from Leon Burnett's abstract for the essay published here. The chapter outlines which follow are for the most part based, where appropriate, on the authors' abstracts/summaries.

CHAPTER I
Cultural Continuities?

Leon Burnett

Leon Burnett is a Reader in Literature and Head of Department of Literature at the University of Essex. His research interests and publications cover modern European poetry, literary translation, the revival of myth in modern culture and Russian fiction before the Soviet era. His work includes a book, *Faces of the Sphinx: Literary Encounters between Russia and the West.*

> Shakespearean fish swam the sea, far away from land;
> Romantic fish swam in nets coming to the hand;
> What are all those fish that lie gasping on the strand?
>
> W.B. Yeats, *Three Movements*

One major concern of Modernism had to do with the problem that authors of the time faced in evaluating the relationship between the present and the past. Indeed so pervasive was this preoccupation that it could be taken to constitute part of the definition of Modernism itself. In this matter, the philosopher and militarist T.E. Hulme (1883-1917) stands as a representative spokesman for an age that saw the need to make a strong case for discontinuity in order to combat the idea, which nineteenth-century positivism had bequeathed, of evolutionary progress in art as in life. In his essay on 'Humanism and the Religious Attitude', published in *Speculations*, we find a powerful attack against the continued affirmation of a humanist position in the twentieth century.[1] Hulme began his essay as he meant to finish it; that is to say, he couched his discourse on a new critical method in the rhetoric of a manifesto:

> One of the main achievements of the nineteenth century was the elaboration and universal application of *continuity*. The destruction of this conception is, on the contrary, an urgent necessity of the present. [...]
> Our principal concern then at the present moment should be the re-establishment of the temper or disposition of mind which can look at a *gap* or chasm without shuddering.[2]

Here, as in other notable examples of the period, a sense of historical divorce between present and past gives rise to the image of spatial fissure: a chasm. We find something akin when the Welsh poet and artist David Jones (1895-1974), looking back upon the late 1920s and early 1930s in his Preface to *The Anathemata*, developed the metaphor of what he referred to as 'The Break', identifying it by reference to two specific locations, the one geographical and the other mythical:

[M]ost now see that in the nineteenth century, Western Man moved across a rubicon which, if as unseen as the 38th Parallel, seems to have been as definitive as the Styx. [...] But it was not the memory-effacing Lethe that was crossed; and consequently, although man has found much to his liking, advantage, and considerable wonderment, he has still retained ineradicable longings for, as it were, the farther shore.[3]

Although Hulme placed a heavy emphasis on discontinuity in his essay, he was prepared to concede that, for an objective view of reality, 'we must make use both of the categories of continuity and discontinuity'.[4] Similarly, Jones, in his allusion to memory, brings out the ambivalences that this concession implies. In his writing, anamnesis comes to stand as a remedy for fracture. The literary image, held in such high store by the modernist poet, is understood to function in much the same way as the symbol did in Ancient Greece, that is to say as a token of a totality that included an absent but complementary element. As Jones put it, 'our Break had reference to something which was affecting the entire world of sacrament and sign'.[5]

The past that writers of the time constructed, whether conceived of as a single unit or represented metonymically by particular authors, particular periods, or particular movements, was postulated upon the existence and survival of texts that were, in a radical sense, *dissimilar* from their own. Dissimilar, yet complementary. The aim of this essay is to examine some of the glosses placed upon this sense of difference in various writings of a period of pluralities and transitions that has been identified as commencing early in the twentieth century, most commonly at some date between 1910 and 1922, and which goes under the name of Modernism. Central to the examples that I shall draw upon is the idea that *intertextuality* acted as a kind of bridge that linked the unattainable past and the inescapable present, although this idea with which we have become familiar (perhaps over familiar) had not yet acquired that appellation. My examples will be concerned mainly with the poetry of the period.

Nowadays, when the topic of intertextuality is addressed, there is an all-too-frequent tendency either to imply that the topic is largely the preserve of certain French theorists or to assume that authority on the subject lies with the French. The names of Kristeva, Barthes, Genette and Riffaterre are the most frequently cited of the so-called 'authorities' (with Saussure often included as a seminal figure whose linguistic theories made it all possible). These, in fact, are the names that form the nexus of Graham Allen's recent volume, *Intertextuality*, published in the New Critical Idiom series.[6]

In addition to the French theorists, two other writers are named in Allen's chapter titles as influential in the field of intertextuality: Mikhail Bakhtin and Harold Bloom. I shall start what I have to say about the relationship between Modernism and Intertextuality with a reference to Bloom or, to be more exact, with a remark made *against* Bloom's postulation concerning the 'anxiety' of influence that is so crucial to his understanding of intertextuality, but much of my subsequent attention will be directed to an examination of the establishment of intertextuality as a critical concept by Bakhtin's Russian compatriots.[7] In the process, I hope to demonstrate that an 'alternative' vision of intertextuality, as illuminating for our understanding of the interaction between literary texts as that offered in the standard Western European view, was evolving as a result of the powerful stimulus of Modernism. Indeed, this Soviet approach, as it has been called, is specifically inter*text*ual in that it accords more respect to the existence of the 'text' (as distinct from the more inclusive sense of 'textuality as discourse' that we find in many of the French approaches).[8]

In an essay only recently translated into English, Joseph Brodsky challenges the proposition, put forward by Harold Bloom and others, that influence is a source of anxiety.[9] In his view, the acknowledgement of influence is not a faint-hearted surrender to precursors who have come to assume the disproportionate and terrifying guise of giants, but a recognition of kinship, affinity and literary evolution. What Brodsky wrote was that

> [a] true poet does not avoid influences or continuity but frequently nurtures them, and emphasizes them in every possible way. There is nothing more pleasant physically (even physiologically) than repeating someone else's lines – whether to oneself or out loud. Fear of influence, fear of dependence, is the fear – the affliction – of a savage, but not of

culture, which is all continuity, all echo. (I wish someone would inform Mr. Harold Bloom.)[10]

Brodsky's own poetry, saturated as it is with references and allusions both to those who wrote in Russian and to those who wrote in other languages, is a testimony to the power of the cultural 'echo' to which he refers in this passage. Brodsky's sensitivity to the multiplicity of voices uttered by his predecessors puts him at one end of what we might call an intertextual spectrum. At the other end, Borges' fable of Pierre Menard's singular ambition to re-write *Don Quixote* may be cited as an example. Menard is, in a sense, the archetypal Modernist, for his attempt to translate Cervantes' seventeenth-century Spanish text into twentieth-century Spanish, employing exactly the same words as the original author, exemplifies the preoccupation mentioned at the start of this essay with the relationship between the present and the past. The narrator of Borges' short story observes:

> To compose the *Quixote* at the beginning of the seventeenth century was a reasonable undertaking, necessary and perhaps even unavoidable; at the beginning of the twentieth, it is almost impossible. It is not in vain that three hundred years have gone by, filled with extremely complex events. Among them, to mention only one, is the *Quixote* itself.[11]

The difference between the perspective offered by Brodsky, the Nobel Prize poet, who regarded fear of influence as the mark of a barbarian, and that of Menard, the fictional embodiment of a Borgesian conceit, is paradigmatic. Intertextuality is, at one extreme, an expression of the 'continuity of existence'[12] and, at the other, a recognition of rupture. More often than not, however, one arrives at an accommodation between anamnesis and fracture, between the present and what lies out of reach in the past on what Jones referred to as the 'farther shore'.

The origin of what might be regarded as the *modern* treatment of an ancient *topos* may be traced to the political exile Alexander Herzen, who, on 1 January 1855, wrote a letter to his fifteen-year-old son (also named Alexander) from Richmond House, Twickenham, in which he warned:

> We do not build, we destroy; we do not proclaim a new revelation, we eliminate the old lie. Modern man, that melancholy *Pontifex Maximus*,

only builds a bridge – it will be for the unknown man of the future to pass over it. You may be there to see him... But do not, I beg, remain on *this shore*.[13]

Other landscapes have included a 'farther shore', inhabited, where it was inhabited at all, by alien figures. Modernism celebrated those alien figures who either stood on the other shore, or else survived in the here and now on this side of a threshold in the form of outsiders torn between 'ineradicable longings' for what was unattainable and an obstinate, if attenuated, sense of belonging. Most of all, however, they commemorated the liminal figure who constructed temporary bridges across the abyss, the 'melancholy *Pontifex Maximus*', the architect of intertextuality.

The sense of alienation and discontinuity, which may be said to constitute the negative pole of the preoccupation with the past, is conjured up in T.S. Eliot's image of the 'familiar compound ghost/ Both intimate and unidentifiable', who challenges the poetic speaker of section II of 'Little Gidding' in the here and now of the mythical present ('this intersection time/ Of meeting nowhere, no before and after'). As in Jones's account of The Break, the geography of 'Little Gidding' extends into the terrain of the mythic. The first section of Eliot's quartet affirms a symbolic connection between present-day England and the 'negative mirror' of elsewhere:[14]

> There are other places
> Which also are the world's end, some at the sea jaws,
> Or over a dark lake, in a desert or a city –
> But this is the nearest, in place and time,
> Now and in England
> [...]
> Here, the intersection of the timeless moment
> Is England and nowhere. Never and always.

These 'other places' have no easily identifiable geographical location, yet they are familiar territory on mythological maps drawn up by authors as diverse as Melville and Virgil, as Sophocles and Dostoevsky. The meeting with the spiritual wanderer, who has left his body 'on a distant shore', in section II of 'Little Gidding', is a threshold encounter, occurring in 'the uncertain hour before the morning' at a place that is described as being 'Between three districts'.[15] The uncanny conjunction of the familiar with the strange, of intimacy and the inability to establish identity, depends upon a recognition of both continuity and discontinuity. It also draws, of course, upon the literary convention that allows the dead to share with the living whatever information they have acquired from their habitation on the 'distant shore':

> what the dead had no speech for, when living,
> They can tell you, being dead: the communication
> Of the dead is tongued with fire beyond the language of the living.

For Eliot, the contemporary landscape consisted largely of a *waste land* that disclosed an 'immense panorama of futility and anarchy'.[16] The 'world of sacrament and sign' to which Jones alluded lay typically in the past and in tradition. In 'East Coker', for example, the 'open field' resounds – at a distance – with echoes of the music of yesteryear, with 'daunsinge, signifying matrimonie –/ A dignified and commodious sacrament'. The ghostly celebrants are identified by their 'heavy feet in clumsy shoes',

> Earth feet, loam feet, lifted in country mirth
> Mirth of those long since under earth
> Nourishing the corn. Keeping time […]

What is located in this moist world of loam, a world in which 'earth' rhymes with 'mirth', is not the sterile condition of *The Waste Land* with its 'mountains of rock without water', where 'Sweat is dry and feet are in the sand', but the 'nourishing' potential for transformation offered by connection and communication.

A counterpart to this lost world is the *Fruchtland* to which Rainer Maria Rilke refers at the end of his second Duino Elegy (and which, with the license of the appropriator, Leishman and Spender translate as a 'little strip of corn-land'):

> Fänden auch wir ein reines, verhaltenes, schmales
> Menschliches, einen unseren Streifen Fruchtlands
> zwischen Strom und Gestein. Denn das eigene Herz übersteigt uns
> noch immer wie jene. Und wir können ihm nicht mehr
> nachschaun in Bilder, die es besänftigen, noch in
> göttliche Körper, in denen es größer sich mäßigt.

> If only we too could discover some pure, contained
> narrow, human, own little strip of corn-land
> in between river and rock! For our own heart still
> > transcends us
> even as theirs did. And we can no longer gaze
> after it now into pacifying image, or godlike
> body, wherein it achieves a grander restraint.[17]

Eliot's 'open field' with its echoes of the past has its latter-day antithesis in the modernity of the 'Unreal City', which he evokes in *The Waste Land* by means of references to the actual streets, bridges and churches of twentieth-century London. From the very opening lines of the first section of this poem, 'The Burial of the Dead', Eliot insists upon an adversity and suspension that finds no panacea within the confines of the text or, by implication, in the modern world. As for Rilke, his *Fruchtland*, which only exists subjunctively (*Fänden ... wir*), sets up the prospect of an imaginary, but limited, human space in contrast to the world of dispossessed divinity, which culminates in his seminal and fragmented cautions on the theme of Orpheus.[18] Continuity, for the modernist writer faced with overwhelming discontinuities, amounted, it would seem, to no more than a synonym for nostalgia – or, at best, a residual possibility of transcendence.[19]

At this point, I would like to introduce the poet who, for me, embodies most fully the spirit of Modernism and who is a key figure, I believe, in the foundation of a distinctive form of intertextuality. I refer to Osip Mandelstam, whom Brodsky acknowledged as one of the most influential of his precursors.[20] The totality of Mandelstam's creative output serves as an enduring legacy to the vitality of intertextuality, from the early poetry that appeared in his first collection of verse, entitled *Stone* (1913), to the late compositions, written in the 1930s, but not published until long after his death, in 1938, from a heart attack while in transit between labour camps in Stalin's Russia. It is the style and structure of his writing, however, more than any dates of composition, that define him as a European Modernist. His poem, 'The Age', is one of Modernism's most powerful lyric evocations of temporal fracture, but it also accommodates the foundation for recovery that is inherent in the very acknowledgement of fracture.

The poem begins:

> My age, my beast, who is able
> To look into your eyes
> And with his blood glue together
> The vertebrae of two centuries?

This is the only question asked in the four-stanza poem, and it is never answered directly (although, as James Greene remarks in a note to his free translation of the poem, the answer is implicitly given in the third stanza: 'the artist, the creator, can do these things').[21] The plight of discontinuity is accepted in the metaphor of the shattered spine that recurs in the final stanza, yet in the course of the poem a tentative belief in a recovery of value and meaning is expressed through the imagery of blood, flute and anatomical suppleness (a child's cartilage, the fontanelle of life). All these images suggest the possibility of amalgamation and future regeneration, while at the same time retaining the potentiality for further destruction. In an extra stanza added by Mandelstam in 1936, the poet's reference to the sea-bed implies, by extension, the existence of a farther shore:

> Blood the constructor gushes
> From the throat of terrestrial things
> And like a burning fish casts
> Onto the shore warm gravel from the sea.[22]

It is in the poetry and the prose of Mandelstam, as much as in any other author of the period, that the interplay between continuity and discontinuity is most finely balanced. Mandelstam championed the marginal and the mythic, for it was at the peripheries (the shore) and beyond (the sea's 'warm gravel') that he sought out what he deemed worth salvaging. Thus, the 'burning fish' in this poem points towards the living word of Christ as *logos*. Mandelstam's poem concludes with the figurative image of 'a beast, once supple' looking at the traces left by its own paws. In singling out *suppleness* as the very quality that has been lost in contemporary Russia, Mandelstam offers a clue to the importance of intertextuality for his poetry and for Modernism. It is the fluidity of the text that allows for, even insists upon, the indeterminacy of boundaries which makes intertextuality not only possible, but ultimately inescapable.

In 'The Twilight of Freedom', an earlier poem of the period, composed of similar ambivalences, Mandelstam responded to the imperative to celebrate the present in a doomed age. The poem commences with the injunction: 'Let us praise, brothers, the twilight of freedom, –/ The great twilight year'.[23] In this composition we find once more the imagery of sea and land, shipwreck and salvation. From a complex of metaphors and allusions that refer to the physical universe (sea, sun and earth) there emerges, in the second half of the poem, the symbol of the floating island: 'Through nets – thick twilight –/ The sun is invisible and the earth is drifting'. The reference here, it would seem, is to the present.[24] However doomed the modern age may appear in poem after poem, the poet demands of its alienated crew, as an act of courage, one final turn of the wheel:

> Well let's try then: an enormous, clumsy,
> Screeching turn of the helm.
> The earth is drifting. Be manful, men.

There is, in such encouragement, another side to the Modernist coin than that of the acceptance of discontinuity and drift, if it is to ring true: it is the call for heroic striving at a time of misfortune.

Responses carry responsibility. What the thunder said in *The Waste Land* – in its repetition of the monosyllabic DA – ends with an invitation for the heart to respond and the hand to control that, in its marine imagery of steerage, presents a parallel to Mandelstam's exhortation:

> *Damyata*: The boat responded
> Gaily, to the hand expert with sail and oar
> The sea was calm, your heart would have responded
> Gaily, when invited, beating obedient
> To controlling hands

What we find stated explicitly in the words of Mandelstam's poetic speaker in 'The Twilight of Freedom' and implicitly in the fable of the meaning of the Thunder in the last section of *The Waste Land* may also be found in the other authors whom I have cited. While revealing an awareness of what David Jones called The Break, each of them also bore witness to the potency of cultural echo, that is to say the ability of language to renew itself. The project of linguistic self-renewal, or what

Mallarmé at the very outset of the Modernist enterprise announced as 'ceding the initiative to words', explains in large measure the appetite for intertextuality that critics and theorists subsequently discovered in authors of the period.

Mandelstam raised the question of continuity in a series of prose pieces written in the early 1920s. He begins one key essay, 'On the Nature of the Word', by defining his area of enquiry in the opening paragraph:

> I would like to pose one question: is Russian literature a unified whole? Is contemporary Russian literature in fact the same as the literature of Nekrasov, Pushkin, Derzhavin, or Simeon Polotsky? If continuity has been preserved, how far back does it go into the past? If Russian literature remains unchanged, what constitutes its unity, what is its essential principle (its so-called criterion for being)?[25]

The answer to these leading questions is contained in the assumption that literature constitutes a homeostatic, philological system. Philology, understood quite literally as 'love of the word', was a recurrent topic in Mandelstam's prose. In 'On the Nature of the Word', he notes with regard to Russian literature:

> We have no Acropolis. Even today our culture is still wandering and not finding its walls. Nevertheless, each word in Dal's dictionary is a kernel of the Acropolis, a small Kremlin, a winged fortress of nominalism, rigged out in the Hellenic spirit for the relentless battle against the formless element, against non-existence, which threatens our history from every side.[26]

As he goes on to explain, it is not 'Hellenization *per se*', but 'an inner Hellenism, domestic Hellenism as it were', which is 'suitable to the spirit of the Russian language':

> Hellenism is the warmth of the hearth experienced as something sacred; it is anything which imparts some of the external world to man [...] Hellenism is a system, in the Bergsonian sense of the term, which man unfolds around himself, like the fan of phenomena freed of their temporal dependence, phenomena subjected through the human 'I' to an inner connection.[27]

Words construct culture. They promise human beings, at some future date, possession of the *Fruchtland*, their 'pure, contained/ narrow, human, own little strip of corn-land'. In a companion essay, Mandelstam also draws upon the imagery of corn and nourishment in concluding that '[g]rain must be scattered through the ether'. The justification for this injunction is found earlier in the essay when the word is equated with bread and flesh:

> [The word] shares the fate of bread and flesh: suffering. People are hungry. The State is even hungrier. But there is something still hungrier: Time. Time wants to devour the State. […] To show compassion for the State which denies the word shall be the contemporary poet's social obligation and heroic feat.[28]

The 'living word' does not 'designate an object', but rather chooses temporarily to *inhabit* 'some objective significance, material thing, or beloved body' around which it wanders freely 'like the soul around an abandoned, but not forgotten body'.[29] Like Eliot's 'communication/ Of the dead […] tongued with fire beyond the language of the living', Mandelstam's *word* has the quality of an aureole. The essay 'On the Nature of the Word' reasserts the claim that 'a word is not a thing', but an image:

> The most appropriate and, in scientific terms, the most correct approach, is to regard a word as an image, that is, as a verbal representation. […] A verbal representation is a complex composite of phenomena, it is a connection, a 'system'.[30]

The repeated reference in this essay to *system* points, on the one hand, to the influence of Bergsonian philosophy (an influence also evident in Hulme, Eliot and other Modernist poets) and, on the other hand to the acceptance of a philological proposition that the cultural richness and harmony of Greek and Roman antiquity survives – through translation, adaptation and other forms of re-writing – in the literatures of modern Europe.[31]

The idea of system that Mandelstam entertains is an open one, freed from temporal restraints, that admits the synchronic presence of all poets and all poetry. Future and past, never and always, are inverted as Mandelstam *awaits* the arrival of the poetry of Ovid, Pushkin and Catullus as 'that which must be, not as that which has already been':

> One often hears: that is good but it belongs to yesterday. But I say: yesterday has not yet been born. It has not really existed. I want Ovid, Pushkin, and Catullus to live once more, and I am not satisfied with the historical Ovid, Pushkin and Catullus.[32]

The word 'belongs' if not to yesterday then certainly to the individual poet. Each word bears the imprint of its author for any listener (or reader) who is 'sensitive to allusion'. Mandelstam, in speaking of the 'true joy of recognition', expressed a sentiment similar to that of Brodsky, when he wrote of feeling a physical (and physiological) pleasure at repeating someone else's lines. For both Russian poets, the word's acoustic properties were paramount.[33] For Mandelstam the 'true joy of recognition' comes through touch and hearing: 'The poem lives through an inner image, that ringing mold of form which anticipates the written poem. There is not yet a single word, but the poem can already be heard'.[34] The precursor, in this respect, resembles the 'familiar, compound ghost' of 'Little Gidding' in that the most powerful and immediate means of communication is *speech*, the spoken not the written word.

The word, Mandelstam contends, is 'brought to life all at once by the breathing of the ages', and 'the most striking thing about speaking is that the speaker does not know the language he is speaking'. Poetry is pentecostal. The poet's 'sacred frenzy' allows him access to 'the language of all times, all cultures'. Poetry, as Brodsky was later to claim of culture, is thus a matter of continuity and echo. For this reason, influence is not affliction but abundance. The poet, Mandelstam wrote, 'has no fear of recurrence'. He is 'free from the burden of memories'.[35]

Mandelstam's remarks on composition and system had a profound effect on how he came to be interpreted when his own poetry was subjected to sustained scrutiny in the 1960s and 1970s. One commentator, in particular, deserves to be distinguished for introducing an intertextual approach to the critical reception of Mandelstam's poetry as a means of explicating what were sometimes obscure allusions. In 1976, Kiril Taranovsky published six essays on Mandelstam that had appeared over the previous decade in various journals and critical collections.[36] The book's unpretentious title did not disguise from its more attentive readers the fact that a radically new method was being proposed in order to explicate the complex imagery of the Russian modernist poet. The sub-title of the first essay in the book – 'The Problem of Context and Subtext' – pointed to the fundamental direction of the new approach.[37] In this essay, Taranovsky drew attention to the recurrence of the same image in different poems by Mandelstam, while identifying the source of various quotations and reminiscences. This led him to observe that

> [a]ll poets have their favorite themes, their favorite images, and even their favorite words. All these recurrent themes and images form inner cycles in the work of a given poet, cycles which very often cannot be placed within exact chronological limits. Moreover, such recurrent themes and images may be characteristic of several poets, often independent of both the so-called poetic schools and even of historical periods. For example, many Russian poets of the twentieth century were fascinated by the image of the ship. [...] Needless to say, we receive more poetic information when we put a poem in a broader context and reveal its links with other texts.[38]

The significance of the 'broader context' is indicated in the sub-title of the second essay in the book: 'The 'Closed' and 'Open' Interpretation of a Poetic Text'.[39] Contextualisation, according to Taranovsky, allows an openness of interpretation that 'helps us decipher those figurative meanings and brings us closer to a deeper understanding of the imagery in the given poem'.[40] In a practical application of his method, Taranovsky demonstrated in both these essays the consistency with which the recurrent motif of air and breathing in Mandelstam's poetry of the twenties and thirties touched on the semantic fields of *Freedom / Non-freedom* and *Poetic Creation/Absence of Creation*.[41] As Taranovsky pointed out, the Formalist critic Yury Tynianov had already in the 1920s commented on the way in which recurrent words and images supplied a key for a whole hierarchy of allusions in Mandelstam's poetry. In reading a particular poem with Tynianov's 'key', as Taranovsky wrote, 'the aesthetic information which we receive from the given text increases'.[42] One consequence of this increase in aesthetic information was the critical construction of larger units to which Mandelstam's short lyric compositions were seen to belong, a form of intertextual continuity.[43]

In this way, the identification of *alien words* within a text, while serving to establish a sense of continuity with other authors, also contributed to the formation of a *context*. The significance of the context, however, would only be appreciated fully when the *relative* importance of the competing texts within the literary composition were ascertained. If one accepted that literary composition could only be considered systemic by virtue of the dynamic distribution of forces within the structure, then it was reasonable to assume that the echoes and allusions, or what Taranovsky referred to as the *subtexts*, were engaged in a struggle for dominance similar to that which took place between other elements in a text. In this respect, Tynianov's notion of *hierarchy* was crucial.[44]

This way of looking at an individual work was shared by Mandelstam himself. In the 1930s, he wrote in his 'Conversation about Dante' that

> a composition is formed not as a result of accumulated particulars, but due to the fact that one detail after another is torn away from the object, leaves it, darts out, or is chipped away from the system to go out into a new functional space or dimension, but each time at a strictly regulated moment and under circumstances which are sufficiently ripe and unique.[45]

Such a view of intertextual functionality, which shifts the emphasis from one of authorial anxiety to that of the homeostasis of the literary system, lies behind Brodsky's rejection of Bloom's view of the tormented artist. It might thus be said that words, rather than poets, 'strain,/ Crack and sometimes break, under the burden'.[46] Mandelstam, in setting out his homeostatic model of literary evolution in 'On the Nature of the Word', attacked the idea of competition between participants:

> Literary forms change, one set of forms yielding its place to another. However, each change, each gain, is accompanied by a loss, a forfeit. In literature nothing is ever 'better', no progress can be made simply because there is no literary machine and no finish line toward which everyone must race as rapidly as possible.[47]

The Modernist dictum articulated in this insistence found support in Eliot, when he wrote: 'There is only the fight to recover what has been lost/ And found and lost again and again: and now, under conditions/ That seem unpropitious'.[48]

It should be evident from what I have already stated about Taranovsky's application of 'context' and 'subtext' that he employed these two words in a way that excludes the kind of usage encountered in other critics who expound methodologies of intertextuality. A phrase such as 'socio-political context'[49] or the understanding of subtext as a subtle, underlying theme that is only present by implication and innuendo would be unacceptable. In Taranovsky, both 'context' and 'subtext' refer solely to textual material. Thus, he offers a definition of *context* as 'a set of texts which contain the same or a similar image', and *subtext* as 'an already existing text (or texts) reflected in a new one'.[50] Acknowledging the importance of *hierarchy* in determining the importance of any subtext, Taranovsky proceeds to suggest that it is possible to distinguish four different kinds of subtext:

(i) that which serves as a simple impulse for the creation of an image;
(ii) a borrowing of a rhythmic figure and the sounds contained therein;
(iii) the text which supports or reveals the poetic message of a later text;
(iv) the text that is treated polemically by the poet.[51]

It is, as Taranovsky pointed out, the identification of (iii) and (iv) that is more likely to contribute to our better understanding of a text.

Taking our cue from Taranovsky, we might respond to Mandelstam and Eliot's rejection of the idea of competition, by observing that intertextuality may imply collaboration (in the convergence of perspective in two or more texts) or conflict (in the divergence of perspective in two or more texts), but not an overcoming, or victory, in which one text supersedes another. A Modernist example of Taranovsky's third category of subtext is found in the indirect reference to Paul Valéry's 'Le Cimetière marin' that Wallace Stevens' poem 'The Poem That Took the Place of a Mountain' contains. Stevens invokes the opening lines of Valéry's poem –

> Ce toit tranquille, où marchent des colombes,
> Entre les pins palpite, entre les tombes;
> Midi le juste y compose de feux
> La mer, la mer, toujours recommencée!

– in the middle stanza of his poem:

> How he had recomposed the pines,
> Shifted the rocks and picked his way among clouds.

It could be said that Stevens' allusion *augments* what Taranovsky refers to as the 'poetic message' insofar as the phrase 'recomposed the pines' echoes the French '*pins*' and '*composé*'. In this example, meaning is 'supported' rather than 'revealed', for the title of the poem has already indicated the modernist, and writerly, theme of the distillation of experience into poetic language as one of *displacement*. The identification of the French subtext does not alter our perception of the poem's import in any fundamental way, but *once recognised*[52] it should warn us against an equation of the 'he' of the poem with a viewpoint associated exclusively with Stevens' own poetics. The polemical intent, if there is any, is reduced to a minimum. We might contrast this convergence between Stevens and Valéry, two modernist poets, on the subject of composition with the divergence over what constitutes seasonal good in two poets of different centuries and different dispositions, signalled in the opening line of *The Waste Land*. Eliot's statement that 'April is the cruellest month' sounds a contentious note that is reinforced by a subtextual allusion to the opening line of Chaucer's Prologue to *The Canterbury Tales* – 'Whan that Aprill with his shoures soote'. The superlative adjective 'cruellest' in the first line of Eliot's poem warns us right at the start that the poetic speaker is out of sorts, but it is only an awareness of the Chaucerian subtext that prepares the reader for the fact that the poet is about to engage in an extensive, revisionary polemic with literary tradition.[53]

Taranovsky's exposure of the transformative effect of the subtext upon a reading of Mandelstam's poetry gave rise to a number of critical studies by later commentators that illuminated obscure spots in the œuvre of the Russian author.[54] Recurrent (and puzzling) images, such as those of the *black sun* or of *dead bees*, which Taranovsky showed to be intertextual allusions, were placed under other microscopes as later scholars initiated searches for further subtexts.[55] This development in research method owed much to the poetic allegiance that Mandelstam himself had acknowledged.

Mandelstam associated himself with the modernist movement or school known as Akmeism (or Acmeism).[56] Akmeism, as defined by Mandelstam, professed itself to be opposed to the sterile self-referentiality of its most immediate – and immoderate – predecessor, Symbolism, which sealed up images in a 'terrifying quadrille of 'correspondences', all nodding to one another'.[57] It sought, if not to deny the existence of the chasm that others had discerned between the present and the past, at least to bridge the gap by establishing new lifelines, new continuities. These continuities were both national and international, both contemporary and historical, driven by an 'active love of literature'[58] that would 'draw the fragile ship of the human word [...] into the open sea of the future'.[59] Repeatedly, there had been periods 'when the moving spirit of Western literature was read with genius', periods when the Spirit of Intertextuality had presided over a festival of continuity that could be said to have confirmed Mandelstam's triumphant assertion that 'the poet has no fear of recurrence and is easily intoxicated on Classical wine':

> Nothing is impossible. As the room of a dying man is open to everyone, so the door of the old world is flung wide open before the crowd. Suddenly everything becomes public property. Come and take your pick. Everything is accessible: all labyrinths, all secret recesses, all forbidden paths.[60]

Modernist poets, 'those emigrants who survived the shipwreck of the nineteenth century and were cast up by the will of fate upon the shores of a new historical continent',[61] were faced with the choice either of the nihilistic capitulation to the chaos of contemporaneity or the Hellenic struggle against formlessness. A capitulation to chaos could be said to be implicit in Hulme's 'cinder theory' that he sketched out for a new Weltanschauung. Language, he wrote, with which we communicate, 'used to excess, becomes a disease, and we get the curious phenomena of men explaining themselves by means of the gossamer web that connects them'.[62] According to Mandelstam, the cure for this disease, when 'new blood [begins once more] to course through the veins',[63] would come in the form of what he understood to be a philological call upon a whole generation of modernists to prepare for the advent of a new European humanism. This was his vision of 'domestic Hellenism', or what he described as 'the relentless battle against the formless element, against non-existence, which threatens our history from every side'.[64]

We are left, then, with the two opposing ideologies of chasm and hearth, that is to say, with the positions held respectively by those who accepted the breakdown of humanism as an inevitable condition of modernity and those who believed that the values of humanism 'have merely withdrawn, concealed themselves like gold currency, but like the gold reserves, they secure contemporary Europe's entire circulation of ideas, and control them the more competently for being underground'.[65] Compelling though the arguments in support of each perspective appear to those already predisposed to a particular orientation, it is certain that they will be submitted repeatedly for revalidation by new and, as yet, unknown factions of the twenty-first century. In this way, theory will continue to construe intertextuality, on the one hand, as a site of conflict and rupture, and to regard it, on the other, as a kind of matrix, a source of renewal and rapture.

> Though the great song return no more
> There's keen delight in what we have:
> The rattle of pebbles on the shore
> Under the receding wave.
> W.B. Yeats, *The Nineteenth Century and After*

NOTES TO CHAPTER I

1. Hulme was killed in action in World War I. His essay 'Humanism and the Religious Attitude' appeared posthumously in T.E. Hulme, *Speculations: Essays on Humanism and the Philosophy of Art*, ed. Herbert Read (London: Routledge & Kegan Paul, 1987 [1924]), pp.1-71.
2. ibid., pp.1-2.
3. David Jones, 'The Preface to *The Anathemata* (1951)', *Epoch and Artist: Selected Writings*; ed. Harman Grisewood (London: Faber and Faber, 1959), p.113.
4. Hulme, op.cit. p.4.
5. Jones, op.cit. p.113.
6. Graham Allen, *Intertextuality* (London: Routledge, 2000).
7. My present concern is not to reiterate the commonly held opinion that Bakhtin's identification of the centrality of dialogism in language utterance was of crucial importance for Kristeva's introduction of *intertextualité* as a theoretical concept (cf. Allen, p.15), but rather to emphasize the prevalence of intertextual, or correlative, approaches in Russian writers from Mandelstam to Brodsky. Nevertheless, it should be noted that, in the contest between those who sought to salvage the category of continuity for literature and those who stressed the fact of cultural disjunction in the Modernist age, Bakhtin stood firmly with the former in his interpretation of *genre*: 'Genre is a representative of creative memory in the process of literary development. Precisely for this reason genre is capable of guaranteeing the *unity* and *uninterrupted continuity* of this development'. (Mikhail Bakhtin, *Problems of Dostoevsky's Poetics*, ed. and trans. Caryl Emerson (Manchester: Manchester University Press, 1984), p.106).
8. See Elaine Rusinko, 'Intertextuality: The Soviet Approach to Subtext', *Dispositio*, IV, 11-12 (1979), pp.213-35.
9. Brodsky's essay 'A Footnote to a Commentary', translated by Jamey Gambrell and Alexander Sumerkin, appears in Stephanie Sandler (ed.), *Rereading Russian Poetry* (New Haven: Yale University Press, 1999), pp.183-201. See *Pis'mo k Goratsiiu* (Moskow: Nash dom - L'Age d'Homme, 1998), pp.121-51 for the original. An edited version of the Gambrell/Sumerkin translation appeared in the *Times Literary Supplement* (27 August 1999), pp.13-16, under the headline 'A Hidden Duet'.
10. Sandler, op.cit. p.184.
11. Letter of 30 September 1934. 'Pierre Menard, Author of the *Quixote*', translated by James E. Irby, is published in Jorge Luis Borges, *Labyrinths: Selected Stories and Other Writings*, ed. Donald A. Yates and James E. Irby (Harmondsworth: Penguin, 1970), pp.62-71 (68). The fact that Pierre Menard destroyed all the drafts of his labour is not without significance.
12. In Chapter XL of *Tess of the d'Urbervilles*, Angel Clare tells Mercy Chant that his scheme to travel to Brazil 'snaps the continuity of existence'.

13. This letter is printed at the start of the Author's Introduction to *From the Other Shore*. See Alexander Herzen, *From the Other Shore and The Russian People and Socialism* (Oxford: Oxford University Press, 1979, p.3). The translation (from the Russian) of *From the Other Shore* is by Moura Budberg.

14. The reference is to Italo Calvino's *Invisible Cities*; trans. William Weaver (London: Vintage, 1997), p.29.

15. The catachresis (*between three*) carries the ironic suggestion that this was a *trivial* encounter.

16. The phrase is taken from Eliot's essay on '*Ulysses*, Order and Myth'. See *The Dial* LXXV (November, 1923), p.5.

17. Rainer Maria Rilke, *Duino Elegies*: The German text with an English translation, introduction and commentary by J.B. Leishman and Stephen Spender (London: Chatto & Windus, 1975), pp.36-39.

18. I discuss some ambivalent aspects of the territory that Rilke staked out as *Fruchtland* in 'Between River and Rock: Landmarks in European Modernism', *The Turn of the Century: Modernism and Modernity in Literature and the Arts*, ed. Christian Berg *et al.* (Berlin: Walter de Gruyter, 1995), pp.199-208.

19. The opening line of the first of the fifty-five Sonnets to Orpheus refers to this transcendence: 'Da stieg ein Baum. O reine Übersteigung!'.

20. See Joseph Brodsky, 'The Child of Civilization', *Less Than One: Selected Essays* (London: Penguin, 1987), pp.123-44.

21. Osip Mandelstam, *Poems chosen and translated by James Greene*: rev. ed. (London: Paul Elek, 1980), p.90. The literal translation of lines from this poem is my own. 'The Age' ('Vek') was first published as a four-stanza poem (of 32 lines) in December 1922. An additional stanza (of 8 lines), written at the same time as the original composition, was included in 1936. For the original, see O. E. Mandel'shtam, *Sobranie sochinenii v chetyrekh tomakh: tom pervyi*, ed. G.P. Struve and B.A. Filippov (Moscow: Terra, 1991), pp.102-03. For the extra stanza, see O.E. Mandel'shtam, *Stikhotvoreniia*, p.132. See Osip Mandelstam, *Selected Poems*; trans. Clarence Brown and W.S. Merwin (London: Oxford University Press, 1973), pp.44-45, for a free translation in which the additional stanza replaces the second stanza of the original poem.

22. The Russian word for 'gravel' (*khriashch*) is the same as that for 'cartilage' or 'gristle'. The Brown-Merwin version attempts to convey this complex word-play by translating the line as 'a hot sand of sea-bones'. Compare the sense of potential peril in the recurrent marine imagery of Eliot's poetry, ranging from the mermaids of 'The Love Song of J. Alfred Prufrock' to the whirlpool of the fourth section of *The Waste Land*, and the 'torn seine' of 'The Dry Salvages'.

23. My translation. 'The Twilight of Freedom' (May 1918) is translated by Brown and Merwin in Osip Mandelstam, *Selected Poems*, p.22. For the original, see Mandel'shtam, op.cit. (1991) p.72.

24. A curiosity, from an intertextual perspective, about the views put forward by Mandelstam, a champion of cultural continuity, and Hulme, who might be regarded as a sceptical opponent, is that they both adopt the same image for contemporary society. Hulme asks (in 'Cinders: A Sketch of a New Weltanschauung'): 'The floating heroic world (built up of moments) and the cindery reality – can they be made to correspond to some fundamental constitution of the world?' op.cit. p.220.

25. The essay 'On the Nature of the Word' is translated by Jane Gary Harris in *Mandelstam: The Complete Critical Prose and Letters*, pp.117-32 (117).

26. ibid., p.126.

27. ibid., pp.127-28.

28. 'The Word and Culture', ibid., pp.112-16 (115). The extract quoted is followed by a six line quotation from his poem 'The Twilight of Freedom'.

29. ibid., p.115.

30. ibid., p.129.

31. See 'On the Nature of the Word', ibid., pp.119-20. The view that Russian literature benefited from the legacy of the classical Greek lexicon that the Slavonic languages inherited in the eleventh century had been articulated by Pushkin a century earlier. In acknowledging this inheritance, Pushkin defined its main quality as 'suppleness' [*gibkost*'], a characteristic (according to Gogol) of Pushkin's own literary style. See Leon Burnett, 'Obval': Pushkin's 'Kubla Khan', *Essays in Poetics*, 6 (1981), pp.22-38 (30-31). Since Mandelstam (in 'The Age') singles out *suppleness* as the very quality that has been lost in contemporary Russia, I would propose the Pushkinian reference as a hitherto undiscovered subtext. The original version of Mandelstam's poem concludes with the figurative image of 'a beast, once supple' looking at the traces left by its own paws.

32. ibid., p.113. Compare the 'new technique […] of the deliberate anachronism and the erroneous attribution' that is mentioned in the last paragraph of 'Pierre Menard: Author of the *Quixote*': 'This technique, whose applications are infinite, prompts us to go through the *Odyssey* as if it were posterior to the *Æneid* […]. To attribute the *Imitatio Christi* to Louis Ferdinand Céline or to James Joyce, is this not a sufficient renovation of its tenuous spiritual indications?', Borges, op.cit. p.71.

33. Mandelstam's 'Conversation about Dante' (*Mandelstam: The Complete Critical Prose and Letters*, pp.397-442) is replete with references to tone, timbre, speech peculiarities. He describes Dante's 'reflexology of speech' as 'the spontaneous psycho-physiological influence of the word' on speaker and auditor. In 'Some Notes on

Poetry' (ibid., pp.165-69), Mandelstam refers to Pasternak's poetry in the following manner: 'To read Pasternak's verse is to clear your throat, to fortify your breathing, to fill your lungs; surely such poetry could provide a cure for tuberculosis' (p.168).

34. ibid., p.116.

35. The quotations in this paragraph are all taken from 'The Word and Culture'.

36. Kiril Taranovsky, *Essays on Mandel'štam* (Cambridge, Mass.: Harvard University Press, 1976).

37. 'Concert at the Railroad Station: The Problem of Context and Subtext', ibid., pp.1-20. 'Concert at the Railroad Station' (1921) is the title of a poem by Mandelstam, which is subjected to a painstaking contextual and subtextual analysis in the course of the essay.

38. Taranovsky, ibid., pp.6-7.

39. 'The Hayloft: The 'Closed' and 'Open' Interpretation of a Poetic Text', ibid., pp.21-47. In this essay, an analysis of 'twin-poems', known as 'The Hayloft', written in 1922, demonstrates 'the polysemantic quality of the texts'.

40. ibid., p.21.

41. ibid., p.33.

42. ibid., p.25.

43. 'Mandel'stam was not a poet of large forms; he did not write long poems or novels. But, as a matter of fact, his entire creative work is one entity, one large form: his unique poetic vision of the world, or – in more modern terms – the genuine poetic model of the world, created by him.' ibid., p.7.

44. Tynianov had written: 'Mandelstam's semantic system is such that *one* image acquires a decisive role for the entire poem, and one verbal series imperceptibly colours all the rest – this is the key to all the hierarchies of images.' Iurii Tynianov, *Arkhaisty i novatory* (Leningrad, 1929, p.570 [my translation]).

45. *Mandelstam: The Complete Critical Prose and Letters*, p.401. A little later in the same essay, Mandelstam concludes that the *Divina Commedia* is 'a stereometric body, one continuous development of the crystallographic theme. It is inconceivable that anyone could grasp with the eye alone or even visually imagine to oneself this form of thirteen thousand facets, so monstrous in its exactitude.' (ibid., p.407).

46. See T.S. Eliot, 'Burnt Norton' V, *Four Quartets*.

47. *Mandelstam: The Complete Critical Prose and Letters*, p.119.

48. T.S. Eliot, 'East Coker' V, *Four Quartets*.

49. The phrase appears on the first page of *Intertextuality: Theories and Practices*, edited by Michael Worton and Judith Still (Manchester: Manchester University Press, 1990).

50. Taranovsky, op.cit. p.18.

51. ibid., p.18.

52. It is important to stress that subtexts do not announce themselves explicitly. The cultural continuity that they assert is only realised by a reading between the lines.

53. In contrast to Eliot's subversive polemic, the opening lines of Meredith's 'The Death of Winter' – 'When April with her wild blue eye/ Comes dancing over the grass' – reinforces cultural continuity in so far as it offers no resistance to the Chaucerian subtext. See George Meredith, *Modern Love and Other Poems* (London: Constable, 1922), p.21.

54. Although the heuristic value of the subtext has been recognised primarily in the exegesis of Mandelstam's poetry, a subtextual approach has been employed by scholars working in other areas of Russian literature. See, for example, Nina Perlina, *Varieties of Poetic Utterance: Quotation in The Brothers Karamazov* (Lanham, MD: University Press of America, 1985) and Pekka Tammi, *Russian Subtexts in Nabokov's Fiction: Four Essays* (Tampere: Tampere University Press, 1999).

55. None of these searches has, so far, been more extensive than the book-length exegesis of two poems, performed by Omry Ronen in *An Approach to Mandel'štam* (Jerusalem: Magnes Press, 1983). Acknowledging the influence of Roman Jakobson, Kiril Taranovsky and Yury Tynianov, Ronen makes the claim that "[s]ubtextual analysis' (i.e. identification and interpretation of subtexts) has become the essential hermeneutic tool in the new approach to Mandel'štam's poetry' (xi). For a discussion of the difficulties inherent in arriving at a conclusive subtext, see Leon Burnett, 'Contours of the Creative Word: Mandel'štam's 'Voz'mi na radost' …' in Perspective', *Slavonic and East European Review*, 70 (1992), pp.18-52.

56. 'The semantic function of the subtext is especially important for the practical purposes of text explication in acmeism. […] The subtextual approach is justified also by the fact that memory is the fundamental concern of acmeism, and literary recollection is the corner-stone, not only of its aesthetic code, but also of its message.' (Ronen, op.cit. xii)

57. *Mandelstam: The Complete Critical Prose and Letters*, p.128.

58. ibid., p.131.

59. ibid., p.132.

60. ibid., p.116.

61. ibid., p.144.

62. Hulme, op.cit. p.217.

63. *Mandelstam: The Complete Critical Prose and Letters*, p.131.

64. ibid., p.126.

65. ibid., p.183.

Woolf Wilde
Nietzsche
          Butor André Gide
      Derek Walcott   Marinetti   Woolf
E. M. Forster Kavafy   Augustine
                Charles Baudelaire
    Aragon   Edgar Allen Poe   Michael Aflaq
Mc Almon   Malraux   Baroja
netti Butor   Kafka   Woolf
            John Dewey   Joyce
  Lorca   Nietzsche
Kafka Benjamin   Kavafy   Woolf   Beckett
  Malraux   John Dos   Proust
William Carlos Williams   Passos Koeppen   Proust   Ez
                      E. M. Forster   Thomas Mann
oyce Benjamin   Baroja   John Dos Passos   Kafka
  Ezra Pound   Michael Aflaq   Beckett
alcott   Koeppen   Butor   F
    Nietzsche Robert Mc Almon Marinetti Aragon   Jo
ett
      Proust   Edg
arinetti   Jol

PART I
MODERNISM AND LITERARY INFLUENCES

CHAPTER II

Intertextual modernity:
Baudelaire and Poe's 'Man of the Crowd'

Emily Salines

Emily Salines is Senior Lecturer in the School of Arts at Middlesex University. Her research interests include 19th century literature, comparative literature and translation studies. She is the author of articles on Baudelaire and on translation.

The aim of this chapter is to explore the complex relationship between intertextuality and modernism through an analysis of Charles Baudelaire's versions of Edgar Allan Poe's 'Man of the Crowd' and the issues these versions raise. Although not part of what is generally called 'High Modernism', Baudelaire (1821-67) is an undisputed central figure in modernism and modernity,[1] his influence radiating across Europe. Baudelaire's own impact on later generations of writers echoes his own dialogue with the Other, and makes him in his own right an important example in a study of modernism and intertextuality. Indeed, this dialogue with the Other, and the centrality of intertextuality in his writings, raise issues which are central to modernist writing. Studying these issues in Baudelaire, therefore, may be a way of understanding both some aspects of his appeal to modernist writers and, more generally, some features of literary modernism.

In this context, Baudelaire's work on and around Edgar Allan Poe's 'Man of the Crowd' is enlightening. Indeed Poe's story is the object of multiple rewritings on the part of Baudelaire: a direct translation, 'L'Homme des foules', first published in January 1855 in *Le Pays* and then published in book form as part of the *Nouvelles Histoires extraordinaires*; then a passage in *Le Peintre de la vie moderne* (first published in 1863 in *Le Figaro*, and then in *L'Art romantique*, 1868), based on the translation; the prose poem 'Les Foules', written roughly in the same period as *Le Peintre de la vie moderne* and first published in 1861 (*Revue fantaisiste*); finally, passages in *Un Mangeur d'opium* (first published in 1860).

Baudelaire's successive versions of 'The Man of the Crowd' are interesting from several points of view. First, the thematics of Poe's text, and, more importantly, Baudelaire's readings and rewritings of it, inaugurate a new aesthetic of the city which is both central to Baudelaire's concerns and very influential for later modernists. Second, Baudelaire's versions illustrate the complexity of intertextual writing, and related issues of authority, originality and transformation, which are also at the core of modernist texts which they thus prefigure. Third, the recurrence of the references to this text in works central to the formulation of a modernist aesthetic (such as *Le Peintre de la vie moderne* and the *Spleen de Paris*) will enable us to relate directly Baudelaire's variations on Poe to modernism.

1. *Baudelaire's variations on 'The Man of the Crowd'*

More than any other story, Poe's 'The Man of the Crowd' is clearly an example of what Baudelaire felt was a 'ressemblance intime' (an intimate resemblance) between himself and the American writer.[2] In this very brief story, a first-person narrator, who enjoys looking at the city crowd, follows a mysterious man who walks around restlessly, and turns out to be incapable of leaving the crowd. The story combines descriptions of the city crowd (of London) and a philosophical reflection on the mysteries of human nature.

The themes of the story are linked to Baudelaire's concerns: the writer as *flâneur* observing the city crowd is of course a central Baudelairean theme. The scenes described in Poe's story echo those in the 'Tableaux parisiens' or *Le Spleen de Paris* (an aspect to which we shall return later). In addition, we have the idea of the loneliness that can be experienced in a crowd: Poe writes about 'feeling in solitude on account of the very denseness of the company around',[3] which again is very close to some passages in *Un Mangeur d'opium* where we read phrases such as 'le Sahara des grandes villes' ('the Sahara of great cities') and other explicit comparisons of the city and the desert:

> Il y a dans le *barathrum* des capitales, comme dans le désert, quelque chose qui fortifie et qui façonne le cœur de l'homme, qui le fortifie d'une autre manière, quand il ne le déprave pas et ne l'affaiblit pas jusqu'à l'abjection et jusqu'au suicide.[4]

> (There is, in the *barathrum* of capital cities, as in the desert, something which fortifies and shapes a man's heart, which fortifies him in a specific way, unless it depraves and weakens him to the point of abjection and suicide.)

Clearly this thematic closeness and perceived affinity are one of the reasons for Baudelaire's repeated visits to and experiments on Poe's text. As already noted, these experiments start with his direct translation of the story, 'L'Homme des foules'.

Like most of Baudelaire's translations of Poe's stories, 'L'Homme des foules' is a relatively close translation. The English text is closely followed by the French text: closeness implies in some instances the choice to follow the English syntax almost word for word. We have for instance clear calques such as 'he did not hesitate in his career' translated by Baudelaire as 'il n'hésita pas dans sa carrière'.[5] Such calques have to be seen in conjunction with the use of English words in the French text (a use which matches Poe's own use of French words within his writing):[6] Baudelaire retains Poe's phrase 'steady old fellows';[7] 'these gentry' is translated as 'cette sorte de gentry',[8] 'what is termed gentility' is translated as 'ce qu'on appelle *gentility*'.[9] In such instances, the target text reveals the presence of the foreign at its core.

Despite such features, 'L'Homme des foules' reads very much like a Baudelairean text. This is of course caused by the concerns of fluency which seem to have dictated Baudelaire's strategy.[10] Fluency, and readability, often taken for granted as necessities in translation, are not as straightforward as it may seem: they can also be seen as an erasing of the foreign characteristics of the source text, a domestication, or an appropriation.

Indeed, the removal from the target text of any characteristics which may disturb the target reader is already a way of hiding the foreign nature of the text. In this respect they are the first step in Baudelaire's integration of Poe's text into his own corpus. In 'L'Homme des foules', there is clearly a tendency towards a modernisation of the language. Poe's latinate and often archaic words are systematically replaced in Baudelaire's version with modern words. Poe's 'habiliments', for instance, is translated by 'vêtements' ('clothes'),[11] 'women of the town' is translated by 'prostituées' ('prostitutes'),[12] 'second-handed roquelaire' by 'manteau évidemment acheté d'occasion' ('evidently second-hand coat') and so on and so forth.[13]

A consequence of Baudelaire's translation choices is that the first readers of Poe in French were struck by the simplicity of his style. An 1856 book review of the *Histoires extraordinaires* reads as follows:

> La phrase, en général, est ferme, nue et sobre, sans agréments et sans surcharges, elle court droit au but, et si une image se rencontre, elle s'en pare sans la chercher.[14]
>
> (Generally the style is firm, plain and sober, without ornament and

73

without excess, it goes straight to the point and if it meets an image, it tackles it without searching for it.)

This impression of simplicity, assigned by the reviewer to Poe's style rather than his translator's (the reviewer states that through the translation 'le public français devient [...] aussi apte à juger les contes de Poë qu'un auditoire américain' (French readers are as able to judge Poe's tales as an American audience)), is contradicted by a close reading of the translation. Despite the translator's invisibility perceived by the reviewer quoted above, some vocabulary choices are typically Baudelairean. Poe's 'avarice' is rendered as 'lésinerie';[15] 'the fiend' becomes 'le démon';[16] 'dangerously pleasant' becomes 'une dangereuse volupté';[17] 'the dim light of an accidental lamp' becomes 'la lueur accidentelle d'un sombre réverbère';[18] 'the most abandoned' becomes 'les plus infâmes'.[19] The translation of the adjective 'wild' is also the occasion for variations: 'the wildest amazement' is translated as 'un effroyable étonnement',[20] and in other instances we have a translation of 'wild' either by 'étrange' or 'effaré': a 'wild and vacant stare' becomes 'un regard fixe, effaré, vide'.[21] 'Turmoil' becomes 'tourbillon'.[22]

In addition, some passages, such as the descriptions of the crowd, have a distinctly Baudelairean tone. In the French text the noun 'foules' is used far more than 'crowd' is in Poe. 'Foule(s)' is used to translate 'crowd', 'the press', 'the mob', and this recurrence betrays Baudelaire's interest in the theme.[23] In the following passage, for example, Poe's text reads as:

> by the time the lamps were well lighted, two dense and continuous tides of population were rushing past the door. At this particular period of the evening I had never before been in a similar situation, and a tumultuous sea of human heads filled me, therefore, with a delicious novelty of emotion.

Baudelaire translates:

> à la tombée de la nuit, la foule s'accrut de minute en minute; et, quand tous les réverbères furent allumés, deux courants de population s'écoulaient, épais et continus, devant la porte. Je ne m'étais jamais senti dans une situation semblable à celle où je me trouvais en ce moment particulier de la soirée, et ce tumultueux océan de têtes humaines me remplissait d'une délicieuse émotion toute nouvelle.[24]

He is not only retaining the metaphor of the human sea, he is also developing it through the choice of the verb 's'écoulaient' for 'rushed', and the translation of 'sea' as 'océan'. The metaphor of the crowd as liquid is highly suggestive: it conjures up the idea of a perfect blending of individuals, a communion with fellow humans as part of a common experience. The Other and the Self become one, or so it seems. At the same time, the image of a perfect blend is contradicted by the position of the narrator, who remains isolated, overseeing the whole, of which the other individuals are not aware. The encounter of the narrator and the wanderer is particularly striking:

> stopping fully in front of the wanderer, [I] gazed at him steadfastly in the face. He noticed me not, but resumed his solemn walk, while I, ceasing to follow, remained absorbed in contemplation.
>
> (m'arrêtant tout droit devant l'homme errant, je le regardai intrépidement en face. Il ne fit pas attention à moi, mais reprit sa solennelle promenade, pendant que, renonçant à le poursuivre, je restais absorbé dans cette contemplation.)[25]

Baudelaire's choice of the verb 'renonçant' ('giving up') suggests a more wilful decision to abandon the search than Poe's neutral 'ceasing'. The choice of 'promenade' conjures up the idea of an idle pursuit which is absent from Poe's 'walk', and in fact goes against the spirit of Poe's story, which focuses on the wanderer's obsession. In Baudelaire's version, then, there is a slight shift from the wanderer as a focus of the story, to the narrator, whose movements seem far more determined. The implications of such a passage as *mise en abyme* of intertextuality will be looked at in a while. Let us however note for the moment the creative dimension of the 'contemplation' triggered by the encounter with the Other, which, as will be seen later, may provide a key to Baudelaire's relationship to his intertexts.

Before this relationship is studied, we must look at Baudelaire's other uses of Poe's 'Man of the Crowd'. The story – and its translation by Baudelaire – are the hypotexts of two passages in *Le Peintre de la vie moderne*.

> Vous souvenez-vous d'un tableau (en vérité, c'est un tableau!) écrit par

la plus puissante plume de cette époque, et qui a pour titre *L'Homme des foules*? Derrière la vitre d'un café, un convalescent, contemplant la foule avec jouissance, se mêle par la pensée, à toutes les pensées qui s'agitent autour de lui. Revenu récemment des ombres de la mort, il aspire avec délices tous les germes et tous les effluves de la vie; comme il a été sur le point de tout oublier, il se souvient et veut avec ardeur se souvenir de tout. Finalement, il se précipite à travers cette foule à la recherche d'un inconnu dont la physionomie entrevue l'a, en un clin d'œil, fasciné. La curiosité est devenue une passion fatale, irrésistible![26]

(Do you remember a picture (it really is a picture!), painted – or rather written – by the most popular pen of our age, and entitled *The Man of the Crowd*? In the window of a coffee-house there sits a convalescent, pleasurably absorbed in gazing at the crowd, and mingling, through the medium of thought, in the turmoil of thought that surrounds him. But lately returned from the valley of the shadow of death, he is rapturously breathing in all the odours and essences of life; as he has been on the brink of total oblivion, he remembers, and fervently desires to remember, everything. Finally he hurls himself headlong into the midst of a throng, in pursuit of an unknown half-glimpsed countenance, that has, in an instant, bewitched him. Curiosity has become a fatal, irresistible, passion!)[27]

La foule est son domaine, comme l'air est celui de l'oiseau, comme l'eau celui du poisson. Sa passion et sa profession, c'est d'*épouser la foule*. Pour le parfait flâneur, pour l'observateur passionné, c'est une immense jouissance que d'élire domicile dans le nombre, dans l'ondoyant, dans le mouvement, dans le fugitif et l'infini.[28]

(The crowd is his element, as the air is that of birds and water of fishes. His passion and his profession are to become one flesh with the crowd. For the perfect *flâneur*, for the passionate spectator, it is an immense joy to set up house in the heart of the multitude, amid the ebb and flow of movement, in the midst of the fugitive and the infinite.)[29]

The first of the two passages presents a summary of Poe's story, and highlights which elements in the story have struck Baudelaire. Whereas the focus of Poe's story was the wanderer walking the street rather than the narrator following him, in *Le Peintre de la vie moderne*, the focus has moved from the wanderer to the observer. The shift noted in the translation has been pushed further. The contemplation already noted in Poe's story and Baudelaire's translation has been transformed into fascination, passion and a pleasure which has strong sexual overtones ('jouissance', 'épouser'). It could be argued that in this shift from contemplation to pleasure there is a move towards a more active role for the *flâneur*, already suggested by the verb 'renonçant' in the passage studied earlier. At the same time, whereas in Poe's story the observer remains detached (and therefore in control of the scene he is viewing), in Baudelaire's rewriting of it he is caught in the crowd, becomes the wanderer rather than the observer.

The above passages are particularly interesting as they seem to represent a middle stage in the gradual integration of Poe's text into Baudelaire's: the hypotext is clearly mentioned, but at the same time, the summary is highly biased, focusing on the themes needed by Baudelaire in his presentation of Guys, and it is of course embedded in *Le Peintre de la vie moderne*, which informs our reading of the passage. Through this direct reference, then, Baudelaire claims the text of the other as his own, rewriting his own translation of Poe into his own text.

'Les Foules', written roughly in the same period as *Le Peintre de la vie moderne*, and first published in 1861 (*Revue fantaisiste*), represents a stage further in this rewriting: the hypotext disappears under the poem, in which Baudelaire explores further the themes which appealed to him in Poe's story:

> Il n'est pas donné à chacun de prendre un bain de multitude: jouir de la foule est un art; et celui-là seul peut faire, aux dépens du genre humain, une ribote de vitalité, à qui une fée a insufflé dans son berceau le goût du travestissement et du masque, la haine du domicile et la passion du voyage.
>
> Multitude, solitude: termes égaux et convertibles pour le poète actif et fécond. Qui ne sait pas peupler sa solitude, ne sait pas non plus être seul dans une foule affairée.
>
> Le poète jouit de cet incomparable privilège, qu'il peut à sa guise être lui-même et autrui. Comme ces âmes errantes qui cherchent un corps, il entre, quand il veut, dans le personnage de chacun. Pour lui seul, tout est vacant; et si de certaines places paraissent lui être fermées, c'est qu'à ses yeux elles ne valent pas la peine d'être visitées.

Le promeneur solitaire et pensif tire une singulière ivresse de cette universelle communion. Celui-là qui épouse facilement la foule connaît des jouissances fiévreuses, dont seront éternellement privés l'égoïste, fermé comme un coffre, et le paresseux, interné comme un mollusque. Il adopte comme siennes toutes les professions, toutes les joies et toutes les misères que la circonstance lui présente.

Ce que les hommes nomment amour est bien petit, bien restreint et bien faible, comparé à cette ineffable orgie, à cette sainte prostitution de l'âme qui se donne toute entière, poésie et charité, à l'imprévu qui se montre, à l'inconnu qui passe.

Il est bon d'apprendre quelque fois aux heureux de ce monde, ne fût-ce que pour humilier un instant leur sot orgueil, qu'il est des bonheurs supérieurs au leur, plus vastes et plus raffinés. Les fondateurs de colonies, les pasteurs de peuples, les prêtres missionnaires exilés au bout du monde, connaissent sans doute quelque chose de ces mystérieuses ivresses; et, au sein de la vaste famille que leur génie s'est faite, ils doivent rire quelque fois de ceux qui les plaignent pour leur fortune si agitée et pour leur vie si chaste.

(Not everyone has the gift of taking a plunge into the multitude: there is an art to enjoying the crowd; and they alone can draw from the human race a feast of vitality on whom a fairy has bestowed, while they were in their cradles, a taste for disguise and masks, a hatred of home life, and a passion for travel.

Multitude and solitude: equal and interchangeable terms for the poet who is active and productive. Those who are not able to people their solitude are equally unable to be alone in a busy crowd.

The poet benefits from an incomparable privilege which allows him to be, at will, himself and others. Like those wandering souls in search of a body, he enters, when he so desires, into the character of each individual. For him alone, everything is vacant; and if certain places appear to be closed to him, that is because in his eyes they are not worth the bother of visiting.

The solitary and pensive stroller finds this universal communion extraordinarily intoxicating. He who finds it easy to espouse the crowd knows feverish pleasures which will be eternally denied to the selfish man, who is as tightly sealed as a strong box, or the lazy man, who is as self-contained as a mollusc. He makes his own all the professions, all the joys, and all the sufferings that chance presents to him.

What men call love is very small, very restricted, and very weak compared with this ineffable orgy, this holy prostitution of the soul which gives itself entirely, poetry and charity, to the unforeseen which reveals itself, to the unknown which happens along.

It is good from time to time to teach the fortunate of this world, if only to humiliate, momentarily, their stupid pride, that there are joys superior to their own, joys which are more immense and more delicate. Founders of colonies, pastors of people, missionary priests living in exile in the world's furthest corners, doubtless know something of this mysterious intoxication; and in the bosom of the vast family their genius has created for itself, they must sometimes laugh at those who pity them for a fate so troubled and an existence so chaste.)[30]

The poem may indeed be read as a development of the often quoted passage of the *Fusées* ('De la concentration et vaporisation du moi, tout est là'), as it explores the relationship of the self to the Other, a combination of openness and closeness ('Multitude, solitude'). *Fusées* also echoes the poem in a more direct way ('Le plaisir d'être dans les foules est une expression mystérieuse de la jouissance de la multiplication du nombre').[31]

'Les Foules' expands on the aspects already noted in *Le Peintre de la vie moderne*. The erotic dimension is emphasised ('jouir de la foule', 'fécond', 'jouit', 'épouse', 'jouissances fiévreuses'). Particularly interesting in this respect is the comparison with love, the encounter with the crowd being likened to an orgy, a holy prostitution, in a typically Baudelairean oxymoron. The theme of the identification with the Other, already present in *Le Peintre de la vie moderne*, is further developed. At the same time, the origins of the poem in Baudelaire's reading of Poe are clear. We have a rewriting of the source text blended with Baudelairean thematics, already started in *Le Peintre de la vie moderne* and brought to completion in this poem. We can indeed identify derivations of elements noted in Poe's story and already transformed in *Le Peintre de la vie moderne*: the water image ('bain de multitude' / 'a plunge into the multitude'), the 'jouissances fiévreuses' / 'feverish pleasures' (which echo Poe's narrator's feverish state), the fascination with the crowd. In addition we have the completion of the application of those elements to Baudelairean concerns already started in *Le Peintre de la vie moderne* – the artist's communication with the multitude, as a *flâneur* fascinated with the crowd. In all these readings of Poe's text by Baudelaire, we have the same expression of the ideal communion between the poet and the world, and the ultimate identification which is the privilege of the poet / artist. The experiences described are very similar: both characters identify with the Other – 'être lui-même et autrui' / 'to be himself and others' ('Les Foules') and 'la recherche d'un inconnu' / 'the search for a stranger' (*Le Peintre de la vie moderne*) are both an opening to the Other. At the same time, the observer's active role is emphasised. The poet is 'actif et fécond'/ 'active and productive', but this fecundity is the result of a taking over of the Other. In this respect, the description of the pleasure derived from the 'bain de multitude' is very significant. 'Faire, aux dépens du genre humain, une ribote de vitalité' / 'draw from the human race a feast of vitality' conjures up quasi-vampiristic impulses, the observer feeding from the energy of his fellow humans. This is reinforced further on, when Baudelaire describes the *flâneur*'s ability to identify with the Other in terms of a possession, with supernatural overtones ('comme ces âmes errantes qui cherchent un corps, il entre, quand il veut, dans le personnage de chacun' / 'like those wandering souls in search of a body, he enters, when he so desires, into the character of each individual'). The *flâneur* not only becomes the Other, he also owns him ('il adopte comme sienne' / 'he makes his own'), in an impulse which seems to prefigure Baudelaire's own ownership of Poe's text as enacted in 'Les Foules'.

Besides the three clear steps in the gradual integration of Poe's text into the Baudelairean corpus witnessed above (from direct translation to a biased summary to an independent prose poem), we can find in other texts more diffuse references to Poe's text and Baudelaire's reading of it. A further stage in this rewriting of Poe's story into the Baudelairean text may be found in *Un Mangeur d'opium*, where the image of the crowd as a sea recurs. Responding to De Quincey's phrase 'the great Mediterranean of Oxford Street', Baudelaire not only chooses to translate directly the phrase by 'grande Méditerranée d'Oxford Street',[32] but we also read, in a passage added to De Quincey's text:

> L'ancien écolier veut revoir cette vie des humbles; il veut se plonger au sein de cette foule de déshérités, comme le nageur embrasse la mer et entre ainsi en contact plus direct avec la nature, il aspire à prendre, pour ainsi dire, un bain de multitude.[33]

(The former student wishes to revisit the humble life of the poor. He wants to dive into the very midst of the disinherited crowd, and as the swimmer embraces the sea, thus entering into the most direct contact, so he wishes, so to speak, to take a bath among the masses.)

The liquid element is once more present ('plonger' / 'dive', 'nageur' / 'swimmer'), and, more importantly the 'bain de multitude' of 'Les Foules' resurfaces, embedded in Baudelaire's adaptation of De Quincey's text, and thereby adding another twist to the intertextual spiral.[34] Poe's text, its translation and various rewritings are concentrated into one single allusion which can be considered as the final stage of Baudelaire's appropriation of the text of the Other.

Similarly, the *Tableaux parisiens* are full of echoes and reminiscences. 'Les Petites Vieilles' (first published in its entirety in 1861), although it openly entertains intertextual links with Victor Hugo (to whom the poem is dedicated), is also very reminiscent of Poe's story:

> Dans les plis sinueux des vieilles capitales
> Où tout, même l'horreur, tourne aux enchantements
> Je guette, obéissant à mes humeurs fatales,
> Des êtres singuliers, décrépits et charmants.
>
> (In the sinuous folds of old capital cities, where everything, even horror, turns to magic, I am constantly on the watch, driven by my ineluctable whims, for certain singular beings, decrepit and delightful.)[35]

This first stanza echoes the figure of the writer as observer noted in all versions of 'L'Homme des foules'. The Paris described as a 'fourmillant tableau' ('swarming scene')[36] is a clear echo of Poe's London (which we find also in *Un Mangeur d'opium* in phrases such as 'les centres les plus *fourmillants* de la vie commune').[37] Similarly, the exclamation 'Ah! Que j'en ai suivi de ces petites vieilles' reminds us of the fascination with the Other already noted in closer transformations of Poe.[38] In this respect, the use of the first person emphasises the presence of Baudelaire's subjectivity and, to some extent, his identification with Poe's narrator, or at least a similar position. The thematic links between this poem and Poe's story reveal one reason for Baudelaire's interest and his need to rewrite it. They may also be seen as the ultimate in Baudelaire's blending of the foreign text into his own writings.

From direct translation to diffuse allusion, we find in the examples explored in the first section of this chapter a whole range of gradual integration of the text of the Other into the Baudelairean text. The dialogue with the foreign which has been highlighted by this study seems motivated by a thematic affinity with the hypotext which in turn is the basis for an appropriation and transformation of that hypotext. Baudelaire's aesthetics of the city and of modernity (as developed in 'Les Foules', *le Peintre de la vie moderne* or the *Tableaux parisiens*) is at least partly derived from a rewriting of earlier texts. This raises issues regarding the relationship between orginality and tradition in modernism, which the second part of this chapter will try to explore.

2. 'Épouvante et ravissement'

As has already been noted in passing, the very thematics of Poe's 'Man of the Crowd' (an encounter which forms the basis of fascination and contemplation) prefigure the dialogue with the foreign which is at the core of both the act of translation and modernist writing. This dialogue is also enacted in a very concrete manner by Poe's style: the text of 'The Man of the Crowd' is sprinkled with quotations and intertextual references (in French, Greek, German, from La Bruyère, Gorgias and Leibnitz), as well as French words throughout the text, which make this text an intensely dialogic one.

This aspect is echoed, as in many of Poe's stories, by the theme of the double – in 'The Man of the Crowd', the narrator follows obsessively the man who has caught his eye ('when suddenly there came into view a countenance (that of a decrepid old man, some sixty-five or seventy years of age) – a countenance which at once arrested and absorbed my whole attention').[39] This encounter with and fascination for the Other is recurrent in many of Poe's stories, and seems to echo the relationship between author and translator, as well as between writer and precursor. It does indeed emphasise the fascination felt by the translator for the author, and the creativity stemming from the encounter: the 'épouvante et ravissement' ('terror and delight') felt by Baudelaire at the discovery of Poe projects him into a re-enactment of the fantastic theme of the double so dear to Poe.[40] Thus the 'contemplation', 'fascination' and even 'passion' inscribed in Baudelaire's man of the crowd may also be seen as his own reaction to his encounter with a literary precursor.

In terms of translation, this 'épouvante et ravissement', or 'incroyable sympathie' as Baudelaire also called it,[41] is highly problematic. It has indeed strong overtones of a Bloomian anxiety of influence, with all the appropriative tendencies this anxiety may trigger. Baudelaire identifies with the admired author and finds himself in his text. The 'épouvante et ravissement' described by Baudelaire are emblematic of his ambivalence at such a discovery. The pleasure of the text is experienced together with a discovery of the impossibility of true originality.

In this respect, the epigraph to 'The Man of the Crowd' is a case in point. Poe's story starts with a paraphrase (in French) of La Bruyère's 'tout notre mal vient de ne pouvoir être seul',[42] which Poe rewrites as 'ce grand malheur de ne pouvoir être seul'. In his translation of Poe's story, Baudelaire further rewrites La Bruyère by adding an exclamation mark to the statement ('Ce grand malheur de ne pouvoir être seul!'). The small modifications operated by the successive readers of La Bruyère's statement are interesting from several points of view. First, they remind us of the impossibility of exact repetition: as Antoine Compagnon shows in *La Seconde Main ou le travail de la citation*, even in the act of quoting, the change in context (whether textual, temporal, or spatial), and the new voice(s) involved through new intertextual relationships mean that the quoted text is transformed by the very act of quotation.[43] In the case of the quotation from La Bruyère, this impossible repetition is enacted by the small transformations made by Poe and Baudelaire. In addition, we could say that these modifications act as a *mise en abyme* of Baudelaire's anxiety of influence: the addition of the exclamation mark, and the increased subjectivity it implies, emphasise his own concerns and at the same time enact the transformative dimension of reading and translation. Baudelaire's empathy with the quotation leads him to add an exclamation mark and thereby blend his voice and La Bruyère's. The 'malheur de ne pouvoir être seul' may thus be read as referring to the anxiety of belonging to a literary tradition, of finding literary brothers. In other words we can read the epigraph as an allegory of Baudelaire's relationship to his source author which blends a sense of identification and one of rivalry. In the quest for the new, central to the Baudelairean quest ('Plonger au fond du gouffre pour trouver du nouveau'), the text of the Other remains an obstacle as well as a help.

Seen from this point of view, the question of affinity in translation raises other – but related – issues too: as Lawrence Venuti notes in *The Translator's Invisibility*, affinity is a subjective feeling, and when applied to a source text, may be a pretext for an appropriation of this source text to the purposes of the translator. Baudelaire's sense of kinship with Poe would then be the starting point of a domestication of the American author to his own poetic and creative purposes. As Valéry writes:

> L'homme ne peut qu'il ne s'approprie ce qui lui semble si exactement *fait pour lui* qu'il le regarde malgré soi comme fait *par lui*… Il tend irrésistiblement à s'emparer de ce qui convient étroitement à sa personne; et le langage même confond sous le nom de *bien* la notion de ce qui est adapté à quelqu'un et le satisfait entièrement avec celle de la propriété de ce quelqu'un.[44]

> (Man cannot but appropriate what seems so exactly *made for him* that he looks at it despite himself as made *by himself*… He tends inexorably to grasp what suits him closely; and language itself joins under the word '*good*' the notion of what is adapted to someone and satisfies him perfectly, and that of that someone's property.)

In the context of a quest for the new, this appropriative dimension of intertextuality is of course problematic, since the existence of literary models and tradition seems to contradict the very concept of novelty. And yet new forms arise from this very tension. If we read Baudelaire's version of 'The Man of the Crowd' metaphorically, the 'giving up' noted earlier ('renonçant à le suivre') gives way to creative 'contemplation'. The failure of imitation and repetition is what stimulates the creation of the new. This relationship between imitation and the new seems to be central to Baudelaire's perception of writing. His most innovative work – *Le Spleen de Paris* – is presented as a failure of imitation:

> Mon point de départ a été *Gaspard de la nuit* d'Aloysius Bertrand, que vous connaissez sans aucun doute; mais j'ai bien vite senti que je ne pouvais pas persévérer dans ce pastiche et que l'œuvre était inimitable. Je *me suis résigné à être moi-même*.[45]

> (My starting point was Aloysius Bertrand's *Gaspard de la nuit*, which you undoubtedly know. But I soon felt that I could not persevere in

this pastiche and that the work could not be imitated. I *became resigned to being myself*.)

The resignation to be oneself is reminiscent of the abandonment of the chase and the ensuing contemplation noted before. The tension between novelty and the literary model emphasised by Baudelaire is precisely what enables him to create a new literary form (the prose poem), and it is through highly hypertextual prose poems such as 'Les Foules' that he reinforces his modern aesthetics of the city. Theories of intertextuality have shown that such tension is integral to literary history. What makes Baudelaire stand out in this respect, however, is the conscious rewriting of his sources and his explicitly intertextual writing as part of a search for an art of modernity, which is resolved through a dialogue with and appropriation of precursors' texts, as I hope to have shown with the example of his use of Poe's 'Man of the Crowd'.

Baudelaire's appeal to modernist writers is grounded in his search for an art of modernity, but also in his dialogue with the foreign. Baudelaire's dialogue with national and international precursors, be they writers, painters, or musicians,[46] could not but appeal to a generation which was itself concerned with an aesthetic based on such a dialogue, with all the transformations and appropriations it involved. In this respect, T.S. Eliot's article 'From Poe to Valéry', which focuses on French readings of Poe by Baudelaire, Mallarmé and Valéry, is a case in point: it emphasises the importance of intertextuality, the transformative dimension of reading and influence, and the centrality of the foreign in literary history, thus providing one more example of the modernists' interest in the foreign and the issues that surround that interest. Eliot's reading of Baudelaire's encounter with Poe is revealing:

> It is certainly possible, in reading something in a language imperfectly understood, for the reader to find what is not there; and when the reader is himself a man of genius, the foreign poem read may, by a happy accident, elicit something important from the depths of his own mind, which he attributes to what he reads. And it is true that in translating Poe's prose into French, Baudelaire effected a striking improvement: he transformed what is often a slipshod and a shoddy English prose into admirable French.[47]

Without entering into the well-worn debate on Baudelaire's knowledge of English or the relative value of Poe as an American writer (as opposed to as a writer translated into French), we can note Eliot's admiration for the transformative dimension of Baudelaire's approach to Poe, which he ascribes to a misreading (we are very close to Bloom's 'anxiety of influence' and misreading theory). Similarly, Eliot praises Baudelaire's 'Le Guignon' (a poem derived from Gray's 'Elegy Written in a Country Churchyard' and Longfellow's 'A Psalm of Life') in terms of the relationship between the French poem and its sources: 'so original is the arrangement of words that we might easily overlook its borrowing from Gray's *Elegy*'.[48] In other words, Eliot's admiration for the poem seems partly due to Baudelaire's successful appropriation of his sources, which grants him originality despite the prominence of these sources as intertexts of the poem. The apparent contradiction between the quest for the new and indebtedness to sources is therefore erased.

Expressed by T.S. Eliot, such views reveal modernist concerns for a dialogue with the foreign. Paul Valéry, whose 'Situation de Baudelaire' (first published in 1929) may be considered as one of the central modernist readings of Baudelaire, provides the other side of the coin. Whereas Eliot focuses on Baudelaire's transformation of Poe, Valéry emphasises the encounter with Edgar Allan Poe as formative and writes of its effect on Baudelaire: 'son talent en est transformé, sa destinée en est magnifiquement changée' ('his talent is transformed, his fate magnificently changed').[49] Valéry's reading of Baudelaire's relationship to Poe's works, which he calls a 'magical contact between two minds',[50] is both a reminder of the deeply intertextual dimension of Baudelaire's writing, and an indirect statement on the importance of intertextuality in modernist literature.

Thus Baudelaire's transformation of his sources seems to announce his rewriting by subsequent writers. For the modernists, this very appeal and its appropriative consequences are a clear sign of Baudelaire's importance in literary history:

> [...] avec Baudelaire, la poésie française sort enfin des frontières de la nation. Elle se fait lire dans le monde; elle s'impose comme la poésie même de la modernité; elle engendre l'imitation, elle féconde de nombreux esprits. Des hommes tels que Swinburne, Gabrielle d'Annunzio, Stefan George, témoignent magnifiquement de l'influence baudelairienne à l'extérieur.[51]

> ([…] with Baudelaire, French poetry finally went out of the nation. It was read in the world. It imposed itself as the poetry of modernity. It engendered imitation, fecundated many minds. Men like Swinburne, Gabrielle d'Annunzio, Stefan George, are magnificent examples of the Baudelairean influence abroad.)

Eliot's reflection on French readings of Poe makes a similar point: 'I find that by trying to look at Poe through the eyes of Baudelaire, Mallarmé and most of all Valéry, I become more thoroughly convinced of his importance, of the importance of his *work* as a whole'.[52]

The transplantation of a national author into an international context, such as that of Poe into the French context, or of Baudelaire into the English context, is inevitably accompanied by a repositioning of that author. As Patricia Clements, who calls Baudelaire the 'begetter of the modern in English literature',[53] notes:

> By the time the modernists were producing their finest works, then, Baudelaire was solidly canonized, part of a conversation that had become almost wholly English. When Eliot recommended him as the exemplar of modern poetry, Baudelaire was a domesticated influence, an aspect now not chiefly of the relation of English literature to French, but of the English tradition itself.[54]

As I hope to have shown, the example of Baudelaire's domestication of Poe and his integration into his own literary corpus – and thereby the French literary tradition – is thus not only an example of his own dialogue with the foreign. It is also symptomatic of the growing importance of international literary links in the prehistory of modernism, an importance which quickly becomes central in modernism and its search for novelty.

NOTES TO CHAPTER II

Notes to Chapter II

1. I am following Walter Gobbers' useful definition of modernism and modernity: 'Personally I would prefer to view 'modernism' as dependent on, and defined by 'modernity', in that 'modernity' denotes a social and cultural climate, summing up at the same time the essence of its character. 'Modernism', for its part, stands for the spirit inherent in modernity, notably the taste of the cult of what is novel, and at the same time for the artistic response to this modernity, or for its artistic mode of expression, perhaps materializing in a movement of literary renewal.', in 'Modernism, Modernity, Avant Garde', in *The Turn of the Century, Modernism and Modernity in Literature and the Arts*, ed. Christian Berg, Frank Durieux, Geert Lernout (Berlin, New York: Walter de Gruyter, 1995), pp.3-16, p.5.
2. Letter to Madame Aupick, 8 March 1854, *Correspondance I* (hereafter referred to as *CI*) (Paris: Gallimard, 1973), p.269.
3. Edgar Allan Poe, 'The Man of the Crowd' (hereafter referred to as *MOC*), in *The Complete Tales and Poems* (New York: Dorset Press, 1989), p.309.
4. *Œuvres Complètes I* (hereafter referred to as *OCI*) (Paris: Gallimard, 1975), p.358. Translations are mine unless otherwise indicated.
5. Respectively 'L'Homme des foules' (hereafter referred to as *HDF*), Edgar Allan Poe, *Œuvres en prose*, trans. Charles Baudelaire, ed. Y.-G. Le Dantec (Paris: Gallimard, 1951), p.332; *MOC*, p.314.
6. See '*ennui*' (p.308), '*bon ton*' (p.309), '*roquelaire*' (p.312).
7. *HDF*, p.325; *MOC*, p.309.
8. *MOC*, p.310; *HDF*, p.325.
9. *MOC*, p.310; *HDF*, p.326.
10. See my book, *Alchemy and Amalgam: Translation in the Works of Charles Baudelaire* (Amsterdam: Rodopi, due out in 2002).
11. *MOC*, p.309; *HDF*, p.324.
12. *MOC*, p.310; *HDF*, p.325.
13. *MOC*, p.311; *HDF*, p.328.
14. 'Edgar Poe Romancier américain', *Figaro*, 27 March 1856 (p.7).
15. *MOC*, p.311; *HDF*, p.328.
16. *MOC*, p.311; *HDF*, p.328.
17. *MOC*, p.312; *HDF*, p.328.
18. *MOC*, p.313; *HDF*, p.331.
19. *MOC*, p.314; *HDF*, p.331.
20. *MOC*, p.314; *HDF*, p.332.
21. *MOC*, p.313; *HDF*, p.330.
22. *MOC*, p.314; *HDF*, p.332.
23. *MOC*, pp.309, 311.

24. *MOC*, p.308; *HDF*, p.324.

25. *MOC*, p.314; *HDF*, p.332.

26. *Œuvres Complètes II* (hereafter referred to as *OCII*), pp.689-90.

27. Translated by Jonathan Mayne, in *The Painter of Modern Life and Other Essays* (London: Phaidon Press, 1964), p.7.

28. *OCII*, p.691.

29. Translation by Jonathan Mayne, op.cit. p.9.

30. Translation by Rosemary Lloyd, in *The Prose Poems and La Fanfarlo* (Oxford: Oxford University Press, 1991), pp.44-45.

31. *OCI*, p.649.

32. ibid., p.460, De Quincey OUP, p.27.

33. *OCI*, p.468.

34. Baudelaire, Poe and De Quincey seem to be in constant dialogue in the city passages of *Un Mangeur d'opium* – references to liquids are frequently entangled with the description of the city. We read, for instance, about the 'tourbillon indifférent d'une grande capitale' (*OCI*, p.468), or the 'vaste perspective de la mer et d'une grande cité' (*OCI*, pp.470-71); the narrator finds his way in the city 'd'après les principes nautiques' and discovers '*terrae incognitae*', he throws himself 'dans la foule et dans le courant humain' (*OCI*, p.470).

35. Translation by Carol Clark, in *Charles Baudelaire, Selected Poems* (Hardmonsworth: Penguin, 1995), p.92.

36. ibid., p.94.

37. *OCI*, p.470 (emphasis added).

38. In 'Les Sept Vieillards', the 'fourmillante cité, cité pleine de rêves/où le spectre en plein jour raccroche le passant' ('O swarming city, city full of dreams, where ghosts accost the passer-by in broad daylight!') (translation by Francis Scarfe, in *Baudelaire, The Complete Verse* (London: Anvill Press, 1986), p.177) may be seen as yet another version of the same theme, while the water imagery highlights another thematic link with Poe:

Vainement ma raison voulait prendre la barre

La tempête en jouant déroutait ses efforts,

Et mon âme dansait, dansait vieille gabarre

Sans mâts, sur une mer monstrueuse et sans bords!

(My reason tried to take over, but in vain: its efforts were all thwarted by the storm, and my soul danced and danced like some old mastless barge heaved on a monstrous shoreless sea.) (translation by Scarfe, p.179).

39. *MOC*, p.311.

40. Letter to Théophile Thoré, around 20 June 1864, *CII*, p.386.
41. Letter to Madame Aupick, 27 March 1852, *CI*, p.191.
42. Jean de La Bruyère, 'De l'homme', *Les Caractères* (Paris: 10/18, p.235). 'All men's misfortunes proceed from their aversion to being alone' (translated by Henri Van Laun (New York: Howard Fertig, 1992), p.307).
43. Antoine Compagnon, *La Seconde Main ou le travail de la citation* (Paris: Seuil, 1979).
44. Paul Valéry, p.608, original emphasis.
45. *CII*, p.208. Emphasis added.
46. This dialogue takes the form of translations, adaptations, and rewritings of English sources, transpositions of paintings, as well as art, literary, and (to a much lesser extent) music criticism.
47. T.S. Eliot, 'From Poe to Valéry', in *To criticize the critics and Other Writings* (London: Faber and Faber, 1965), pp.27-43, (p.36).
48. T.S. Eliot, 'Baudelaire', in *Collected Essays* (London: Faber and Faber, 1932), pp.419-30 (p.425).
49. Paul Valéry, 'Situation de Baudelaire', in *Œuvres* (Paris: NRF (Bibliothèque de la Pléiade), 1957), p.599.
50. 'ce magique contact de deux esprits', *ibid.*, p.499.
51. *ibid.*, p.598.
52. T.S. Eliot, 'From Poe to Valéry', p.42, original emphasis.
53. Patricia Clements, *Baudelaire and the English Tradition* (Princeton, New Jersey: Princeton University Press, 1985), p.4.
54. *ibid.*, pp.7-8.

CHAPTER III

Intertextual Sun-worshippers:
Marinetti's *Mafarka* and Nietzsche's *Zarathustra*

Carol Diethe

Carol Diethe lectured in the History of Ideas at Middlesex University until 1997 and is currently a Research Fellow there. She is also the Treasurer of the Friedrich Nietzsche Society, which she helped to found in 1989, serving as its first Secretary. Her publications include translations of Nietzsche's *On the Genealogy of Morality*, 1994, and Marinetti's *Mafarka the Futurist*, 1997. Her *Nietzsche's Women: Beyond the Whip*, 1996, has also been published in German, 2000. She has also compiled a *Historical Dictionary of Nietzscheanism*, 1999.

In 1915, in an essay entitled 'Contro i professori' ('Against the Professors'), Marinetti wrote, with a degree of guile which will be discussed in the following pages: 'I feel I really have to demonstrate here that the critics have been completely wrong in considering us as new Nietzscheans'.[1] In the same essay, Marinetti accuses Nietzsche of hankering after the past, in company with all other professors, and castigates him for allowing his *Übermensch*, about whom so much is promised for the future, to descend to the level of paganism and mythology. Marinetti's comment that Nietzsche's *Übermensch* is 'generated from the philosophical cult of Greek tragedy' is reinforced by the statement that he is made up of 'the elegance and beauty of Apollo, the strength of Mars and the dizziness of Dionysus'.[2] Of course, in *The Birth of Tragedy* (1872), where Greek gods abound, Nietzsche makes no mention of the *Übermensch*, whilst in *Thus Spoke Zarathustra* (1883-5) there is no direct mention of Greek gods in relation to the *Übermensch*. Yet in spite of this erroneous – and, according to McGinn,[3] – probably deliberate conflation of what are actually two distinct strands in Nietzsche's thought, Marinetti was right to highlight the paradox inherent in Nietzsche's desire to deflect our gaze away from contemporary society by referring us to the qualities in antique Greece which he wished to see reinstated by future generations, such as hardness and courage.

What I shall seek to demonstrate here is that there is a very similar paradox in Marinetti's own portrayal of Mafarka in *Mafarka the Futurist*; we shall find that this man of the future exists amid an aura of the past. In spite of Marinetti's disclaimer, it is widely acknowledged that Nietzsche had a profound effect on the Futurists[4] and we shall find the influence of Nietzsche's *Thus Spoke Zarathustra*, in particular, indelibly printed on Marinetti's novel. Already, in the mid-1960s, Armin Arnold set down a check list for examples of Nietzscheanism in *Mafarka the Futurist*: this included Mafarka's love of danger, his death wish and his superhuman strivings.[5] The point I would stress is that from the turn of the century, Nietzsche was all things to all people:

everyone took from him what they wanted. This is still true today: and it was certainly true of Marinetti.

Although in this chapter I shall chiefly examine Marinetti's frequent adoption of a Zarathustran stance (or what he understood to be a Zarathustran stance) in *Mafarka the Futurist*, only to abandon it, there are other similarities which should be mentioned at the outset. The language and punctuation are sometimes remarkably similar. Both Nietzsche and Marinetti use three dots as a fairly routine way of ending a passage, so that closure is avoided. Both writers use repetition to great effect. Nietzsche introduces the notion of the *Übermensch* only after a sonorous string of sentences which all begin with 'I love him who ...'.[6] Marinetti habitually repeats words for effect, as a glance at the quotations in this chapter will confirm. This ruse of rhetorical repetition is very reminiscent of the Old Testament, to say nothing of Nietzsche's sustained spoof on the New Testament throughout *Thus Spoke Zarathustra*. The iconoclast Marinetti likewise confuses his reader as to his intent by revelling in an acoustic bedlam when the Mullahs call the faithful to prayer: 'Allah, Allah, Allah'.[7]

This, and the constant references to animals from oxen to jackals in *Mafarka the Futurist* and the eagle, serpent and camel in *Thus Spoke Zarathustra*, give the flavour and feel of the Middle East even without Zarathustra's mockery of the Mount of Olives (*Za III*: 'On the Mount of Olives', p.193ff) or Marinetti's evocation of the magnificent funerary temples and rock-hewn tombs of Thebes in Chapter 8 ('The Hypogea'). Marinetti's experience of Alexandria, where he grew up, provides material for a constant supply of similes. Nietzsche, who had never been further South than Italy, displays a similar facility in conjuring up an exotic background. More often than Marinetti, he uses straightforward metaphors rather than similes. Compare the beginning of 'The Mount of Olives': 'Winter, an ill guest, sits in my house; my hands are blue from his friendly handshake', with the description of a victorious Mafarka sitting among his War-giraffes 'like an admiral among the tall masts of his fleet' (*MF* p.75). Both Nietzsche and Marinetti choose colours to express mood, and both allow their imaginations full rein. We follow Zarathustra and Mafarka to far-flung locations and, with them, are exposed to the elements.

In a way similar to *Thus Spoke Zarathustra*, which is divided into four parts which differ markedly in content and tone, *Mafarka the*

Futurist falls naturally into two distinct parts consisting of the chapters which lead up to the death of Magamal (Mafarka's younger brother) depicting Mafarka as a bullish warlord and latter-day Antar[8] capable of every treacherous ploy, and the chapters after the death of Magamal which portray a changed Mafarka, a recluse who communes with the elements and with inanimate objects such as the branches of trees, and who shuns his fellow men. This chastened Mafarka is the man who most resembles Nietzsche's Zarathustra in his disillusionment about mankind in general and in his wish, not just to see a new type of man emerge, but to actually create that new being. Gazourmah's belligerence matches that of his father earlier in the novel – the Mafarka who won battles and gave thanks for good omens:

> You protect me, O winged God, God of speed and frantic spasm, God of sweat, death rattle and death pangs! […] I give you thanks! Allah!, Look here! … I kneel and kiss your feet! (*MF* p.75)

By worshipping Allah and the Sun in the same breath, Mafarka displays a primitivism very much in vogue (especially in painting, as with the Fauves), but it is equally true that at the time Marinetti wrote his novel, any mention of sun-worshipping would be construed as a clear reference to *Thus Spoke Zarathustra*, which begins with Zarathustra's hubristic address to the Sun: 'Great Star! What would your happiness be, if you had not those for whom you shine?' (*Za I*: 'Zarathustra's Prologue', p.39). This hubris, which contains its own resonance of Goethe's poem *Prometheus*,[9] will in its turn be echoed later in Marinetti's novel when Gazourmah declares himself to be the master of the Sun: 'Oh Sun, my slave […] On your knees! … Kiss my feet!' (*MF* p.199).

What we are witnessing in tracing Nietzsche's intertextual influence is the way a myth enters a culture. At the turn of the century, there were all sorts of interest groups – nudists, vegetarians, campaigners for free love and so on – who claimed allegiance to a Nietzsche they themselves had constructed.[10] From the turn of the century, Nietzsche enthusiasts could usually be defined by whether they were influenced most by *The Birth of Tragedy* (in which case they often manifested Dionysian abandonment with much gusto)[11] or *Thus Spoke Zarathustra*, in which case a certain belligerence was felt to be *de rigueur*. Marinetti belonged very firmly to the latter camp. Of course Nietzsche, by naming his protagonist Zarathustra after the historical fire-worshipping Persian prophet Zoroaster, who was born around 660 BC and who is described in the *Avesta* as exhorting his followers to fight evil and pursue what is good, deliberately anchored his book in an indeterminate span of time in antiquity, an impression which the reader retains in spite of the work's oblique references to the present and its many exhortations about the future. In a similar fashion, Mafarka, by apostrophising the Sun and other stars (amongst them Sirius, the brightest star in the sky and Vega, the second brightest in the Northern hemisphere, *MF* p.36), evokes not only Zoroastrians but more specifically their African descendants, the star-worshipping Sabians.[12] True to these ancestors, Mafarka glories in the starry sky as he waits for the dawn to arrive: 'And you, our own Sun, you're taking your own good time this morning to hoist yourself on to the horizon …' (*MF* 35-36).

The North African backdrop also provides a possible link with Marinetti's pronounced misogyny, which in the novel is much more crude than anything suggested by Nietzsche. As a boy in Alexandria, Marinetti would probably have heard rumours about the homosexual culture at nearby Siwa, which even countenanced homosexual 'marriages' or bonded pairs. These probably originated as an aid to morale in battle rather than as an outright rejection of women. The men involved, known as the *zaggalah*,[13] still populated Siwa in spite of official Koranic disapproval of homosexuality, so that the oasis was notorious as a sort of homosexual red-light district. But even if Marinetti had been immune to the stories circulating about the *zaggalah* at Siwa, the fact remains that women were second-class citizens in the North Africa of Marinetti's youth, something which possibly influenced his inclusion of scorn for woman in his literary programme. This coincided with the profound unease towards female sexuality which characterised the literature, music and painting of the European avant-garde around the *fin de siècle*, a tradition which Marinetti both assimilated and challenged when he joined the French literary scene in the early years of the century. Contempt for woman, whose guile is described as infinitely dangerous to man, pervades Marinetti's novel, which sets out to show that man can procreate without the need for the participation of any woman. It will now be my task to assess to what extent Nietzsche might have influenced this attitude.

It remains a conundrum that Nietzsche, and after him almost the entire literary and artistic avant-garde (including the Futurists), chose to align with the interests of the declared enemy, the chauvinistic bourgeoisie, in a systematic attack on feminism. Marinetti's own ambivalent stance is typical; he admired the Suffragettes because they were engaged in a fight (in fact, their window-breaking tactics were at the centre of national debate during his visit to Britain in 1912)[14] but, with characteristic inconsistency, denied that women should be awarded emancipation. Nietzsche, too, was implacably opposed to feminism because he shared the belief, common at the time, that the feminist was a freak, a lesbian who could not or would not bear children. She belonged to 'the underprivileged whose most fundamental instinct is revenge'.[15] Nietzsche's own position on the woman question was based on his belief that heroes had emerged in pre-Socratic Greece because their mothers had been able to devote themselves completely to their offspring. The impoverishment in women's lives which this must have entailed does not appear to have occurred to him, so sure was he that society itself was thereby enriched. As Diana Behler has pointed out, Nietzsche envisaged these women as vegetating in the shadows but held in a certain awe; once the state began to decline in ancient Greece, the domestic role of woman came to be seen as 'possessing the healing power of nature for the state'.[16] Nietzsche's tone in the early fragment on the Greek woman (written in 1872) lacks the brittle edge it would later develop:

> The Hellenic woman as mother had to live in obscurity, because the political instinct together with its highest aim demanded it. She *had* to vegetate like a plant, in the narrow circle [...] Women have indeed really the power to make good to a certain extent the deficiencies of the State – ever faithful to their nature, which I have compared to sleep.[17]

In spite of Nietzsche's apparently backward-looking position on woman's place in society, he did not share the Wilhelmine prudery which sought to insist upon the genteel woman's lack of sex drive; in fact, he believed that women were sexually driven, but that this meant they were in pursuit of men for one thing only, a child. This view of woman as manipulator jars somewhat with his comment that girls should not be brought up in ignorance of the facts of life[18] – a recognition, then, that young women were manipulated by their educators. Be that as it may, Nietzsche vigorously opposed women's scholastic aspirations, something which automatically put him in opposition to feminists of every faction in Germany, who were united only in their call for better educational opportunities for women.[19] The fact that Nietzsche simultaneously conducted warm friendships with some of the most scholarly of these feminists is analogous to Marinetti's similar tendency to ignore his own preaching, and indeed, for all the anti-woman rhetoric in *Mafarka the Futurist*, Marinetti appears to have been the model husband and *pater familias*. As he explains in his preface to *Mafarka the Futurist*, having just raised the topic of scorn for women: '[...] it isn't woman's animal value that I'm talking about, but her sentimental importance' (*MF* p.1-2). However, he then proceeds to write about woman's animal nature in the novel at some length, retaining Nietzsche's ideal of Oriental seclusion in the exotic description of Magamal's bride, Ouarabelli-Charchar, but also relishing the descriptions of hetari-type slave women whom Mafarka proceeds to abuse. The age-old distinctions of woman as housewife or whore survive intact in this self-styled 'great fire-brand novel' (*MF* p.1), as indeed they do in Nietzsche's thought.

In *Mafarka the Futurist*, then, Marinetti creates a sense of antiquity not only through references to solar worship but also through the atmosphere of male sexual dominance pervading the novel. In addition, Marinetti adopts the same attitude towards female sexuality as Nietzsche, who had already characterised it as animalistically unfettered when not bridled by the customs of society, and potentially hazardous to the male, though one should also note that such a view had been peddled by Flaubert in *Salammbô* (1862), itself a strong influence on *Mafarka the Futurist*.[20] Marinetti thus portrays nearly all the female characters in the novel as being in a permanent state of sexual arousal. His underlying doctrine that women are redundant, even for procreation – announced provocatively in the preface to *Mafarka the Futurist* but dormant as a theme until the closing chapters – makes it a logical step for him to portray their sexual desire as both predatory and self-destructive. Female sexuality is thus presented as little short of a death wish, with the raped Biba, for example, begging her rapist: 'Mahmood, Mahmood, kill me, kill me like this!' (*MF* p.25).

Mafarka himself displays savage misogyny in throwing his deposed uncle's favourite dancers to the sharks, crying 'Curse you! Curse you! [...] All the poison of hell is in your eyes, and the saliva on your lips shines to kill … yes, to kill as well as daggers, or still better!' (*MF* p.102).

Death, sex and violence towards women are thus constantly linked throughout the novel, from the notorious rape scene, the centre of attack during the novel's obscenity trials in 1910 (which Marinetti characteristically milked for their publicity value) to Magamal's ill-fated nuptials, which end with his immolation of Ouarabelli-Charchar in a rabid frenzy on what was supposed to be her bridal night. Such instances entitle one to suggest that Marinetti's novel was the most misogynist publication of the European avant-garde,[21] though it was not without rivals in the field, such as Kokoschka's *Mörder, Hoffnung der Frauen* (*Murderer, Hope of Women*) (1909-17). Indeed, from the turn of the 19th century, depictions of the power of the potentially destructive *femme fatale* had been commonplace in literature, paintings and films.

Although some of the misogyny in *Mafarka the Futurist*, as well as much of the ribald humour such as that surrounding the tale of Mafarka's miraculously elongated penis, goes back to Rabelais,[22] Marinetti's fellow Modernists were much more likely to pin it down to the influence of the recently deceased Nietzsche. It was widely believed that Nietzsche, through his comments on the predatory nature of female sexuality, had endorsed violence towards woman as a sort of justified pre-emptive strike. In particular, whilst he was still alive (though by then in his benighted state), controversy raged round his delphic comment in *Thus Spoke Zarathustra*, in the mouth of an old crone: 'Are you visiting women? Do not forget your whip!' (*Za I*: 'Of Old and Young Women', p.93).[23] Nietzsche's contemporaries tended to take this as indicative of his own point of view, but various recent readings have sought to downplay the misogyny of this particular passage; in particular, Annemarie Pieper has stressed that the crone does not make it conclusively clear that the whip would be used on the woman rather than the other way round[24] (though I would argue that the suggestion that man has anything to fear from his visit to a woman then becomes equally problematic.)[25] It is, however, convincing that the crone comes off best in her encounter with Zarathustra, who is usually accustomed to having the last word but on this occasion is silenced. Speculative critics like Hermann-Josef Schmidt are inclined to trace such passages back to emotional disturbances in Nietzsche's early years.[26] Nietzsche remained deliberately elusive and, like Marinetti, no doubt anticipated disputes about his meaning with considerable relish.

At all events, Marinetti depicts the wraith-like Coloubbi in *Mafarka the Futurist* as a doomed yet dangerous *femme fatale* familiar from Nietzsche's pronouncements,[27] though her ethereal substance might also suggest an interpretation of her function in line with current trends which speak of Nietzsche's use of the term 'woman' as a trope (for example, woman as truth).[28] Coloubbi raises other issues closer to home, such as Marinetti's obsessive desire to debunk romantic love. Suffice it to say here that Marinetti and his contemporaries interpreted female sexuality in line with what were commonly perceived as Nietzschean precepts summed up in Zarathustra's remark: 'For the woman, the man is a means: the end is always the child' (*Za I*: 'Of Old and Young Women', p.91). Coloubbi seems to bear this out by declaring that, simply by having watched Gazourmah's birth (in other words, by having witnessed the fateful and fatal kiss by which Mafarka breathes life into his artefact), she is thereby co-parent of Gazourmah, his mother, something which infuriates Mafarka and his 'son' in equal measure. Although Marinetti almost certainly knew nothing of Otto Weininger's *Geschlecht und Charakter* (*Sex and Character*, 1903), it is noteworthy that in this work a similar view of long-distance fecundation is mooted – Weininger advises men to be wary of their gaze, since women can be impregnated even without coitus: 'The woman is impregnated not only through the genital tract but through every fibre of her being'.[29] Weininger himself firmly believed he was following Nietzsche's precepts when he declared: 'The maternal woman regards the sexual relations as a means to an end'.[30] Gazourmah's brutal reaction to Coloubbi's lustful advance is to fly straight into her, an act of cruelty which will have cosmic consequences at the close of the novel: 'You've crushed my heart under your ribs of bronze! ... It is the Earth you've killed in killing me! ... Soon you will hear her first death throes.' (*MF* p.202). In order for us to assess the importance of the murder of Coloubbi, we must recall the official Futurist standpoint on woman's maternal function:

> For Futurism there was only one woman – the mother – who with her immense natural energy conquered and absorbed the totality of the world; while the beloved male was the father – Marinetti – accumulator of a vital charge as a being capable of performing the possible and impossible through his infinite fertility.[31]

Naturally, the above description of woman as Earth Mother conflicts with the fantastic venture upon which Mafarka is engaged, since it is Mafarka's express purpose to create a son without the aid of woman. Perhaps the cataclysmic end to the novel which follows the despatch of Coloubbi represents Marinetti's own acknowledgement that to make female reproduction redundant would spell out the end of the world as we know it.

The novel also strains against its own anti-woman logic by portraying Mafarka as a dutiful son communing with the spirit of his mother. The function in the novel of Langourama, a caryatid woken from the sleep of death, is only intelligible if one realises the depth of feeling the Futurists invested in affirming woman's mothering role: Marinetti in *Mafarka the Futurist* provides a notable exception to this by stating in the Preface that childbirth is passé, yet Mafarka himself is devoted to his dead mother to an unnatural degree. The Freudian hints, that there could be a longer tale to tell of this relationship between Mafarka and his mother, whose spirit whispers: '… I'm offering my lips beneath the wood of the coffin … Yes! Yes! I can feel the heat of your lips! …' (*MF* p.194), indicate Marinetti's own ambivalence on the matter, with the mother revered on principle, but represented nevertheless as an encumbrance who arouses feelings of guilt in Mafarka. I do not, however, share Kaplan's view that Mafarka takes on a female role and becomes a 'martyred mother' by bringing Gazourmah into the world, complete with a birthing topology which Kaplan refers to as 'an obviously uterine landscape'[32] – Mafarka's journey down the corridors of the Hypogeum in search of his mother's coffin (*MF* p.193) – and that he becomes weak and effeminate thereby. It is much more likely that, rather than descending to such 'feminisation' through some error of judgement which necessitates Gazourmah's arrival 'to rescue the narrative',[33] Marinetti is echoing Nietzsche's symbolic use of the birth metaphor in *Thus Spoke Zarathustra*: 'For the creator himself to be the child new-born he must also be willing to be the mother and endure the mother's pain' (*Za II*: 'On the Blissful Islands', p.111). This would align with Graybeal's argument that pregnancy is 'Nietzsche's image for creation, for fertility, for the possibility of the new'.[34] In situating Langourama in a coffin carried by Mafarka, Marinetti graphically portrays the burden she creates for her son. This 'weight', being both physical and metaphysical, is similar to Tereza's suitcase full of unresolved childhood conflicts (particularly with regard to her mother) in Milan Kundera's novel *The Unbearable Lightness of Being* (1984), itself inspired by Nietzsche, as the title indicates.[35] A very great deal has recently been written about Nietzsche's faulty relationship with his mother,[36] and it is probably fair to suggest that his difficulties with Franziska found their way into his writing, though the relationship of a writer to his/her text is always contentious. Kelly Oliver has stressed that Nietzsche 'continually struggles to separate from the maternal' in his work.[37] This is also true of Mafarka, though Marinetti's own relationship with his mother does not appear to have been as fraught and intense as that of Nietzsche and Franziska. What is certain is that Marinetti himself felt an irrational burden of guilt when his elder brother Leone, his mother's favourite, died whilst Marinetti was a student.[38]

As mentioned at the outset, we must be sceptical about Marinetti's denial of the influence of Nietzsche on Futurism. Marinetti was certainly much less interested in Nietzsche's serious philosophical challenge to moral precepts than in his ideas on *amor fati* and the will to power, which Nietzsche introduced in *Thus Spoke Zarathustra*: 'Only where life is, there is also will: not will to life, but – so I teach you – will to power!' (*Za II*: 'Of Self-Overcoming', p.138). In addition, *Der Wille zur Macht* (*The Will to Power*), Elisabeth Förster-Nietzsche's compilation of Nietzsche's rejected jottings, had appeared in 1901.[39] Marinetti manipulates Nietzsche's theory on the will to power after his own manner. In the ninth chapter of *Mafarka the Futurist* ('Futurist Address'), in which Mafarka's men have come in sailing ships to look for him, and in doing so have placed themselves in great danger, Mafarka reveals to them his 'religion of externalised Will and Heroism', which will be discussed below. Having apparently followed Zarathustra's advice on the creativity of the self, Mafarka declares to his men: 'At last, here I am as I wanted to be: destined for suicide, and ready for the birth of the god that each man carries in his heart!' (*MF* p.148). The problem is that Mafarka has not created himself, he has created Gazourmah. The difficult thing for the Nietzschean *Übermensch* is to *live*, not to die: for him, the war is not against others, but against the self. Marinetti appears to have taken at face value Nietzsche's proposition that cruelty is an integral part of 'higher culture',[40] and similarly, Nietzsche's apparent endorsement of war in

Zarathustra's command: 'You should love peace as a means to new wars' (*Za I*: 'Of War and Warriors', p.74). Both in *Mafarka the Futurist* (*MF* p.2) and 'The Founding and Manifesto of Futurism', Marinetti refers to war as 'the world's only hygiene'.[41] Marinetti, like many of his contemporaries who used Nietzschean pronouncements as a battle cry in the period prior to the Great War, preferred to accept a belligerent Zarathustra rather than interrogate Nietzsche's actual text. After all, who *is* the enemy in *Thus Spoke Zarathustra*? Not other people so much as other ideas and negative thoughts like *ressentiment*. Zarathustra tells his brothers in war:

> You are not great enough not to know hatred and envy. So be great enough not to be ashamed of them! And if you cannot be saints of knowledge, at least be its warriors ... You should seek your enemy, you should wage your war – a war for your opinions. (*Za I*: 'Of War and Warriors', p.74)

The subtlety of Nietzsche's text was lost on a generation gripped by war fervour and dazzled by Georges Sorel's seductive pronouncements, in *Réflections sur la violence* (1908), on the function of violence in society. Marinetti's descent into Fascism will not be dealt with here, though Barbara Spackmann has used *Mafarka the Futurist* as the principal text for a discussion of the link between the Italian dash for colonies – the Italian war with Libya took place in Tripoli in 1911 – and male exercise of power over women.[42]

As indicated already, Mafarka undergoes a paradigm shift from ruthless warrior to a nomad wild with grief, but he is not reborn in the Nietzschean sense of self-overcoming (*Za III*: 'Of Old and New Law-Tables', p.216: 'Man is something that must be overcome'). What, then, of Gazourmah, less a New Man in Expressionist mode than a computer ahead of his time? Gazourmah is indeed problematic, since he fulfils two purposes which are not necessarily linked: he is the mechanical apotheosis of the human will as well as being the vehicle for Marinetti's anti-woman diatribe. In the latter capacity, he is remarkably effective, since the creation of Gazourmah is all the more insulting to women in the light of the Futurist view that child-bearing is a woman's sole function. Mafarka's exultant comment goes far beyond Nietzsche's worst misogyny:

Oh! The joy of having given birth to you like this – handsome, free of all the blemishes that come from the inefficient vulva and bias us to old age and death! (*MF* p.188)

In Gazourmah's other capacity as embodiment of will, Marinetti is able to go beyond Nietzsche's rejection of science because he has a superior knowledge of aviation, the *dernier cri* when he was at work on his novel. When Zarathustra/ Nietzsche looks into the sky, it makes him want to fly; Mafarka/Marinetti knows how this can be achieved. If we recall earlier remarks made on the subject of sun worship, it becomes clear that neither Nietzsche nor Marinetti were interested in the beauty of the sun or sky for aesthetic or emotional satisfaction alone, but as a springboard for their theories on the human will. In the beautiful section 'Before Sunrise' in *Thus Spoke Zarathustra*, Nietzsche, using Zarathustra as mouthpiece, exults in the blue sky as he waits for the dawn:

> And all my wandering and mountain-climbing: it was merely a necessity and an expedient of my clumsiness: my whole will desires only to fly, to fly into you! (*Za III*: 'Before Sunrise', p.185)

Marinetti, obsessed with flight, makes Gazourmah a 'living aeroplane' by an act of Mafarka's will, significantly enough at sunrise. Though Mafarka has formerly worshipped the Sun, Gazourmah is the Sun's enemy and the moment of his birth is not auspicious: 'There in the furthest distance, on the limit of the horizon, the Sun, that smouldering serpent, stabbed into space with his poisonous golden tongue …' (*MF* p.196). If sunrise befits the birth metaphor used by both Nietzsche and Marinetti, the ways part thereafter, with Zarathustra/Nietzsche pursuing an agenda of moral regeneration which will ultimately benefit mankind by producing a race of *Übermenschen*, while Mafarka harbours 'designs to conquer the sun and to engineer the prototype of a perfected, mechanised race'.[43] Mafarka uses pseudo-science based on solar energy to bring about this new life and in this respect is the direct literary heir to Mary Shelley's Baron Frankenstein.

I would now like to indicate briefly the influence to be detected in *Mafarka the Futurist* of Henri Bergson, himself a Nietzschean, whom Marinetti greatly admired, specifically endorsing his idea that 'life is a current sent through matter, drawing from it what it can'.[44] In 1907, Bergson's *L'Évolution créatrice* (*Creative Evolution*) had been published; Marinetti almost certainly read this in French, though in 1909, the year in which Marinetti's *Mafarka the Futurist* appeared, Giovanni Papini published a selection of Bergson's work in Italian under the title *Filosofia dell'intuizione* (*The Philosophy of Intuition*). In outlining the essentials of *élan vital*, Bergson posited that solar energy was stored in every living organism, to be released in a series of small explosions governed by the will. This notion helps to make sense of the otherwise cryptic passage in the novel in which Mafarka seeks to explain his 'religion of externalised Will and everyday Heroism':

> Here's my thought, clenched like my fist ... Just as there are countless fragments of organic matter whirling round the Sun, receiving its light and remaining attached to it by invisible but indestructible links and by a filial loyalty; likewise, each of us receives continual light from the universe, and is sometimes enriched by memories and sensations it received on its pilgrimage, during the infinite transformations that its immortal matter has passed through! ... (*MF* p.146)

The involuntary process described by Bergson, whereby irradiated particles produce life by means of constant explosions so imperceptible that the impression is one of constant flux, also meant that 'there are no things, there are only actions ... In reality, life is movement'.[45] What Marinetti extrapolated from these ideas is that inanimate objects are pervaded by the same force as that which pervades animate subjects; this gave him the springboard for the assumption, which of course he could not prove, that matter can think. We should pause to consider recent theories on artificial intelligence and 'the ghost in the machine' before dismissing Marinetti's ideas outright. Mafarka's Gazourmah had soared into space long before K9 stepped into the Tardis with Dr Who, to say nothing of current research into virtual reality.

With such a fascination for matter, Marinetti drew away from Nietzsche's influence, with its rigour in calling for an interrogation of all values[46] and gave himself up to the pleasure of speculating on technical wizardry; it should not go unremarked that in *Mafarka the Futurist*, Marinetti omitted to deal with the doctrine of Eternal Return. Moreover, Marinetti uses Nietzsche's notion of will to power selectively, shying away from its use for redeeming the past,[47] however sophisticated this concept might be, since the past is something he rejects outright. However, as we have seen, in this area Marinetti was more successful in theory than in practice, since like Nietzsche, whom he accuses of defending the greatness and beauty of the antique past, Marinetti also manifested a deep and perhaps unconscious respect and fascination for the pagan culture of pre-Islamic North Africa. In addition, Marinetti's hero Mafarka is patently unable to escape the burden of the past in the form of family ties, as already discussed. Furthermore, the Bergsonian dynamic which informs the spirit of much that is superficially 'scientific' in *Mafarka the Futurist* is itself specifically based on the principle that the present always contains the past.[48]

I would suggest that the reason Marinetti steered clear of tackling Nietzsche's doctrine of Eternal Return – wisely, one could argue – was that he wished to graft the machine aesthetic onto both a Nietzschean mastery of the will and a Bergsonian vitalism (a connection also made by Sorel).[49] As John White has shown, Marinetti developed a 'new matter-orientated aesthetics'[50] which went beyond what Bergson had posited: 'Bergson's critique of intelligence, as it is outmanœuvred by life, readily widens in Marinetti's case to a full-scale primitivist anti-intellectualism'.[51] Hence Marinetti's rejection of books, libraries and everything to do with scholarship so that he could be utterly objective towards matter, the essence of which he saw as 'courage, will power and absolute force',[52] echoing Bergson's view of matter as vital, as 'necessity itself'.[53] In effect, Marinetti attempted to pressgang Futurism into rendering a thing's interior force. Mafarka is shown to be a man who can perceive the fundamental essence of matter as mental energy when he tells Gazourmah: 'I created you thus, with all the force of my despair, for the intensity of creative energy varies as the scale of the despair that engenders it' (*MF* p.195). Bergson had transposed Nietzschean will to power into 'vital impulse' so that 'life ... is unceasing creation'.[54] Marinetti, rejecting Nietzsche's *Übermensch* as *passé*, pushed Bergsonian will-laden *élan vital* to its limits:

> Let us pursue each minute of our lives in splendour, by acts of impetuous will, risk upon risk, constantly courting the Death that will immortalise the fragments of our remembering matter, in all their beauty, with a rough kiss! (*MF* p.147)

What Marinetti does which goes far beyond anything Nietzsche contemplated is posit the apotheosis of will as a physical force: 'Our will must come out of us so as to take hold of matter and change it to our fancy. So we can shape everything around us and endlessly renew the face of the earth' (*MF* p.146). The trouble with statements such as this is that they are palpably impossible to fulfil, rather like Jesus' statement about faith which can move mountains. Even so, Marinetti's real point – that we can do anything if we try – deserves consideration, though it is immediately contaminated by the misogynist call for men to circumvent woman's procreative capacity: the very next line reads: 'Soon, if you appeal to your will, you too will give birth without resorting to woman's vulva' (*MF* p.146). Marinetti's misogyny in this novel, which, as I have discussed, rests on a foundation built by Nietzsche even if it does not inhabit the same house, should be condemned and rejected, but his portrait of Mafarka as a man who tries to reach for the stars is worthy of our serious attention. In the end, what really separates Marinetti from Nietzsche is seriousness of purpose. Both men badly wanted to shock the bourgeoisie and were seduced into misogyny in the process. However Nietzsche, having defined the problems which beset European culture, at least proffered his own cure, while Marinetti, in *Mafarka the Futurist*, his longest piece of prose, could ultimately find no more convincing an outcome for his novel that an apocalyptic destruction of the planet. Thus Marinetti, the great iconoclast, falls back on the hackneyed Doomsday scenario familiar to man since the Book of Revelations, but as a true innovator and man of the moment he leaves the reader's ear ringing with 'the soaring flight of all the songs of Earth' as Gazourmah's wings beat 'the great dream of total music' (*MF* p.205), a contemporary allusion to Mahler's symphony *Das Lied von der Erde* (*Song of the Earth*) (1908).[55]

NOTES TO CHAPTER III

1. F.T. Marinetti, *Guerra sola igiene del mondo*: 'Contro i professori' (1915), in *Teoria e invenzione futurista*, ed. Luciano De Mario, 4 vols (Milan: Mondadori, 1968), II, p.262.

2. ibid., p.263.

3. Robert E. McGinn, 'Verwandlungen von Nietzsches Übermenschen in der Literatur des Mittelmeerraumes: d'Annunzio, Marinetti und Kazantzakis', in *Nietzsche-Studien*, 10/11 (1981/82), pp.597-614. McGinn surmises that the two errors made by Marinetti lay in assuming that the *Übermensch* expressed the young Nietzsche's interest in Greek gods and that Nietzsche wished to see a return to heathen mythology as found in Greco-Roman antiquity. Whether these were deliberate errors on Marinetti's part remains a matter for conjecture.

4. Günther Berghaus, *Futurism and Politics Between Anarchist Rebellion and Fascist Reaction, 1909-1914* (Providence and Oxford: Berghahn, 1996), pp.22-25.

5. Armin Arnold, *Die Literatur des Expressionismus* (Stuttgart, Berlin, Cologne and Mainz: Kohlhammmer, 1971 [1966]), p.69.

6. Friedrich Nietzsche, *Thus Spoke Zarathustra*, trans. R.J. Hollingdale (Harmondsworth: Penguin, 1969), Part I: 'Zarathustra's Prologue'/4, p.44f. Henceforth cited in the text as *Za* with the relevant section and page reference.

7. F.T. Marinetti, *Mafarka the Futurist*, trans. Carol Diethe (London: Middlesex University Press, 1997), p.7, henceforth cited in the text as *MF* with the page reference. I am indebted to the help and encouragement of my colleague Raynalle Udris in preparing the translation.

8. Though the mediæval fourteenth-century stories centring on the exploits of the historical sixth-century Bedouin poet Antar probably contain little fact, they are as popular in Arabian culture as *The Arabian Nights* and enjoyed a vogue in Europe in the nineteenth century, especially in France (with Renan and Lamartine in particular). See H.T. Norris, *The Adventures of Antar* (Warminster: Aris and Phillips, 1980).

9. J.W. von Goethe's *Prometheus* was written in Autumn 1774. In the second stanza, Prometheus mocks the Gods who only exist through the superstition of the unfortunate and weak.

10. Steven Aschheim, *The Nietzsche Legacy in Germany 1890-1990* (Berkeley and Los Angeles: University of California Press, 1992), *passim*.

11. A typical example would be *Die Kosmiker*. See Carol Diethe, *Historical Dictionary of Nietzscheanism* (Lanham MD and London: Scarecrow, 1999), p.137ff. See also the entries in the same volume for Marinetti, Futurism, Zarathustra etc.

12. The Sabians were Arabs who worshipped the fixed stars and planets. Tribes would choose to worship a particular star, such as the sun or Sirius. Solar worship was

widespread in North Africa and the Middle East from ancient times, much of it, like the worship of Ra (the sun) in Egypt, having originated in the East.

13. In Marinetti's day the *zaggalah* in Siwa (originally warriors, *zagal*=club) were still an openly homosexual brotherhood. See Walter Cleine, *Notes on the People of Siwah (sic) and El Garah in the Libyan Desert* (Wisconsin: George Banta, 1936) [General Series in Anthropology 4], p.19 and Ahmed Fakhri, *The Oases of Egypt* (Cairo: American University of Cairo Press, 1973), pp.43-44.

14. For details of Marinetti's visits to London see Lawrence Rainey, 'The Creation of the Avant-Garde: F.T. Marinetti and Ezra Pound', in *Modernism/Modernity* I, 3, 1994, pp.195-220.

15. Friedrich Nietzsche, *Ecce Homo*, 'Why I Write Such Good Books: 5', in *Basic Writings of Nietzsche*, trans. Walter Kaufmann (New York: Modern Library, 1968), p.723 [p.h. 1908].

16. Diana Behler, 'Nietzsche's View of Woman in Classical Greece', in *Nietzsche-Studien*, 18, 1989, 359-376, p.372.

17. Friedrich Nietzsche, 'Nachgelassenes Fragment, 1871' translated as 'The Greek Woman' by Maximilian Mügge in *Early Greek Philosophy and Other Essays* (London and Edinburgh: T.N. Foulis, 1911), p.23 (original emphasis).

18. Friedrich Nietzsche, *The Joyful Wisdom*, trans. Thomas Common, in Kurt Reinhardt ed. (New York: Ungar, 1973), II: 71, p.104.

19. See Carol Diethe, *Nietzsche's Women: Beyond the Whip* (Berlin: de Gruyter, 1996), p.73ff.

20. See the Introduction to my translation of *Mafarka the Futurist*, p.XVff.

21. See my chapter 'Sex and the Superman. An Analysis of the Pornographic Content of Marinetti's *Mafarka le futuriste*', in Gary Day and Clive Bloom (eds), *Perspectives on Pornography: Sexuality in Film and Literature* (London: Macmillan, 1988), pp.159-74.

22. See Rabelais' *Gargantua et Pantagruel*, Book 11, Ch 1, for a humorous description of the emergence, in ancient times, of physical deformities such as elongated penises so long they could be used as belts. This is obviously the inspiration for Marinetti's tale of Mafarka's elongated penis, which he coils up like a rope (*MF* p.47).

23. See Carol Diethe, op.cit. (1996) pp.63-66 for a discussion of this phrase.

24. Annemarie Pieper, *'Ein Seil geknüpft zwischen Tier und Übermensch'. Philosophische Erläuterungen zu Nietzsches erstem Zarathustra* (Stuttgart: Klett-cotta, 1990), p.312.

25. Is it really just a coincidence that Nietzsche endorses the following Florentine saying as true to life: 'buona femmina e mala femmina vuol bastone' (both a good and bad woman want the stick)? Friedrich Nietzsche, *Beyond Good and Evil*, op.cit. (1968) p.279.

26. See note 35. For a critical discussion of Schmidt's views see my comments in *Nietzsche's Women: Beyond the Whip*, p.65.

27. For example *Beyond Good and Evil*, VII: 239, p.359:

> What inspires respect for woman, and often enough even fear, is her *nature*, which is more 'natural' than man's, the genuine, cunning suppleness of a beast of prey, the tiger's claw under the glove, the naïveté of her egoism, her uneducability and inner wildness, the incomprehensibility, scope and movement of her desires and virtues – What, in spite of all fear, elicits pity for this dangerous and beautiful cat 'woman' is that she appears to suffer more, to be more vulnerable, more in need of love, and more condemned to disappointment than any other animal. (original emphasis).

28. See Ronald Lehrer, *Nietzsche's Presence in Freud's Life and Thought* (New York: State University Press, 1995), Ch 13: 'Woman, Truth and Perspectivism' for a good overview of the area.

29. Otto Weininger, *Sex and Character*, trans. anon. (London: Heinemann, 1906 [1903]), p.233.

30. ibid., p.231. Weininger draws a distinction between the 'maternal woman' and the prostitute.

31. 'G.C', 'Love and Sexuality' in *Futurism and Futurisms*, ed. Pontus Hulten (New York: Abbeville, 1986), pp.503-04, p.504.

32. Alice Yaeger Kaplan, *Reproductions of Banality: Fascism, Literature and French Intellectual Life* (Minneapolis: University of Minnesota Press, 1994), p.83.

33. ibid., p.83.

34. Jean Graybeal, *Language and 'the Feminine' in Nietzsche and Heidegger* (Bloomington: Indiana University Press, 1990), p.47. See also Carol Diethe, 'Nietzsche and the Woman Question', in *History of European Ideas*, XI, 1989, pp.865-79.

35. Milan Kundera, *The Unbearable Lightness of Being* (Harmondsworth: Penguin, 1984), p.5. In the world of eternal return the weight of unbearable responsibility lies heavy on every move we make. That is why Nietzsche called the idea of eternal return the heaviest of burdens (*das schwerste Gewicht*).

36. Two works which criticise Franziska – too harshly, in my view – are Jørgen Kjaer, *Friedrich Nietzsche. Die Zerstörung der Humanität durch Mutterliebe* (*Friedrich Nietzsche: The Destruction of Humanity Through Mother Love*) (Opladen: Westdeutscherverlag, 1990) and Klaus Goch, *Nietzsche über die Frauen* (*Nietzsche on Women*) (Frankfurt am Main and Leipzig: 1992). Some interesting speculation on the matter can be found in Hermann-Josef Schmidt, *Nietzsche absconditus oder Spurenlesen bei Nietzsche* (*Nietzsche Absconditus or Reading Traces in Nietzsche*), 2 vols (Berlin-Aschaffenburg: IBDK, 1991), II, pp.899-908.

37. Kelly Oliver, 'Nietzsche's Abjection', in Peter J. Burgard (ed.), *Nietzsche and the*

Feminine (Charlottesville and London: University Press of Virginia, 1994), pp.53-67, p.58. In note 8, p.55, Oliver writes: 'Although psychoanalysis can provide an interesting and useful way to read texts, I am wary of extending that analysis to a diagnosis of the author's actual psychological problems.'

38. R.W. Flint, *Marinetti. Selected Writings* (London: Secker and Warburg, 1971), p.10.

39. For a history of the text of *Der Wille zur Macht* (*The Will to Power*) (1901), purportedly by Friedrich Nietzsche, see *Historical Dictionary of Nietzscheanism*, p.152ff.

40. *Beyond Good and Evil*, VII: 229, p.348.

41. F.T. Marinetti, 'The Founding and Manifesto of Futurism', in Flint, op.cit. pp.39-44, p.42:

> We will glorify war – the world's only hygiene – militarism, patriotism, the destructive gesture of freedom-bringers, beautiful ideas worth dying for, and scorn for woman.

42. Barbara Spackmann, 'Mafarka and Son: Marinetti's Homophobic Economics', in *Modernism and Modernity*, I, 3, 1994, pp.89-107.

43. Günter Berghaus, *Italian Futurist Theatre 1909-1944* (Oxford: Clarendon, 1998), p.500.

44. Henri Bergson, *Creative Evolution*, trans. Arthur Mitchell (London: Macmillan, 1913), p.280.

45. ibid., pp.261, 263.

46. Friedrich Nietzsche, *On the Genealogy of Morality*, trans. Carol Diethe (Cambridge: Cambridge University Press, 1994), I: 17, p.37:

> *All* sciences, from now on, must prepare the way for the future work of the philosopher: this work being understood to mean that the philosopher has to solve the *problem of values* and that he has to decide on the *hierarchy of values*. (original emphasis).

47. *Za II*: 'Of Redemption', p.161:

> To redeem the past and to transform every 'It was' into an 'I wanted it thus!' – that alone do I call redemption […] 'It was': that is what the will's teeth-gnashing and most lonely affliction is called. Powerless against that which has been done, the will is an angry spectator of all things past. The will cannot will backwards; that it cannot break time and time's desire – that is the will's most lonely affliction.

48. Bergson, op.cit. p.2:

> My mental state, as it advances on the road of time, is continually swelling with the duration which it accumulates: it goes on increasing – rolling upon itself, as a snowball in the snow … the truth is that we change without ceasing, and that the state itself is nothing but change.

49. Berghaus, *Futurism and Politics*, p.32: 'The hero has in himself the intuitive *élan vital* and the *Wille zur Macht* …'.

50. John J. White, *Literary Futurism. Aspects of the First Avant-Garde* (Oxford: Clarendon, 1990), p.337.

51. ibid., p.336.

52. F.T. Marinetti, 'Technical Manifesto of Futurist Literature' (1912), in Flint, op.cit. pp.84-89, p.88.

53. Bergson, op.cit. p.278.

54. ibid., p.24.

55. Mahler died in 1909, never having heard this symphony played.

CHAPTER IV

The Waste Land and The Death of the Author:
Intertextuality and the Politics of Modernism

Edward Neill

Edward Neill was a Senior Lecturer at Middlesex University. He has interests in the areas of 18th, 19th and 20th century literature, including the work of Jane Austen, Thomas Hardy, modernist poetry and theory. He has published widely in academic journals including the *Critical Quarterly, Victorian Poetry, Essays in Criticism, Victorian Literature and Culture, English,* the *Cambridge Quarterly, Textual Practice,* and the *Oxford Literary Review,* and reviews quite regularly in the *Times Higher Education Supplement.* In 1999 he published two books, *The Politics of Jane Austen* and *Trial by Ordeal? Hardy and the Critic.*

Ironically, as professedly a purveyor of poetic difficulty[1] to at least the professorial masses, T.S. Eliot became, astonishingly quickly, the most famous, the most discussed and the most successful poet of the Anglophone world. As early as 1938 Wallace Stevens was wondering, only a little maliciously, in a *Harvard Advocate* symposium devoted to its most famous literary alumnus, just what there was to say about him any more.[2]

Although it would be inaccurate (as well as unkind) to speak of a waste land of critical commentary on Eliot at the very moment at which one seems poised to add to it, it might be less than kind to force the reader to traverse that conspicuously unattractive territory. We are not about to join those Burbanks with literary Baedekers[3] who tour Eliot country in chartered buses.[4] Innocently battening on a poetry already too much discussed, too much explained,[5] commentators on Eliot's poetry seem nevertheless to have had the experience but missed the meaning,[6] too confident, perhaps, that his stream of consciousness would not contain the boulders of ideology. (Perhaps the 'stream' itself turned out to be something of a 'solution'.)

Yet Eliot's poetic achievement stands in the shadow of his dark familiar, Ezra Pound, whose tragic history[7] seems to underwrite or underline the suspicion that the discursive convoy for the poetics of modernism secretes an unlikeable politics which human power cannot remove,[8] and that the poetry itself has, lodged in its capillaries, what Keats called 'a palpable design on us'.[9] Indeed, Anthony Easthope has translated and extended the Keatsian apprehension to a more generalised and seemingly ineluctable idea of poetry 'as' discourse[10] (which is certainly a word with a penumbra). Modernism, even of Eliot's type, is apparently, in Milton's idiom 'pawing to get free' of this ideological tendentiousness, but is still, in effect, affiliated to many of the 'traditional' features he deprecates. Yet he appears, rather strangely, to ignore this.

Is art not merely 'among the ideologies', in Althusser's idiom,[11] but succumbing to them? Probably the reader's estimate of modernism itself depends on her/his answer to this question. Even, or perhaps especially, intertextuality, with its sense of impersonal structures 'one' inhabits like a ghost in the machine, it seems, may be discourse, according to analysts like Fairclough and Mills,[12] and Foucault, describing the world of discourse, makes it sound a little like intertextuality:

> So many authors who know or do not know one another ... pillage one another, meet without knowing it and obstinately intersect their unique discourses in a web of which they are not the masters, of which they cannot see the whole, and of whose breadth they have a very inadequate idea.[13]

Is modernist intertextuality a prison-house of language? Is its role for the poet (the word itself being 'feminine in form, masculine in gender' in its Latin original), permissive or appropriative, passive or active? Reassuringly, it seems that at least *The Waste Land* is saved by having no 'Author-God' in sight; as a sort of panopticon without portfolio, the poem seems to help itself by a Saussurean negativity, being not quite by Eliot, not quite by Pound. It was designed to have designs, but someone, wielding a blue pencil perhaps, lost the blueprint, and it became much stronger.

Eliot indeed emerges as, in some respects, almost an inept reader of his own poem: for example, he wished to delete the lines which now constitute section four, 'Death by Water', until Pound pointed out that the rest of the poem carefully prepares for it.[14] He was indebted to Pound not merely as editor, but also as salesman and literary entrepreneur, and Lawrence Rainey well describes how he induced editors of *The Dial* and the *Little Review* to pant for a poem, sight unseen, which he had already persuaded them was the modernist masterpiece they craved.[15]

For all I know Jürgen Habermas' apparent claim, but made in words of Daniel Bell whose tone and import he will shortly dispute, that modernism is 'dominant but dead'[16] may be a 'sentiment to which every bosom now returns an echo', to echo formerly dominant Dr Johnson.[17] (The dominance comes from a desolating sense that, as Terry Eagleton cheekily puts it, 'they had *The Cantos*; we have Jonathan Culler',[18] or, as Dryden put it in a formula we can transpose – feeling his age to be, if more 'polite' than the Age of Shakespeare, perhaps a little effete in its cosy Covent Garden coffee houses – 'Theirs was the giant-race before the flood'.)

Perhaps Habermas, despite his nostalgia for the Enlightenment project, might actually want us to wish this strangely-designated cultural modernism dead in any case, presumably because the politics of modernism, modernism as discourse, has been, persistently and apparently paradoxically, associated with reactionary mischief.[19] Whether modernist poems necessarily secrete this is still a fascinating question, and indeed a voice in what might be called the ur-text of *The Waste Land* certainly seems to think so, intoning 'he do the police in different voices',[20] as a warning, perhaps, to deviant readers, to keep out, by a Dickensian Sibyl.

Must we concede that the distinction by Frank Lentricchia (borrowed from Wallace Stevens) between 'Ariel and the Police', between poetry and discursive regimes,[21] has indeed crumbled away in *The Waste Land*, and its darkly carceral imaginings, 'thinking of a prison', are so cramped by crookedness, custom and fear[22] that it is perhaps hardly surprising that succeeding generations have finally chosen to seek notes towards a definition of culture in other times and other places? Or is it that the poem is confirming rather than dissenting from Hardy's diagnosis? The poetry itself seems heavily invested, not merely in Sir Philip Sidney's point that 'the poet nothing affirmeth', but rather that the poet isn't really there even to deny that he affirms something. The effects of *montage* and *collage The Waste Land* achieves through 'juxtaposition without copulae'[23] seem specifically designed to resist the prisings and prosings of critics.

Specifically, if intertextuality and the death of the author are the watchwords of subsequent theory, aren't they transparently derived from such modernist practice, as Nicholas Zurbrugg seems to be suggesting,[24] and is it not indeed rather difficult to know which offers hermeneutics to (which) other? If theory helps you with modernism, modernism, it seems, already secretes the theory which is invoked to 'explain' it. Those phrases and fragments which compose the Barthesian text by blending and clashing, 'none of them original',[25] seem present, correct and conspicuous in the disfigured mosaic of *The Waste Land*.

With the author's absence from its linguistic role-call and the intertextual allusiveness of its cultural echo-chamber, the poem is suspended between voice and presence and text and absence, between its sense of itself as a body of sound or a multitude of writings. The method of presentation also seems designed to create a hermeneutic leeway which offers appeasements to a reader left cold by Eliot's forensic pontifications, his particular ideological investments, and the 'antique drum' which he could never quite bring himself to relinquish.[26]

Of course part of the awkwardness of this 'poetry as discourse' idea is that Eliot also has 'discourse' *as such*, no doubt about it: it is said, for example, that *Notes towards a Definition of Culture* (1948) led Raymond Williams by negative reaction to his long prose revolution, one of considerable moment, and the wheel is still turning.[27] One should note that one might be led to infer from this that Eliot was composing something like a Last Night of the Proms in prose, whereas it is at least interesting that his attitude to his adopted land, even at this relatively late stage, is one of vinegary alienation, and his famous metonymic catalogue of things English, from pickled beetroot and cabbage cut into sections to the music of Elgar,[28] confirms his status as *metoikos* or resident alien, as he was inclined to sign himself.[29] Even if Eliot was never quite in the running as what Edward Said calls a specular border intellectual,[30] his implied critical negation, bracing as Scunthorpe, makes him seem a slightly more volatile 'ideological' property than his current reputation suggests. Does our sense of this 'volatility' extend into the poetry itself? Even if, despite its unpredictable postures, Eliot the critic and social thinker is a rather desperate case, it isn't the inevitable convoy for the poetry, and *The Waste Land* in particular, that it may once have seemed to be.

It has been pointed out (in apparent riposte to I.A. Richards, who claimed that *The Waste Land* had effected a severance between poetry and belief),[31] that a Buddhist is as immanent as a Christian in *The Waste Land* ('The Fire Sermon' and all that), but, unless you are Glen Hoddle, you are unlikely to find this idea terribly exciting, especially as the notes to 'The Fire Sermon' coolly detail the spiritual refrigeration supplied by eastern and western asceticism (*Collected Poems 1909-1962*, p.74). My feeling is that, although the poem is not there to offer segmented solidarities, the overdetermined sense of the death of the author permits the reader, slouching towards the Unreal City to be born, whether as Marxist, feminist, psychoanalytic or even a postcolonial critic, to find something in the poem which speaks to the constituencies they address.

After all, *The Waste Land* unforgettably presents the intolerable conditions of modern commercial civilisation, the seduction and betrayal of lowly and lonely womenfolk by 'the loitering heirs of city directors' (in 'The Fire Sermon', *The Waste Land*, l.180), the intolerable conditions of working class existence: 'she's had nine already and nearly died of young George' ('A Game of Chess', *The Waste Land*, l.160); while the failure of a 'transcendental ego',[32] even in the form of a Dante or a Tiresias to take charge of the poem's cultural echo chamber, saves the reader from being 'bullied ... by the whims of an egotist',[33] as Keats puts it, even a transcendental one. It speaks also of the flimsy illusoriness of national identity and ethnic affiliation (*'bin gar keine Russin', stamm aus Litauen, echt Deutsch'*, as the voice of deluded racial righteousness puts it in 'The Burial of the Dead').[34]

Indeed, even where the political extrudes, in the form of the reference to Coriolanus in part five of the poem – 'Only at nightfall, aetherial rumours,/ Revive for a moment a broken Coriolanus' in 'What the Thunder Said' (*The Waste Land*, ll.415-6), the manner of invocation exudes muffled subtleties which commit one to nothing. This is, typically, a highly pondered or alembicated linguistic assaying which makes for reversible, alternating currents of positive and negative valorisation – 'revived' for a moment only, and at 'nightfall' which represents the mode of 'unreason' or the end of vision or the end of history.

Coriolanus is held in the imagination of a potential acolyte, as, perhaps, the 'other' of the speaker's timidity, by faintly ironic, if Virgilian, 'aetherial rumours'. These are possibly influenced by the racier moments of Pound's more obviously comic imitations of Propertius (1919).[35] Thus the 'truly strong man' idea (as taken up by Auden in his '1929' poem)[36] may seem merely a straw man, a snare, a delusion, at most a figure surrounded by what Derrida calls 'useless pathos'. Yet Eliot was fascinated by the figure of Coriolanus, by Shakespeare's play, and by the Beethoven overture which inspired the 'Coriolan' sequence he wrote (1931-2).[37]

But although a cult of Coriolanus may be felt to be cognate with the cult of what R.P. Blackmur called 'Caesarism in Rome and Berlin',[38] and a production of *Coriolanus* in Paris in the early thirties is said to have caused riots, we must contrast the possum-like caution of Eliot's poetic secretions here with Pound's enthusiastic incorporation of Mussolini, his Caesar/Coriolanus and his 'perfect man'[39] presumably, in his *Cantos*, 'the Boss' glimpsed in a moment of reciprocal regard for the Cantos themselves in Canto 41 (both of them reaching a mirror/stage at the same moment, as it were): '*'Ma questo ... e divertente'*; catching the point before the aesthetes had got there'.[40] If Fascism entails, as Benjamin has famously remarked, the aestheticising of politics, Pound responds eagerly with an unguarded and inverse politicising of his aesthetics to accommodate Fascism in the form of the *Duce*, though (to be fair) some critics, like C.K. Stead, have found his impetuous commitments more attractive than Eliot's 'master of the subtle school'[41] velleities and ideological feinting and fencing.[42]

This seems to work well in the poem, however, and the indeterminate semantic wobblings save the Coriolanus references from seeming insidious. This indeterminacy also helps define a metrical policy, the celebrated 'no *vers* is *libre* for the man who wants to do a good job'.[43] His idea that one select a metrical pattern and approach and withdraw from it is a suggestive insinuation of rhythmical teasing which might open on a Derridean theme of deferral and '*différance*'.[44]

Indeterminacy or undecidability of genre also seems set to keep the reader on his toes here: unwilling to precipitate out its positive terms and conditions, as not quite satire, not quite narrative, less than wholly epic, intermittently lyric, novelesque in colloquiality and knowing mimicry, all its modes are somehow qualified or, as one might say, *sous rature*, eluding positive definition and fixed position.

In this connection it may also be possible to add a nuance in pointing out that a 'gay' (or 'queer') studies critic might also find something in *The Waste Land* to his/her taste, although in this case the author, apparently safely sequestered from his poem, let slip the dogs of war on hearing of a 'homoerotic' reading. This was in an article by John Peter in *Essays in Criticism* in 1952,[45] and Eliot promptly had solicitors fire off some unpleasant correspondence to him, the journal publishers, and to the editor, F.W. Bateson, who was forced to destroy remaining copies of the journal.[46] Unfortunately, however, Peter involves himself with 'Phlebas the Phoenician' here (in Part Four of the poem), but it is surely the emotional intensity and tremulousness to be found in the 'Hyacinth girl' section of part one of the poem, in which an intense erotico-religious experience is elliptically recorded (Hyacinth being a beautiful Greek youth),[47] which is the one to ponder. F.W. Bateson himself, the friendly (if mischievous) editor of *Essays in Criticism*, pointed out, in discussing the forced omission of the article from some of the copies of the journal, that Lord Tennyson's extensively recorded 'lad's love' for A.H. Hallam in *In Memoriam* did not preclude his assuming the mantle of Eminent Victorian.

Certainly Eliot's homophobic response to the piece hardly precludes what might be called suspicions, except that this might entail insinuations of culpability where none was incurred in the first place. To be homophobic (as his resort to legal means to 'clear his name' here suggests he was being) even, or especially, about what might be descried as his own homoerotic impulses, would merely define the limiting terms of his own self-respect rather than the absence of the impulses themselves. To assume the possibility at least of such an emotional 'core' experience would confirm the sense of 'hermeneutic leeway' we have already explored in relation to other postmodern forms of critical response.

But Eliot's 'out-rage' in the face of the *Essays in Criticism* article also raises fascinating questions of literary ownership as well as of hermeneutic licence (and licensing). Dropping his mask of what Joyce might have called pluterperfect imperturbability (assumed in the face of his impersonality theory), the poet, as Mallarmé might put it, 'arose with naked sword'[48] in an embarrassing 'propria persona' intent on the proprieties. This seems odd in any case, and especially as he appears to have made such elaborate arrangements for his own funeral in the poem itself, rehearsing that Death of the Author which Barthes defined as part of the entry into the condition of language itself,[49] which Eliot seemed eager to assist at: the soubriquet of 'undertaker' bestowed by Lady Ottoline Morrell on Eliot is particularly helpful if you realise that his role was largely that of arranging his own funeral. That achieved, his poem floats free of the rather dismally mundane shell of traditional intellectualism[50] with which he sought to surround it.

It is, then, paradoxically because its author is so firmly interred in the soil of his own literary allotment, even if modernism must be imagined as no longer dominant, that we are also allowed to imagine it as being at least undead. As critics, however, we may still finally turn out to be like those large, friendly dogs counselled against in part one of *The Waste Land* who, most reprehensibly, keep digging up the corpse just to see how it's getting on ('progressing') in part one of the poem, sternly entitled 'The *Burial* of the Dead', which we may read off as an invitation to consider *The Waste Land* itself as a sumptuous piece of literary undertaking by a 'prince of morticians'.[51]

Yet its funer(e)al pyrotechnics were not entirely of his own contriving, and we may speculate whether the dedication of the poem to Ezra Pound as *il miglior fabbro* actually salutes him as the better craftsman in relation not only to his own work, but to the fabrication or forging of *The Waste Land* itself.

Pound, it seems, was needed to shunt Eliot on a little from what might be called 'hypomodernism' to 'hypermodernism'.[52] The typescript drafts of the poem which turned up in 1968, three years after Eliot's own death, show him to have been constantly tempted by linear narrative, full-blown blowsy parody or pastiche, 'full frontal' satire, a wholly recognisable protagonist possibly known, somewhat unguardedly, as 'Tom', a broadly signalled and surprisingly unsubtle relationship to *The Odyssey*, *The Æneid* and Dante's mediæval equivalent of classical epic, the whole to be unified in the consciousness of Somebody who speaks, if not from a position of authority, at least from a provisionally authorial position. This Somebody had a pronounced tendency to dish out beakish and weakly Baudelairean wiggings which inspire Pound to great heights of marginal rudeness.[53]

All this cold-feet conformism was eradicated by Ezra in what seems to be a primal scene of literary de(con)struction. A shearsman of sorts, in Wallace Stevens' idiom, Pound, in his matchless ability to litter the cutting-room floor with those fragments unworthy to be shored against one's ruins (*The Waste Land*, l.430), shows modernism's devotion to the *atelier* and Pound's particular thrill at finding *Dichten*, which I take to be a German word having to do with the production of poems, glossed as *condensare*, to condense.[54] Indeed, although High Modernism seems much closer to Adorno than Benjamin, the emphasis on a kind of literary *montage* suggests the modern techniques of production of which Benjamin could presumably approve. Pound's intervention made the poem more radically modernist, more taxing and more taxonomically indeterminate. He happily smudged the lines of that genre affiliation which for modernism is always *sous rature* as imparting forms of ideological fixity. Although within sight of all of them, what one finds one has 'entered' is not quite a narrative, not quite an epic, heteroglossic as a novel, but of course, not quite that either. The text wears on its sleeve its exoskeleton of allusiveness while actually submerging its profoundest influences.

The Poundian intervention, then, paradoxically, helps prevent, *inter alia*, authoritative voiceovers which control responses, so that, for example, as Anthony Easthope puts it, in the 'final' version of *The Waste Land* the 'ego' is merely 'a point in a process', not fixed in any definite relation to London, Dante, the Punic wars ... and Webster's play, *The White Devil* in the section of part one he examines'.[55] Eliot himself may hardly have given up the attempt to have an 'ego with attitude' in the poem, but the poem succeeds precisely as the 'attitude' (or attitudinising) fails, and the poet cannot be a god in his own intertextual machine, but must be, in a special sense, deus *ex* machina.

The attempt to smuggle in what might be called a transcendental ego in the form of 'I, Tiresias', or 'I' as Tiresias', meets with little success, although the 'Notes' to the poem urge his claims with marginal or 'parergonal' heckling which we might be wise to ignore.[56] Ezra proclaimed that 'one's incult pleasure',[57] (the words 'one's incult' are working hard to demonstrate that one is far from being that), would be unspoiled by 'one's' muddling the sources a little. It is quite in line with this to be, as Frank Lentricchia puts it, bored rather than gratified by the similarly reductive formula to the effect that all the women in the poem are one woman and all the men one man.[58] The 'motto' of the poem is, decidedly, not 'e pluribus unum', as Eliot seems to want it to be, but 'I will show you differences', and this heteroglossia derives from its depersonalised intertextuality. Is the poem's reach well out of the poet's grasp? That this in itself makes for a political pluralism may be doubted, as friend Pound's *Cantos*, amazingly heteroglossic as they are after the Bakhtin model, speaking to us in a bewildering variety of tones, registers and Babylonish dialects, are not exactly 'dialogic' in the sense that implies the direct political rebuke to monologic political dispensations Bakhtin has been seen as deliberately articulating.[59]

As a kind of anti-Benthamite panopticon *The Waste Land* invites you to a 'What The Prophet Saw', but you have more power to interpret the results than the formula seems to be suggesting. Perhaps the 'Notes' are a bit insidious in this respect, the mortified author engaging in a little light heckling *d'outre-tombe*. But if the 'Notes' are, in a sense, parergonal, might we be allowed to re-write them in order to make the poem say something a little different to whatever the original notes are insinuating?

For example, if a note had informed us that the typist and clerk episode in 'The Fire Sermon' was not instant sex, but *marriage* as seen from the perspective of Edmund in *King Lear*, who postulated a 'dull, stale, tired bed' as the inevitable outcome of circumstances of prolonged domestication, how different would the episode have been? Would it then have become, as students say, more realistic? (One-night stands, after all, however louche and reprehensible they might be deemed, if not necessarily by the participants, are reputed to be rather exciting.) And does the reference to the Goldsmith poem which appears to suggest that a woman betrayed by a *man* behaving badly should kill *herself*[60] entail the inference that putting a record on the gramophone is automatically, so to speak, a worse way of responding? Did the poet allow for the possibility of this question, or as the signs say in New Jersey, do we even have to bother to ask? As the god-man of his own poem, the poet is indeed something of a *Deus Absconditus*, and we prefer it that way.

Interestingly, Conrad Aiken, friend and minor poet, consulted the psychologist Homer Lane over the emotional brouhaha in or of the poem. He received the advice that his (Aiken's) friend should loosen up a little, as, as he put it, 'he thinks he's God'.[61] Having this reported back to him is said to have made Eliot himself become incandescent with rage, which does not dispel any suspicions one might entertain about the possible accuracy of this particular psychological pot-shot. Even if the poem does contain the promise or the threat of 'Tradition and the Individual Talent' to put the Mind of Europe on the line, not even the Mind of Europe should be in too much of a hurry to reach 'What the Thunder Said', a primal act of goddish/godlike bellowing which abrogates difference.

Slightly goddish in tone also is 'A crowd flowed over London Bridge, so many/ I had not thought death had undone so many' of 'The Burial of the Dead' (ll.62-3). The notes enjoin remembrance of Dante but amnesia of Blake[62] at this point, perhaps because Blake, in writing of 'the Accuser who is the God of this world' is a more humdrum ally in a poem about London, as well as a superb analyst of the dubious social effects of religious orthodoxies. The 'I' of the poem is trying to form itself as a transcendental ego, to become some kind of 'visually submissive' phenomenologist, but remains an importer of concepts, 'itself creating what it sees', in the words of a fascinating phrase by Cowper appropriated by Jane Austen,[63] as Blake's speaker in the 'London' poem, who himself supplies 'marks of weakness, marks of woe', seems so pointedly to be doing.

In fact, withdrawn from their Dantean context, the Eliot lines seem to be sounding the note of Arnold in his Rugby Chapel poem, which contrasts his recently dead father with those who 'their lives to some unmeaning taskwork give'[64] – apparently a snooty assessment of a pustularly proletarian 'purposiveness without purpose' at work. But Eliot's lines might also speak to the condition of those who come after and know about the insidiousness of interpellation and the pressures of hegemony, secreting the compassion he formally disavowed in a flight from sentimentality more convincingly mimed by 'hard men' of modernity like Pound and Lewis which was all too uncritically relayed by scholars of modernism like Hugh Kenner. (Similarly, 'the moral outrage of Tiresias' as 'Peeping *Tom*' [sic] seems curiously unalert to the fact that Tiresias is himself outrageous, a sort of perversion of the Conradian hest 'above all to make you *see*'.)

What we see, here, then, is finally what might be called 'I''s problem, or the problem of the 'I', an 'I' which here talks only to Dante or God,[65] cognate with 'I, Tiresias' or the voice of hysterical moralism which follows the cosmopolitan opening of the poem – 'What are the roots that clutch, what branches grow/ Out of this stony rubbish?', a puritanism in excess of its 'object' (the opening of the poem contains desultory chit-chat without being clearly reprehensible). (Auden finds a marxising transposition of this sort of 'effetely cosmopolitan' scene which makes a lot more sense in terms of its combination of analysis and implied criticism).[66] Here the Voice of the Accuser is seen to be stronger than the idea that there is something to reprehend, but that itself is finally part of the poem's 'strength'.

In fact the poem's exoskeleton of allusion is made all the bonier by its surprising notes. According to Eliot in one of his moments of deft but suggestive buffoonery, they became so popular that the poem became a parasite on them rather than the other way round, and the publication of the poem in 1922 without notes in the *Criterion* and *The Dial*, but with them for the small publishers Boni and Liveright,[67] raises fascinating questions of not only what Kant and Derrida would call parergonality, or framing for the text, but also of hermeneutic control and discursive closure. Kant also suggests the image of the 'cut' which establishes the 'inside' and the 'outside' of the work.[68] We might associate this with the cutting-room floor of that Poundian *atelier*, where the *rejectamenta*, as Wallace Stevens might have called them, bear silent witness to the difficulties in deciding what's 'in', what out, in a more agonisedly pragmatic fashion.

As for the 'Notes', then, one might legitimately demand the poem be read without them,[69] especially as Eliot persistently compares a poem to a body of sound, at one point desiring an audience which could neither read nor write, and he writes constantly of 'the auditory imagination', 'the music of poetry', *'Four Quartets'* and so on.

But one might also call attention to what the notes don't mention and thus to their possible strategic functions. For example, they don't mention any of the major contemporary influences on the poem: Joyce's *Ulysses*, itself published in 1922 – but Eliot had been reading (and proofreading) the 'novel' since 1917[70] – Conrad's *Heart of Darkness*[71] – and Stravinsky's *Rite of Spring*,[72] which contained just the right combination of what Richard Wolin calls the avant garde requirement of 'provocation' and 'aesthetics' which *The Waste Land* seems similarly to have caught: thus the poem functioned ambiguously in the minds of its first readers as pure poem or pure provocation respectively.[73]

The way Eliot 'crosses' his intertextual references still compels admiration, and even a short citation like 'My people humble people who expect/Nothing' ('The Fire Sermon', ll.304-5) seems to stir in an 'interior monologue' style like that of Joyce's Leopold Bloom in *Ulysses* with a Conradian resonance and a hint of Webster, but it would be difficult to pick out or pick up on all of this: for example, Chaucer's 'Prologue' (to the *Canterbury Tales*) isn't alluded to either, although its opening lines about April and the natural promptings which culminate in the line 'than longen folk to goon on pilgrimages' seem relevant, all too relevant, too like explicit elucidation, I suppose, in the pompous but apposite phrasing of F.R. Leavis (the 'modern world has no appropriate social equivalent for the natural urgings').

The point is that one can then play this game for oneself, and perhaps the word 'game' doesn't seem, finally, all that inappropriate either to a poem which seems to mingle luddism and ludism, and I think Hemingway was right to admire the poem without feeling able to take it entirely seriously. Indeed, *The Waste Land*'s attempt at expressionist scream or 'hysterical sublimity' is shadowed by the insistent need to make the reader work at making verbal connections, in 'hints followed by guesses'.[74] Indeed, this might be felt to recall the substance of Dr Johnson's perennially penetrating observation on the elaborate *decor* and decorum of Milton's eruditely assembled 'Elegy' for Edward King, so instantly metamorphosed to 'Lycidas', that 'where there is leisure for fiction there is little grief',[75] although the scrambled citations at the conclusion of Eliot's poem may suggest anguish as they invite ingenuity, and it is at least interesting that the most 'emotional' parts of the poem find their feelings convoyed (if not conveyed) by ancestral voices as they enumerate old themes.

Intertextuality may accommodate the fruits of an almost unwitting mimicry at micro-level – for example, there seems to be a previously unnoticed use of Racine in the 'Hyacinth girl' passage discussed previously, which seems to be a telescoping of the lines in *Britannicus* ('*J'ai voulu lui parler, et ma voix s'est perdue…*' [2.2.]) and *Phèdre* ('*Mes yeux ne voyaient plus, je ne pouvais parler…*' [1.3])[76]: 'I could not/Speak, my eyes failed, I was neither/Living nor dead…', although Eliot's free-ish verse and headlong enjambements do something original with the original material.

Intertextuality, however, is distinguishable both from minute and perceptible resemblance, contrived allusiveness and conscious craftsmanship. Just as the Death of the Author (see note 49) was predicated by Barthes on The Birth of the Reader, texts which unite or achieve a kind of Venn diagram congruence in the reader's mind are examples of intertextuality. We have seen how the 'Notes' to *The Waste Land* achieve a kind of strategic function and exclude much that might have been included, and they were perhaps excluded for a similarly 'strategic' reason.

Interestingly, at the 'macro'-level a major precursor for the poem seems to be Shelley's 'Triumph of Life', a poem found in (soaked) manuscript after his 'Death by Water' in the Bay of Lerici,[77] a vision poem influenced by many poets including Dante, Milton and Shakespeare offering a dismayed and surprisingly anti-'Romantic' vision of the power of life in the form of desire, passion and emotional derangements to overcome the essential effort of self-overcoming. It particularly seems to have it in for Rousseau, a favourite target of Eliot's anti-Romantic mentor Irving Babbitt, and this awareness of the profound congruence of his own and Shelley's poem here survives any surfaced awareness for Eliot himself, intertextuality once more overcoming the ghost in its machine.

The Waste Land, then, is nothing if not 'Spelt from Sybil's Leaves',[78] the title of a Gerard Manley Hopkins poem, attentive to what Baudelaire would have called the '*confuses paroles*'[79] of nature where Eliot's poem is more attuned to folios. 'Spelt from Sibyl's Leaves' would certainly be a good alternative title for the poem, particularly in the light of its epigraph from Petronius, in which the Sibyl, rather like Swift's Struldbrugs or Tennyson's Tithonous,[80] remains undead rather than simply immortal. Indeed, the poem is perhaps to be read in terms of the citation from *Measure for Measure* (3.1.5) which stands as epigraph to 'Gerontion' (1920), in a speech which counsels Claudio, extremely guilty of making love to his girlfriend, to be 'absolute for death'.

This is an idea which Eliot himself seems at times to be a little keen on. Indeed part four of *The Waste Land*, 'Death by Water', seems *inter alia* to offer a watery euthanasia as a final solution for spiritual drought. At least, the tranquil detachment in the tone of part four seems at odds with the idea, following on the identification of somebody, by some kind of surreal interpellation, as a Phoenicean, in part one of the poem ('You who were with me in the ships at Mylae!'), that we (or somebody) should '*fear* death by water' [my emphasis], as Madame Sosostris put it.

Although there seems to be a traditional air of religious menace about the injunction to '*Consider* Phlebas' [my emphasis], the tranquil pleasure with which we are made to contemplate his lot is perhaps designed to make us behold with some envy his release or relief from the horrors of having or being a body, with its demeaning desires and sordid requirements, very much underscored in the French version of the lines from Eliot's own poem, '*Dans le Restaurant*', from which Part Four was (surprisingly) translated.[81]

In this poem, in which the Phlebas section follows the protagonist's encounter with an old waiter who inspires physical disgust yet insists on telling of a paedophile-like encounter with a girl he tickles, experiencing a delirious sense of pleasure thereby, the revolted diner is humiliated by his inability to dissociate his own experiences and emotions from those of the disgusting (but also disgustingly candid) waiter. Eliot seems to be creating himself as his own French precursor here, the final trick of the intertextual poet *par excellence*, at once repressing and repossessing himself.

Curiously though, in repossessing himself he had, in a way, to call on others, and, in a rather special way, to revoke his own poetic licence. If *The Waste Land* is finally about absences, the most significant absence is finally that of the poet himself. This was, in fact, 'overdetermined' by his exhibitionistic surrender to the impersonal structures of language, and his more modest compliance with Pound's overconfident but highly perceptive strictures and interventions. There was of course an area of congruence in their 'foreign flotations': both had 'gone native' in Europe in a Jamesian 'joint stock' venture, seeking cultural capital in cultural capitals.

As a result, perhaps the most remarkable feature of the poem is the complete repression of its ultimately 'American' extraction, so full of the plenitude and the emptiness of 'Europe' as an Ithaca (New York?) the American voyager[82] happily never quite makes it to. This finally suggests, perhaps, the virtually colonial anxieties which inhabit its apparently magisterial cultural appropriations and the grand larcenies of its artistic kleptomania, ambiguous as to whether it is host or parasite of its materials[83] as it subjects the desiccations of Europe to what might be called a little 'colonic irrigation'.

However, it can still be argued that although such modernists as Pound and Eliot remain extremely impressive in their desire not to repeat themselves, it is at least arguable that their compulsion to repeat everyone else becomes excessive and, in the end, limiting. Although the poem stakes everything on not being 'discursive', it's difficult to see how such an impressive *bricolage* of historically 'pre-*fabbro*-cated' linguistic materials wouldn't finally attract at least a discursive convoy of a highly conservative type. But, as we have seen, possibly owing to the rather strange conditions of its 'cultural production', there appears to be some sort of evidence that *The Waste Land* at least resists that sort of wholesale recuperation.

NOTES TO CHAPTER IV

Notes to Chapter IV

1. T.S. Eliot, 'The Metaphysical Poets': 'Our civilisation comprehends great variety and complexity, and this variety and complexity, playing upon a refined and complex sensibility, must produce refined and complex results'; see Frank Kermode (ed.), *Selected Prose of T.S. Eliot* (London: Faber and Faber, 1975), p.65.
2. Wallace Stevens, 'Homage to T.S. Eliot', *Harvard Advocate*, 125 (1938), p.41.
3. See *T.S. Eliot: A Collection of Critical Essays*, ed. Hugh Kenner (Englewood Cliffs, N.J.: Prentice-Hall, 1961), pp.1-14.
4. 'Burbank with a Baedeker: Bleistein with a Cigar', a 'quatrain' poem of Eliot's *Selected Poems* (London: Faber and Faber, 1961), pp.34-35.
5. From Eliot's 'Ash Wednesday', *Selected Poems*, p.84.
6. 'The Dry Salvages', part 2, in (e.g.) *Collected Poems 1909-1962* (London: Faber and Faber, 1963), p.194.
7. See 'The Cage', in Hugh Kenner, *The Pound Era* (London: Faber and Faber, 1972), pp.60-495.
8. 'Little Gidding', pt.4 *Complete Poems and Plays*, p.196.
9. See 'Letter to J.H. Reynolds, 3 Feb. 1818', in *John Keats* ['The Oxford Authors'], ed. Elizabeth Cook (Oxford: Oxford University Press, 1990), p.377.
10. See Anthony Easthope, *Poetry as Discourse* (London: Methuen, 1982).
11. See e.g. Terry Eagleton, *Criticism and Ideology: A Study in Marxist Literary Theory* (London: New Left Books, 1976), pp.82-84.
12. 'Intertextuality is one of the discursive mechanisms which brings about a change within discourses' (Sarah Mills, *Discourse* (London: Routledge, 1997), p.154); cf. Norman Fairclough, *Discourse and Social Change* (London: Polity, 1992).
13. Michel Foucault, *The Archaeology of Knowledge*, trans. A.M. Sheridan Smith (New York: Harper and Row, 1976), pp.126-27.
14. See *The Letters of Ezra Pound, 1907-1941*, ed. D.D. Paige (London: Faber and Faber, 1951), p.237. ('I DO advise keeping Phlebas ... In fact I more'n advise'.).
15. See Lawrence Rainey, 'The Price of Modernism: Publishing *The Waste Land*' in *T.S. Eliot: The Modernist in History*, ed. Ronald Bush (Cambridge: Cambridge University Press, 1991), pp.91-133.
16. See 'Modernity vs. Postmodernity', *New German Critique*, 22 (1981), pp.13-30; also George Trey, *Solidarity and Difference: The Politics of Enlightenment in the Aftermath of Modernity* (Albany, N.Y.: State University of New York Press, 1998), p.4. To follow the plot here, we should also note what a strange example of 'modernism' T.S. Eliot is (though he is regularly placed as a prime example of a modernist). Habermas's argument that 'neoconservatism is confused in its understanding of the relation between culture and society', pursued in relation to Daniel Bell, is also relevant to the thought and theory of T.S. Eliot himself. See *Habermas and the*

Unfinished Project of Modernity: Critical Essays on 'The Philosophical Discourse of Modernity', ed. Maurizio Passerin d'Entrèves and Seyla Benhabib (Oxford: Polity, 1996), p.3.

17. Samuel Johnson, 'Thomas Gray', in *Lives of the English Poets (1779-81)* (London: J.M. Dent, 1925), p.392.

18. See 'The End of English', reprinted in *The Eagleton Reader*, ed. Stephen Regan (Oxford: Blackwell, 1998), p.277.

19. Particularly early in the field, and probably cued by William Empson, was John R. Harrison, *The Reactionaries* (London: Gollancz, 1966). For Habermas, this contradicts the idea that modernism might form an artistic convoy to his commitment to its culmination of an Enlightenment 'project'(ile). As Maurizio Passerin D'Entrèves points out, 'by drawing the distinction between *societal* modernisation and *cultural* modernisation, and showing how the former is responsible for those pathological syndromes mistakenly attributed to the latter, Habermas is able to rebut the claims of neoconservative critics of modernity', in *Habermas and the Unfinished Project of Modernity*, p.3.

20. See *T.S. Eliot: The Waste Land; A Facsimile and Transcript of the Original Drafts Including the Annotations of Ezra Pound*, ed. Valerie Eliot (London: Faber and Faber, 1971), pp.5-21; the quotation is from Dickens' *Our Mutual Friend*, ch.16; see also Calvin Bedient, *He Do the Police in Different Voices: 'The Waste Land' and its Protagonist* (Chicago: University of Chicago Press, 1986).

21. Frank Lentricchia, *Ariel and the Police: Michel Foucault, William James, Wallace Stevens* (Brighton: Harvester, 1988).

22. Thomas Hardy, 'In Tenebris, 2', *Collected Poems* (London: Macmillan, 1968), p.154.

23. See Hugh Kenner, *The Invisible Poet: T.S. Eliot* (London: Methuen, 1965), p.128.

24. Nicholas Zurbrugg, 'Baudrillard, Modernism and Postmodernism', in *Baudrillard: A Critical Reader*, ed. Douglas Kellner (Oxford: Blackwell, 1994), pp.227-55.

25. See 'The Death of the Author', in *Image-Music-Text*, trans. and ed. Stephen Heath (London: Fontana, 1977), pp.142-48.

26. In 'Little Gidding, III', in *Four Quartets* (*Complete Poems and Plays* (London: Faber and Faber 1969)), p.196.

27. Cornel West also points out approvingly that we read the poems of Eliot and others despite their 'official' affiliations in 'The New Cultural Politics of Difference', *The Cultural Studies Reader*, ed. Simon During (London: Routledge, 1993), p.213.

28. Eliot defines culture as 'all the characteristic activities and interests of a people: Derby Day, Henley Regatta, Cowes, the twelfth of August, a cup final, the dog races,

the pin table, the dart board, Wensleydale cheese, boiled cabbage cut into sections, beetroot in vinegar, nineteenth century Gothic churches and the music of Elgar'. *Notes Towards the Definition of Culture* (1948); see (e.g.) *Selected Prose of T.S. Eliot*, ed. Frank Kermode (London: Faber and Faber, 1975), p.298.

29. Lyndall Gordon, *Eliot's New Life* (Oxford: Oxford University Press, 1988), p.208.

30. See Abdul JanMohammed, 'Worldliness-Without-World, Homelessness-as-Home: Towards a Definition of the Specular Border Intellectual', in *The Edward Said Reader* (Oxford: Blackwell, 1992), pp.96-120.

31. As cited in Stephen Spender, *The Destructive Element: A Study of Modern Writers and Beliefs* (London: Jonathan Cape, 1935), p.144.

32. See (e.g.) discussion of Sartre on Husserl in Eric Matthews, *Twentieth Century French Philosophy* (Oxford: Oxford University Press, 1996), p.62.

33. *John Keats* ('The Oxford Authors'), ed. Elizabeth Cook, p.376.

34. i.e. 'I am not Russian at all; I come from Lithuania; I am a real German': see (e.g.) B.C. Southam, *A Student's Guide to the Selected Poems of T.S. Eliot* (Sixth edition) (London: Faber and Faber, 1994), p.142.

35. See Ezra Pound, *Selected Poems 1908-1959* (London: Faber and Faber, 1975), pp.79-97.

36. W.H. Auden, *Collected Poems* (London: Faber and Faber, 1976), p.50.

37. Including 'Triumphal March' and 'Difficulties of a Statesman'; in *Collected Poems, 1909-1962*, pp.125-29.

38. R.P. Blackmur, cited in Paul A. Bové, *Mastering Discourse: The Politics of Intellectual Culture* (London: Duke University Press, 1992), p.186.

39. From Yeats's 'In Memory of Major Robert Gregory', *The Poems*, ed. Daniel Albright, (London: J.M.Dent, 1990), pp.181-84.

40. See Ezra Pound, *The Cantos* (London: Faber and Faber, 1975), p.202.

41. See C.K. Stead, *Pound, Yeats, Eliot and the Modernist Movement* (New Brunswick: Rutgers, 1984).

42. 'Mr Eliot's Sunday Morning Service', *Collected Poems 1909-1962*, p.48.

43. Quoted and noted by Ezra Pound in *Literary Essays* (London: Faber and Faber, 1954), p.12.

44. See e.g. *Textualities: Between Hermeneutics and Deconstruction*, ed. Hugh J. Silverman (London: Routledge, 1994), p.91.

45. See John Peter, 'A New Interpretation of T.S. Eliot's *Waste Land*', *Essays in Criticism*, 2 (1952), pp.242-66.

46. F. W. Bateson: in a note explaining the omission of the article (subsequently restored in xerox in the copy of this number of 'E in C' inspected in the University of London library).

47. In fact 'Hyacinths' was a lightly-coded name for young male homosexual 'partners' in Byron's time: see Benita Eisler, *Byron: Child of Passion, Fool of Fame* (London: Hamish Hamilton, 1999), p.199.

48. See 'Le Tombeau d'Edgar Poe', in *Œuvres Complètes* (Paris: Gallimard, 1945), p.70.

49. See 'The Death of the Author', in *Image-Music-Text*, trans. and ed. Stephen Heath (London: Fontana, 1977), pp.142-48: (e.g.) 'Writing is that neutral, composite, oblique space where our subject slips away, the negative where all identity is lost, starting with the very identity of the body writing' (p.142); also suggestive for the movement into a modern sense of language as authority is James Risser's summary of the import of his work here in an essay, 'Reading the Text', in *Gadamer and Hermeneutics: Science, Culture, Literature*, ed. Hugh J. Silverman (London: Routledge, 1991), pp.93-105: 'But who really owns the text? Barthes thinks we do not have to search far for our answer, for it has already appeared in the work of Mallarmé. The French symbolist poet suggested that because of the possibilities adhering in the poem, the poet is often surprised to find more has been written than was known by the author. The author as well as the reader can take pleasure in discovering new extensions of meaning. Consequently, Mallarmé tells us that we must 'cede the initiative to words': 'to write is to reach the point where it is not me who acts, but language... language speaks, not the author''; see also *The Death and Return of the Author: Criticism and Subjectivity in Barthes, Foucault and Derrida*, second edition (Edinburgh: Edinburgh University Press, 1998), by Sean Burke, in which he attempts to qualify the idea, as, in a very different scholarly register, does Jack Stillinger in *Multiple Authorship and the Myth of Solitary Genius* (Oxford: Oxford University Press, 1991).

50. Gramsci's phrase, as discussed (e.g.) in *The Eagleton Reader*, ed. Stephen Regan, p.171.

51. Ezra Pound, 'Canto 80', in *The Cantos of Ezra Pound* (London: Faber and Faber, 1975), p.498.

52. 'Hypomodernism': a coinage – a world premiere for this word (?); 'hypermodernism': not used in literary discussion but employed in the literature of chess, and in the 1920s, when masters like Nimzowitsch made 'mysterious' moves (in fact soundly based on traditional 'openings', etc.) which proved to be profoundly innovative.

53. It is interesting for evidence of Eliot's reliance on these linguistic transfusions that the whole of part four of the poem apart from the short 'narrative' of the fate of Phlebas was deleted by Pound. See *The Waste Land: A Facsimile and Transcript of the Original Drafts*, ed. Valerie Eliot (London: Faber and Faber, 1971).

54. See, e.g. 'The Invention of Language', in Hugh Kenner, *The Pound Era* (London: Faber and Faber, 1972), pp.94-120.

Notes to Chapter IV

55. Anthony Easthope, *Englishness and National Culture* (London: Routledge, 1999), p.181.
56. See (e.g.) David Carroll, *Paraesthetics* (London: Methuen, 1987), pp.131-54.
57. See Hugh Kenner, *The Invisible Poet: T.S. Eliot*, p.131.
58. See Frank Lentricchia, *Modernist Quartet* (Cambridge: Cambridge University Press, 1994), p.272.
59. See Tom Cohen, 'The Ideology of Dialogue: The Bakhtin/De Man (Dis)connection', *Cultural Critique* 33 (Spring, 1996), pp.41-86.
60. The 'Notes' refer to the 'Song' in Goldsmith's *Vicar of Wakefield*, in which the 'lovely woman' is to 'bring repentance' to her betraying lover by 'dying': *Collected Poems 1909-1962*, p.73.
61. See Conrad Aiken, 'An Anatomy of Melancholy', in *T.S. Eliot: The Man and his Work*, ed. Allen Tate (London: Chatto and Windus, 1967), p.195.
62. Cf. e.g. 'London': 'I wander thro' each charter'd street/ Near where the charter'd Thames does flow,/ And mark in every face I meet/ Marks of weakness, marks of woe.' *Selected Poems*, ed. David V. Erdman (New York: New American Library, 1976), p.144.
63. William Cowper, *The Task*, bk. 4 l.290. Cited in *Emma*, by Jane Austen (1816), vol.3, ch.5.
64. In fact the theme of that poem contrasts such with the spirit of his redoubtable father, but the line itself is in 'A Summer Night' (1852); see Matthew Arnold *Poetical Works*, ed. C.B. Tinker and H.F. Lowry (London: Oxford University Press, 1950), p.243.
65. Partly intended to stir memories of Boston as 'the land of the bean and the cod,/ Where Lowells talk only to Cabots,/ And Cabots talk only to god.' Although neither a Lowell nor a Cabot, Eliot too was part of this 'American aristocracy'.
66. See Cleanth Brooks, 'Auden's Imagery', in *Auden: A Collection of Critical Essays*, ed. Monroe K. Spears (Englewood Cliffs, N.J.: Prentice-Hall, 1987), pp.18-20.
67. See *The Waste Land: A Facsimile and Transcript of the Original Drafts*, ed. Valerie Eliot (London: Faber and Faber, 1971), esp. p.30.
68. See (e.g.) David Carroll, *Paraesthetics* (London: Methuen, 1987), pp.131-54.
69. Hugh Kenner's opinion, for example, in *The Invisible Poet*, p.129.
70. See B.C. Southam, *A Student's Guide to the Selected Poems*, p.130.
71. ibid., p.129.
72. ibid., p.134.
73. See Richard Wolin, summarising Peter Bürger in *Labyrinths: Explorations in the Critical History of Ideas* (Amherst: University of Massachusetts Press, 1995), p.19.
74. See 'Little Gidding', pt.V, *Complete Poems and Plays*, p.190.

75. Samuel Johnson, 'John Milton', in *Lives of the English Poets*, p.96.

76. First spotted in *A Barthes Reader*, ed. Susan Sontag (London: Jonathan Cape, 1982), p.182.

77. See P.B. Shelley, *Selected Poems*, ed. Timothy Webb (London: J.M. Dent, 1977), pp.171-88.

78. See, e.g., *The Poems of Gerard Manley Hopkins*, ed. W.H. Gardner and N.H. Mackenzie, fourth edition (London: Oxford University Press, 1970), pp.97-98.

79. Charles Baudelaire, 'Correspondances', in *Œuvres Complètes* (vol. 1) (Gallimard: NRF, 1975), p.11.

80. See *The Poems of Tennyson*, ed. Christopher Ricks (London: Longman, 1969), p.1112 ('Me only cruel immortality/ Consumes'); for 'Struldbrugs', see 'A Voyage to Laputa', in *Gulliver's Travels* (Oxford: Basil Blackwell, 1959), Ch.10, pp.207-14.

81. 'Dans le Restaurant', *Complete Poems and Plays*, pp.51-52.

82. See, e.g. *Three Voyagers in Search of Europe: Henry James, Ezra Pound, and T.S. Eliot*, by Alan Holder (Philadelphia: University of Philadelphia Press, 1966).

83. See J. Hillis Miller, 'The Critic as Host', in *Theory Now and Then* (Hemel Hempstead: Harvester Wheatsheaf, 1991), pp.143-70.

CHAPTER V

'If one word did not cease to exist
when it has sounded...':
Some Augustinian Presences in Beckett

David Houston Jones

David Houston Jones is College Lecturer in French at St John's College, Oxford. He studied comparative literature at the University of Warwick and subsequently completed a PhD in modern French literature at Darwin College, Cambridge, and taught at the University of Paris VIII (St Denis). He is the author of a book entitled *The Body Abject: Self and Text in Jean Genet and Samuel Beckett*, 2000 and of articles on Genet and Beckett including a contribution to *Powerful Bodies: Performance in French Cultural Studies*, ed. by Peter Collier and Victoria Best, 1999.

Beckett's work is exemplary of the distressed intertextual relations frequently seen to be at work in and between Modernist texts. Not only does it pose, with particular urgency, questions which are at the forefront of contemporary debates on intertextuality, ruthlessly interrogating the 'proper' boundaries of the text and the questionable referential capacities of language, but the underlying dialectic of sameness and alterity is relentlessly foregrounded.[1] While intertextual echoes abound in Beckett, their sources are frequently obscured by a fragmentary mode of quotation, and Biblical references, in particular, are twisted out of context to apparently parodic effect. Beckett's allusions to Augustine seem to indicate a teleological exploitation of sources: even when references surface in identifiable form, Beckett's writing seems to put an unacceptable loading on the Christian doctrinal framework within which Augustine intended his work to be read. This paper investigates both the complex predicament of the versions of Augustine which appear in Beckett and the deeper formal or stylistic affinity which may be traced between their work. Both have important consequences for contemporary critical notions of textual authority and intertextual referentiality.

In a number of works, and most famously in *Waiting for Godot / En attendant Godot*, Beckett refers to the two thieves who were to be crucified alongside Christ:

> One is supposed to have been saved and the other…
> [*He searches for the contrary of saved*]… damned.
> […]
> How is it that of the four Evangelists only one speaks of a thief being saved. The four of them were there – or thereabouts – and only one speaks of a thief being saved.[2]

Not only does the textual evidence for the anecdote, in the Gospels, assume immediate importance in its telling, but Beckett elsewhere accords the version found in the writings of St Augustine a special status:

> I am interested in the shape of ideas even if I do not believe in them. There is a wonderful sentence in Augustine. I wish I could remember the Latin. It is even finer in Latin than in English. 'Do not despair; one of the thieves was saved. Do not presume; one of the thieves was damned'. That sentence has a wonderful shape. It is the shape that matters.[3]

This famous remark, made to Harold Hobson in an interview, is a key both to the importance of Augustine in Beckett and to a certain practice of writing which, in Beckett's fiction, devolves textual authority to a peculiarly intertextual and reflexive domain. Beckett scholars have long sought the original in Augustine, in English translations and in glosses on the Gospels, producing likely candidates in Alexander MacLaren's *Expositions of Holy Scripture* and even in the works of the Elizabethan Robert Greene.[4] The most likely source, however, must be that identified in Augustine's *Epistola* by McMillan and Fehsenfeld:

> Tres cruces in loco uno erant: In una latro liberandus: in alia latro damnadus: in media christus: alterum liberatur: alterum damnatur[5].

Despite the importance of the discovery, the question remains as to the role and status of the fragments of Augustine which punctuate Beckett's work. Although Beckett appears to pay homage to the 'wonderful shape' of Augustine's phrase, his work appears to retrospectively deform it: as readers we cannot help subsequently adding Beckett's gloss, 'It is the shape that matters', to its elegant surface. Apparently innocuous, the remark goes against the grain of Augustine's writings, which consistently attack the submersion of proper Christian messages in elaborate formal trappings. This is one of the chief concerns of the *Confessions*, the text which tells the story of Augustine's Christian conversion (and which, I argue, contains important correspondences with Beckett's Trilogy). The conversion, as well as being a cardinal autobiographical event, is also the condition and *raison d'être* of the narrative, allowing Augustine's narrator to accede to a state of enlightenment sufficient to praise God's grace by written means, and to describe, in particular, the iniquities of his past life. Among the most prominent of these is the sin of 'loquaciousness', the loading of discourse with elaborate rhetoric. As for Beckett, the development of Augustine's sensibility appears to have been accompanied by a distrust of 'excessive' forms of language and, as for Beckett, its imperatives prompted the resignation of an academic post. Augustine describes, in book IX of the *Confessions*, how his conversion only delays an immediate renunciation of the teaching of rhetoric and literature in deference to practical necessity and consideration for his students:

> I made a decision 'in your sight' (Ps. 18:15) not to break off teaching with an abrupt renunciation, but quietly to retire from my post as a salesman of words in the markets of rhetoric. I did not wish my pupils, who were giving their minds not to your law (Ps. 118:70) nor to your peace, but to frenzied lies and lawcourt squabbles, to buy from my mouth weapons for their madness. Fortunately there were only a few days left before the Vintage Vacation. I decided to put up with them so that I could resign with due formality. Redeemed by you, I was not now going to return to putting my skills up for sale.[6]

Augustine's stand against the vacuous excesses of rhetoric is well-known. If the hawking of valueless wares is his dominant description of the conceits of contemporary oratory and literature, over-absorption in reading and the placing of an excessive value on narrative is equally derided ('What is more pitiable than a wretch without pity for himself who weeps over the death of Dido dying for love of Æneas, but not weeping over himself dying for his lack of love for you, my God').[7] The central paradox of the *Confessions*, however, is the prominence of Augustine's distinctive, and frequently elaborate, literary style. The text's opening, following a dense series of Biblical quotations, sets up a complex logical problem concerning the possibility of addressing or praising God in language:

> 'Grant me Lord to know and understand' (Ps. 118:34,73,144) which comes first – to call upon you or to praise you, and whether knowing you precedes calling upon you. But who calls upon you when he does not know you? For an ignorant person might call upon someone else instead of the right one. But surely you may be called upon in prayer that you may be known. Yet 'how shall they call upon him in whom they have not believed? And how shall they believe without a preacher?' (Rom. 10:14). 'They will praise the Lord who seek him' (Ps. 21:27).[8]

The solution to the dilemma is at the same time a rhetorical flourish and a demotion of language: 'In seeking him they find him, and in finding they will praise him. Lord, I would seek you, calling upon you – and calling upon you is an act of believing in you'. The certainty of the opening quotation, 'You are great, Lord, and highly to be praised', dissolves into a fraught equivocation concerning the linguistic framing of worship, only to be rescued in a formulation which transcends the terms of the question. Implicitly addressing the limitations of human discourse, the narrator sets up the verbs 'know', 'call' and 'understand' precisely in order to undercut them with a synthetic or 'neither-nor' response. Rather than simply posing a redundant question, however, this complex narrative operation is central to the structure of the *Confessions*, which constantly pursues an interrogation of the means of confession and the profession of faith which resounds disconcertingly with contemporary enquiries into narratorial authority and the prospect of referentiality. The narrator's proposition of professedly inadequate terms ('to call upon you or to praise you...?'), allowing Augustine's text to finally emerge from its screen of Biblical quotation at the end of the first paragraph, evokes an elaborate abdication of authority. And yet it is Augustine's peculiarly self-effacing and rigorous deference to the Word which cannot be framed in earthly language that lends his work such impact and importance.

A similarly reflexive interrogation of the global purpose of the *Confessions* occurs at the opening of book XI, where the relationship of verbal enunciation and divine power is examined:

> Lord, eternity is yours, so you cannot be ignorant of what I tell you. Your vision of occurrences in time is not temporally conditioned. Why then do I set before you an ordered account of so many things? It is certainly not through me that you know them. But I am stirring up love for you in myself and in those who read this, so that we may all say 'Great is the Lord and highly worthy to be praised' (Ps. 47:1).[9]

Why, indeed, *does* Augustine's narrator present a chronological account of his life and conversion, if God's time and presence are infinite? Not only is it wholly unnecessary to itemise human affairs which are already part of Divine schemes, but they are already *known* to an omnipotent God. The instability concerning the intended audience of the *Confessions* amounts to something like a rhetorical switch: supposedly addressed to God, the narrative is actually aimed at human readers. This disingenuous turn concerning the genesis and conditions of narrative constitutes one of the affinities between Augustine and Beckett to which I want to draw attention. The reflexive check to which Augustine's narrative subjects itself here is not only escaped, it actually achieves an important structural effect: although the questioning of narrative premises has an implosive quality, the resolution or postponement in which it culminates is clearly not the same thing as a narrative in which this questioning does not take place. The exploitation of this difference is one of the key tactics of Beckett's prose Trilogy. Reading the famous opening of *The Unnamable*, it is tempting to conclude that Beckett's text is built up entirely in the reflexive zone designated by the interrogation of narrative premises: 'Where now? Who now? When now? Unquestioning. I, say I. Unbelieving. Questions, hypotheses, call them that'.[10] The stark unravelling of narrative takes precisely those questions which are conventionally the province of the reader, deciphering a text, as its matter. To rephrase Beckett's remark on Augustine, the form matters here to the extent that it has itself become the sole subject of narrative.

James Olney indicates an interesting correspondence between the two authors in terms of Augustine's questioning of the narrative impulse, which becomes, in Beckett, 'irrational and illogical, compulsive, obsessional, repetitive, unwilled and often unwanted but not to be denied'.[11] In an interesting analysis of *Company* and *Krapp's Last Tape*, Olney proposes that Beckett and Augustine both collide with the same fundamental formal problem in differingly autobiographical works: the narration of immemorial events, and specifically birth:

> What the narrative of *Company* succeeds in doing by beginning with this absolutely unverifiable event is not only to cast great doubt on everything else the voice tells of a past but to render impossible the assertion of 'I' in the recalling of these unrecallable events. If you cannot say 'born upon such and such a day', you cannot say 'I' either: if you cannot remember the event, you cannot narrate out of the continuity of being that 'I' implies. Augustine gets around this as best he can by writing, not of his birth to be sure but of his early infancy.[12]

While this appears true, the inward scrutiny directed at narrative genesis is much more severe than a simple uncertainty resulting from the absence of reliable memory. If birth is categorically immemorial, many of Beckett's characters (as Olney notes) claim precisely to remember it:

for Mr Hackett in *Watt*, the pain of birth is acutely present:

> That is a thing I have often wondered, said Mr. Hackett, what it feels like to have the string cut.
> For the mother or the child? said Goff.
> For the mother, said Mr. Hackett. I was not found under a cabbage, I believe.[13]

In *Watt*, as in many of Beckett's texts, birth and sex designate a parodic thematic complex in which mothers are held eternally responsible for inflicting the life-sentence of birth. In an unexpected echo of Beckett's remark on form, however, textual construction here proves peculiarly interpenetrated with thematics: a key corroboration of the equation of birth with suffering and atrocity occurs in the fragmentary annexe entitled *Addenda* at the end of the book, in the unexplained remark 'Never been properly born'.[14] The remark is itself a textual fragment in the construction of *Watt*, neither fully participating in the unity of the main text nor definitively outside it, but acquires an intertextual aspect in its recurrence in *All That Fall*:

> *Mrs Rooney:* 'I remember once attending a lecture by one of these new mind doctors. I forget what you call them [...] I remember his telling us the story of a little girl, very strange and unhappy in her ways [...] The only thing wrong with her as far as he could see was that she was dying [...] Then he suddenly raised his head and exclaimed, as if he had had a revelation, The trouble with her was she had never really been born!'[15]

The insistent recurrence is itself expressive of a formal disturbance: the larger unity of Beckett's work is undercut and destabilised by the insidious presence of the image of the transgressive and psychically disastrous birth. This motif of perverted biology signs the process whereby the proper containment of content within textual limits gives way to a principle of intertextual replication.[16]

Augustine's narrative in the *Confessions* proves peculiarly susceptible to self-interruption precisely when it touches upon birth and biological derivation. Its scheme follows a clear progression in book IX following Augustine's conversion until the death of his mother, Monica, is announced:

> While we were at Ostia by the mouths of the Tiber, my mother died. I pass over many events because I write in great haste. Accept my confessions and thanksgivings, my God, for innumerable things even though I do not specifically mention them. But I shall not pass over whatever my soul may bring to birth concerning your servant, who brought me to birth both in her body so that I was born into the light of time, and in her heart so that I was born into the light of eternity.[17]

If the announcement is motivated by the chronological occurrence of Monica's death during the move back to Africa following the conversion, it subsequently diverts the narrative from its sequential scheme and into an extended reflection on Monica's life and character (IX.viii-IX.xii). A reassessment of the project of the *Confessions* like that seen above is simultaneously triggered, as the narrator adds to his list of personal failings that of omitting to mention various events (in praise or in repentance, as appropriate). Having previously established, as we have seen, that all such events are simultaneously present to Divine consciousness, Augustine's narrator nevertheless persists in enumerating them, both according to a chronological scheme and in terms of their importance relative to the development of his Christian faith. The latter is the surface-level cause of the digression: Monica is described as having given birth to Augustine both physically and spiritually.

Straightforward and familiar as the formulation appears, the encounter of physical birth and the soul is the site of a deeply-felt equivocation in the *Confessions*. Godliness hovers between an innate quality and an acquired disposition, as is hinted immediately after the reference to Monica's death: 'You created her, and her father and mother did not know what kind of character their child would have'.[18] The admission of ignorance concerning birth and infancy at the opening of the narrative, 'I do not know where I came from',[19] like the commemoration of both the narrator's parents at the end of book IX, addresses the soul as well as physical origins: '[…] all who read this book may remember at your altar Monica your servant and Patrick her late husband, through whose physical bond you brought me into this life without my knowing how'.[20] If the passage into 'this life' is to be celebrated, it is because the narrator sees it as leading to true faith (it would otherwise be a mere biological fact), even as itself implicated in the infusing of the body with spiritual essence. (The pious commemoration of the 'heredity' of Augustine's faith is undercut, however, by the fact that Patrick, his father, was not a Christian.) As in Beckett's writing, biological origins model a deeply-felt anxiety concerning narrative motivation and textual genesis. Details of infancy and even of one's own birth may be retrieved from trusted third parties, but the dilemma of how the soul is united with the body punctuates the *Confessions* with a disabling indeterminacy. The unvoiced question plays around the text's opening and recurs at moments like that of Monica's death in which physical origins are conflated with those of the text and of the Christian belief which is its key event. If the narrator is asking 'Who am I?' at the text's opening, there persists, in addition to the question's function of introducing the chronological presentation of Augustine's life, the unresolved problem of whether the conversion was possible as a result of principles and beliefs learnt, for example from Monica, or due to an essence present in the soul from birth or conception.

Augustine's famous indecision on the question may well have preoccupied Beckett. Although it is not my intention here to document direct allusions to Augustine in Beckett,[21] the manner of Beckett's reference to it is highly significant in view of the formal affinities which his work shows with that of Augustine. The uncontextualised remark 'the foetal soul is born full grown', referring to the Manichee belief that the soul was united with the embryo due to heredity, appears, like the comment on impossible birth, in the *Addenda* to the novel *Watt*.[22] If birth occupies a position of provocative uncertainty and anguish in Beckett, the formal replication of this uncertainty (the *Addenda*) is explicitly preoccupied with the question which played the same role in Augustine's work.

The disruptive potential of the thematics of biological derivation becomes particularly acute in the relationship of Molloy and his mother in Beckett's *Molloy*. Not only is their encounter early in the book characterised by a phobic insistence on the remembrance of birth ('her who brought me into the world, through the hole in her arse if my memory is correct'),[23] it involves an equivocation concerning naming which leads to a radical loss of faith in the expressive capacities of language:

> I called her Mag, when I had to call her something. And I called her
> Mag because for me, without my knowing why, the letter g abolished

the syllable Ma, and as it were spat upon it, better than any other letter would have done.[24]

The necessity of naming the mother-figure introduces a larger-scale engagement with the fraught imperative of linguistic communication: Mag chatters away continually and incomprehensibly ('She jabbered away with a clatter of dentures and most of the time didn't realise what she was saying' – p.18) while Molloy invents a code based on knocking on her skull ('One knock meant yes, two no, three I don't know, four money, five goodbye' – p.18). Narrative inclines ever more closely towards the frank impossibility of signification, the aborted act of naming giving way to a failed gestural scheme as the four knocks to signify money are replaced by another system ('this consisted in replacing the four knocks of my index knuckle by one or more (according to my needs) thumps of the fist, on her skull' – p.19). However degraded the means of its expression, 'money' has taken on the status of a key signifier: the self-cancelling dynamic of the narrative now denies this too, however, as it is revealed that, despite all the preceding manœuvres, money is not the object of the episode ('In any case I didn't come for money' – p.19). Like Augustine's implosive rhetoric, Beckett's narrative is increasingly absorbed into the questionable possibility of saying: its principal subject is a ghastly involuted scrutiny of its own conditions. Molloy's pronouncement of the name 'Mag' mounts a fundamental challenge to narrative sequentiality: not only does it launch the elaborate false trail of the aborted gestures leading to the fake motivation of 'money', but it vaunts its own absolute logical gratuity: 'Besides, for me the question did not arise [...] of whether to call her Ma, Mag or the Countess Caca, she having for countless years been deaf as a post' – p.18).

The principal move or figure of the passage is the principle of retrospective negation by which the 'money' device is cancelled, and by which the act of naming, the motivational force behind the whole episode, is revealed to be essentially redundant. The sense of a ruthlessly self-antagonistic narrative mode grows when it is realised that the same movement is contained *within* the pronouncement of the name: although 'g' follows and supplements 'Ma', it is described as negating this first syllable. How can what has already been voiced be modified by a subsequent sound? Although this may be seen to be possible on a literal level, the second sound assimilating what might have signified in its own right as merely part of another signifier, the extreme emphasis of the verb 'abolish' evokes a more sinister operation whereby, like the reverse motive logic of the following passage, the very existence of the preceding sound is somehow cancelled. A striking parallel occurs in the second part of *Molloy*, in which Moran is meditating on his knowledge of Molloy, which seems to come to him from some distant recess of his brain, like a sensation of *déjà vu*: 'Molloy, or Mellose, was no stranger to me. [...] Perhaps I had invented him, I mean found him ready-made in my head' (p.103). The uncertainty surrounding the name is emphasised when Moran shifts to the subject of 'Mother Molloy':

> Mother Molloy, or Mellose, was not completely foreign to me either, it seemed. But she was much less alive than her son, who God knows was far from being so. After all perhaps I knew nothing of mother Molloy, or Mollose, save in so far as such a son might bear, like a scurf of placenta, her stamp.
>
> Of these two names, Molloy and Mollose, the second seemed to me perhaps the more correct. But barely. What I heard, in my soul I suppose, where the acoustics are so bad, was a first syllable, Mol, very clear, followed almost at once by a second, very thick, as though gobbled by the first, and which might have been oy as it might have been ose, or one, or even oc. (p.103)

In a shocking reversal of the principles of heredity, the mother-figure appears to be derived from Molloy himself: the degree to which she is alive is assessed purely by reference to Molloy, and knowledge of her is deduced solely from the supposition that if Molloy existed, his mother must exist to the extent that he would resemble her. If this relationship operates according to the founding of statements on empty or false premises which is so crucial to narrative motivation in Beckett, its wilfully disabled predication again invokes a problematic oral enunciation. Here, if the first sound is unmistakably distinct (but actually the soft and *indistinct* 'Mol'), how can it be responsible for cancelling and obscuring the second, for having 'gobbled' it? While the second sound might itself be so soft as to be easily mistaken for others (as could easily be the case for 'oy', 'ose' or 'one'), its specificity can hardly be eroded by a preceding certainty. Beckett reduces sounds to a pretext by which a larger problematic of differentiation may be articulated: just as Molloy and Mother Molloy do not refer to any identifiable essence, their bodily dereliction and extravagantly handicapped communication serve to articulate a disassembling motion in language itself. Like Augustine, Beckett is concerned to exploit language's perpetual failure to signify: his determination to 'fail again, fail better' is fundamentally compatible with the rhetorical inwardness of the *Confessions*, and with Augustine's central, constraining belief that 'words are inadequate to convey an ineffable Godhead'.[25] The crucial dilemma in Augustine's writings is precisely this:

> [i]n relation to God's Word, the voice whose syllables arrive and pass away must be 'distantly other' (II.vi.8). How then is that Word to be approached, heard, known, confessed?[26]

If Augustine and Beckett would be expected to represent fundamentally different standpoints to Christian doctrine, they both respond to the prospect of linguistic failure by making it one of the essential subjects of their work. Like Beckett's situation of narrative in a posthumous domain like that normally occupied by interpretation ('Où irais-je, si je pouvais aller, que serais-je, si je pouvais être, que dirais-je, si j'avais une voix, qui parle ainsi, se disant moi?', 'Where would I go, if I could go, who would I be, if I could be, what would I say, if I had a voice, who says this, saying it's me?'),[27] Augustine's project in the *Confessions* avidly embraces the shortcomings of language. This project takes place firmly in the context of its value to Christian faith, of course: language proves itself inadequate because it is insufficient to praise God (as well as quite incapable of evoking the Divine), and human acts of narration are utterly redundant in the face of God's omniscient knowledge, as Augustine admits: 'If anything I say to men is right, that is what you have first heard from me. Moreover, you hear nothing true from my lips which you have not first told me'.[28] Like the perverse, inwardly subsiding entropy of Beckett's Trilogy, proceeding by 'aporia pure and simple' (p.267), Augustine's narrative takes place amidst the collapse of the conditions which guarantee and justify its existence. The background to the question of the viability of narrative and of linguistic expression at large in Augustine is unquestionably the monumental presence of the Logos. If the fallen, human, lower-case version of the Word is precisely the punctual instance of the voicing of sounds, Augustine specifically meditates the nature of speech as he charts his spiritual development in book IV:

> Not everything grows old, but everything dies. So when things rise and emerge into existence, the faster they grow to be, the quicker they rush towards non-being. That is the law limiting their being. So much have you given them, namely to be parts of things which do not all have their being at the same moment, but by passing away and by successiveness, they all form the whole of which they are parts. That is the way our speech is constructed by sounds which are significant. What we say would not be complete if one word did not cease to exist when it has sounded its constituent parts, so that it can be succeeded by another.[29]

There is a very interesting interaction to be observed between Augustine's analysis of the role of the transience of sounds in the ultimate unity of the Creation and Beckett's extravagantly aborted speech acts. Although, in Augustine, sounds only render fleeting and debased intimations of the 'whole', this occurs precisely in their disappearance in order to make way for successive sounds and in the more general abnegation thereby evoked, which man would positively desire, if his intellect had not been impaired by the Fall, in order to appreciate the 'whole'.[30] This orderly fading is crucially disabled in Beckett, so that the pronunciation of the sound 'g' obscures the syllable 'Ma', while 'Mol' pre-emptively silences the indeterminate sound which may be 'one', 'ose', 'oy', or 'oc'. This is, then, the very amplification of Babel which Augustine imagines, the proper distinction between words and their interrelationships eroded by a mode of speech which strains sequentiality until language begins to collapse into a series of bodily noises. While proper communication for Augustine (in so far as that is possible in a fallen world) is predicated on the timely dissolution of words' temporary plenitude into silence, in Beckett the failure of speech brings about an ironised form of presence in which, like Mother Molloy's babble or the Unnamable's torrent of words, the voice can never properly be said to be silent.

While it might appear foolhardy to invoke the spectre of the Logos in relation to a body of work as profoundly intertextual and anti-monolithic as that of Beckett, this very intertextuality is the sign not of an assimilation or appropriation of discourses, but of a resolute permeability whereby texts like those of Augustine are engaged with as much by formal affinity as by allusion. The very distinctive shape arising from Augustine's writing is uniquely provocative in Beckett: the meditations on the momentary accommodation of form in sounds in the *Confessions* are sharply reminiscent of Beckett's remarks on the need to find a form to contain the ever more intransigent 'mess'. Not only is Beckett fascinated by the 'form' which he observes in Augustine, but his work displays formal unease at precisely the same point as that of Augustine. Birth, origins and reproduction constitute the site of an analogous anxiety in Beckett and Augustine which is reflected in reflexivity, self-disempowering rhetoricity and large-scale formal disruption. The abdication which this involves, not only of narrative authority but of textual propriety altogether, triggers something like an intratextual devolution. The defining thematic of anxiety at origins attains such intensity that it is no longer only a thematic. The texts in which it is dealt with testify, finally, to a sort of textual incapacity: in Beckett, reference to the birth and motherhood complex becomes so dense and so frequent that the establishment of a viable textual base from which intertextual reference may be conducted is seriously threatened. The quest for the source of Beckett's reference to the two thieves in Augustine, then, curiously mirrors the textual equivocation around origins which both authors' work manifests. If Beckett claims to wish to remember Augustine's Latin 'original' (which itself refers to Luke 23 and Mark 15), its obscurity nevertheless participates in the anxious disposition whereby generative sites are alternately laid bare and disgustedly hidden from view in his writing. The inappropriable profusion into which readable meaning dissolves in Beckett and Augustine is uniquely implicated in notions of source and origin, and yet refuses to conceptualise these notions. If Mother Molloy exists only to the extent that the son to whom she has given birth must resemble her, Beckett's narrative aporia recalls the humbling confrontation in Augustine with the inarticulable presence of divine mystery; both are inevitably and unendingly preoccupied with the impossible imperative of narration. While Beckett's Unnamable imagines a final but infinitely postponed resolution to his obligation to narrate, in which he would finally 'have them carry me into my story, the words that remain, my old story, which I've forgotten, far from here, through the noise, through the door, into the silence' (p.381), Augustine's narrator closes his confession in the same image of openness and proliferation: 'Only you can be asked, only you can be begged, only on your door can we knock [...] that is how it is received, how it is found, how the door is opened' (XIII.xxxviii (53), p.305). Both persist in the avowedly impossible narration of the ineffable, whose final goal is the silence which lies beyond its distressed, failing, and yet resurgent core of murmurs.

NOTES TO CHAPTER V

1. On intertextuality and notions of difference and alterity in contemporary theory, see Judith Still and Michael Worton (eds), *Intertextuality: Theories and Practices* (Manchester: Manchester University Press, 1990), pp.1-2, 14-33.
2. Beckett, *Waiting for Godot*, in *Complete Dramatic Works* (London: Faber and Faber, 1986), p.14.
3. Beckett, quoted in Harold Hobson, 'Samuel Beckett: Dramatist of the Year', *International Theatre Annual*, no.1 (1956), 153-155 (p.153).
4. See David Green, 'A Note on Augustine's Thieves', *Journal of Beckett Studies*, 3, no.2 (1994), pp.77-78, and Chris Ackerley, 'Do Not Despair: Samuel Beckett and Robert Greene', *Journal of Beckett Studies*, 6, no.1 (1997), pp.119-24.
5. 'In a place were three crosses. On one, a thief marked out to be saved; on another, a thief marked out to be condemned; and in the middle, Christ. For the one to be saved was one to be condemned' - Augustine, *Epistola* XLVIII (translation mine). The passage is quoted in Dougald McMillan and Martha Fehsenfeld, *Beckett in the Theatre: the Author as Practical Playwright and Director* vol. 1: From *Waiting for Godot* to *Krapp's Last Tape* (London: John Calder, 1988), p.59, where it is described as 'the closest approximation' to what Beckett (wrongly) ascribed to Augustine's *Confessions* in an interview in 1979.
6. Augustine, *Confessions*, IX / ii (2), trans. Henry Chadwick (Oxford: Oxford University Press, 1991), pp.155-56.
7. ibid., I.ix (21), p.15.
8. ibid., I.i (1), p.3.
9. ibid., XI.i (1), p.221.
10. Beckett, *The Unnamable*, in *The Beckett Trilogy* (London: Picador, 1976), p.267.
11. James Olney, 'Memory and Narrative Imperative: St. Augustine and Samuel Beckett', *New Literary History* 24, no.4 (Autumn 1993), 857-880 (p.858).
12. ibid., p.862.
13. Beckett, *Watt* (London: John Calder, 1963), p.12.
14. ibid., p.248.
15. *All That Fall*, in Beckett, *The Complete Dramatic Works*, op.cit. pp.195-96.
16. Also see Vladimir's and Estragon's remarks in *En attendant Godot*, 'Si on se repentait?' [...] 'D'être né?' (in *Théâtre I* (Paris: Éditions de Minuit, 1971), p.13), and the formulation 'J'ai renoncé avant de naître, ce n'est pas possible autrement', in *Pour finir encore et autres foirades* (Paris: Éditions de Minuit, 1976), p.38.
17. Augustine, *Confessions*, IX.viii (17), p.166.
18. ibid., IX.viii (17), p.166.
19. ibid., I.vi (7), p.6.
20. ibid., IX.xiii (37), p.178.

21. Mary Bryden identifies many important echoes of and allusions to Augustine in Beckett's *Dream of Fair to Middling Women*. See Bryden, *Samuel Beckett and the Idea of God* (London: Macmillan, 1998), pp.77-96.

22. Beckett, *Watt*, p.248.

23. Beckett, *Molloy*, in *The Beckett Trilogy*, p.17.

24. ibid., p.18.

25. Anne Howland Schotter, 'Vernacular Style and the Word of God: the Incarnational Art of *Pearl*', in P.S. Hawkins and A.H. Schotter (eds), *Ineffability: Naming the Unnamable from Dante to Beckett* (New York: AMS, 1984), 23-34 (pp.23-24).

26. Ralph Flores, *The Rhetoric of Doubtful Authority: Deconstructive Readings of Self-Questioning Narratives, St. Augustine to Faulkner* (Ithaca and London: Cornell University Press, 1984), p.49.

27. Beckett, *Nouvelles et Textes pour rien*, IV, (Paris: Éditions de Minuit, 1958), p.139, Beckett, *Texts for Nothing*, IV, (London: Calder, 1974), p. 22.

28. Augustine, *Confessions*, X.ii (2), p.179.

29. ibid., IV.x (15), pp.61-62.

30. 'if your physical perception were capable of comprehending the whole […] you would wish everything here present to pass away, so that the totality of things could provide you with greater pleasure' – ibid., IV.x (17), p.63.

CHAPTER VI

Rites of Passage:
Intertextuality and the Metaphysics of Space
in Aragon, Benjamin, Butor and Koeppen

Eric Robertson

Eric Robertson is a Lecturer in French at Royal Holloway, University of London. His main research interests are in twentieth-century French and comparative literature, visual arts, and literary bilingualism. Author of *Writing Between the Lines*, 1995 on René Schickele, and co-editor of *Yvan Goll and Claire Goll: Texts and Contexts*, 1997, he has published articles and chapters predominantly on the interaction of text and image (Arp, Cendrars, R. and S. Delaunay, Goll, Michaux).

> Der Vater des Surrealismus war Dada,
> seine Mutter war eine Passage.
>
> Walter Benjamin
>
> Métaphysique des lieux, c'est vous qui bercez les enfants, c'est vous qui peuplez leurs rêves.
>
> Louis Aragon

In dealing with Michel Butor's *La Modification* and Wolfgang Koeppen's *Der Tod in Rom* (*Death in Rome*), we are faced with a peculiarly multi-layered intertextuality.¹ For not only are these novels related to one another by what Gérard Genette terms hypertextuality,² but both works also form part of a broader transtextual network operating on several levels. Most overtly, *Der Tod in Rom* compels us to take into account Thomas Mann's *Der Tod in Venedig* (*Death in Venice*), which the conception and the title of Koeppen's work consciously recall. This tripartite relationship is extended further by the fact that Mann's novella is strewn with references to Plato's *Symposium* and *Phaedrus* and Plutarch's *Eròtikos*, while the dream sequences in *La Modification* contain allusions to Julian the Apostate, the legend of the Great Huntsman, and Virgil's *Æneid*, all of which connections have been extensively documented.³

Besides a marked similarity of style, what aligns *La Modification* and *Der Tod in Rom* is above all their shared emphasis on the urban space as a conduit linking the individual psyche and history. It is this too which reveals both novels to be surprisingly indebted to two iconic works of inter-war Modernism, namely Walter Benjamin's monumental study of Paris, *Das Passagen-Werk* (*The Arcades Project*), and Louis Aragon's Surrealist narrative *Le Paysan de Paris* (*Paris Peasant*), which not only employ an intertextual montage structure, but are themselves connected intertextually.⁴ In charting these routes, the present essay will examine some of the principal ways in which the notion of passage, both as place and as action, not only informs the structure of Koeppen's and Butor's texts, but also serves as a connecting vessel which links them conceptually to the discourses of Aragon and Benjamin.

It is a commonplace that the very structure of the *nouveau roman* as a genre is intertextual: in Butor's *Passage de Milan*, the multi-layered construction of the block of flats operates as a *mise en abyme* of the stratifications of the narrative itself, and of textuality in a wider sense.[5] In this respect, Koeppen's highly autoreferential fiction aligns itself closely to that of Butor. Published in 1954, Koeppen's text explores the search for new values in Germany in the aftermath of the Second World War; that this historical and political agenda implicated Koeppen in experimentation of a literary kind is clear from the book's self-reflexivity, a feature it shares with *La Modification*. Published three years after Koeppen's text, Butor's work is widely regarded as a landmark of the *nouveau roman* in its radical experimentation and its highly unconventional use of the second-person narrative voice. Besides their choice of modern-day Rome as setting, the two novels share some important structural and stylistic features: their strikingly unconventional syntax, their extensive use of inner monologue and their multiple time levels all reveal close similarities. For all that geophysical space in the *nouveau roman* often functions as a *mise en abyme* of the text's own structure, the geographical milieu in these works transcends the mere formalism that this would imply. What links these two novels, both to each other and to Aragon's and Benjamin's exegeses, is above all their exploration of what Butor has termed *le génie du lieu*,[6] the power of a particular place to generate resonances in the subjective consciousness. This fascination with geographic locations and their interconnectedness with mental space recalls the Surrealists' exploration of the modern urban milieu as a productive point of contact between external reality and the subjective imagination.

An important link between the four narratives under discussion is to be found in the figure of the *flâneur*, first celebrated by Baudelaire, and injected with new life by Surrealist narratives such as André Breton's *Nadja* and *Les Vases communicants*, and Louis Aragon's *Le Paysan de Paris*. Developing the aimlessness of *flânerie* into a strategy for escaping the confines of the conscious mind, Breton and Aragon show how certain environments can sensitise the willing participant to what Breton terms 'objective chance', and to the marvellous. Rather than the open spaces familiar to the tourist, they are particularly fascinated by the covered galleries around the Place de l'Opéra which had largely been condemned to dereliction or demolition by Haussmann's extensive restructuring of the city. In the long first section of *Le Paysan de Paris*, entitled 'Le Passage de l'Opéra', Aragon describes the particular attraction which draws him towards the enclosed spaces of transit and commerce that had formerly dominated this part of the city: 'How oddly this light suffuses the covered arcades which abound in Paris in the vicinity of the main boulevards and which are rather disturbingly named *passages*, as though no one had the right to linger for more than an instant in those sunless corridors'.[7] These are for Aragon no less than 'the true sanctuaries of a cult of the ephemeral, the ghostly landscape of damnable pleasures and professions, places that were incomprehensible yesterday and that tomorrow will never know'.[8] In wandering through these dark and unsalubrious passages, the modern-day *flâneur* can find in even their most unprepossessing recesses the entry key to an underworld of sensual pleasure and self-discovery.

Both the arcades themselves and Aragon's literary exploration of them exercised a strong fascination for Walter Benjamin, who devoted a considerable proportion of his literary output to a long-standing and wide-ranging critique of French culture and literature.[9] In particular, repeated references to *Le Paysan de Paris* are to be found in the myriad notes constituting *Das Passagen-Werk*, whose very construction was to be based on the montage of intertextual fragments:

> Method of this project: literary montage. I needn't say anything. Merely show. I shall purloin no valuables, appropriate no ingenious formulations. But the rags, the refuse – these I will not inventory but allow, in the only way possible, to come into their own: by making use of them.[10]

In thematic terms, Benjamin's and Aragon's texts are analogous in their foregrounding of the dream: many of Benjamin's notes on the arcades were intended to form part of a section entitled 'Traumhaus' ('House of Dreams'). In one such fragment, he likens the entrances of the arcades to the thresholds of a realm whose precise function is initially unclear, but whose presence is unmistakably portentous: 'These gateways – the entrances to the arcades – are thresholds. No stone step serves to mark them. But this marking is accomplished by the expectant posture of the handful of people. Tightly measured paces reflect the fact, altogether unknowingly, that a decision lies ahead'.[11] Clearly, this visualisation of the arcades as a modern-day Styx owes much to Aragon's metaphorical use of geophysical and architectural allusions: indeed, shortly after the passage cited above, Benjamin quotes Aragon's evocation of the passages as 'the true sanctuaries of a cult of the ephemeral';[12] over three hundred pages further on, he cites a fragment from a text by Amédée Kermel who, nearly a century before Aragon, muses on the acute sense of unease which befalls the visitor before the passage de l'Opéra: the person who ventures inside does so 'as if he were penetrating into the temple of God'.[13] Benjamin, for his part, observes that a letter box stands outside the entrance to the arcades as if to offer the intrepid visitor 'a last chance to give a sign to the world one is leaving behind'.[14] It is through such metonymies that Benjamin, like Aragon and Kermel before him, reveals the arcades and other enclosed spaces to be 'the houses of the collective dream'.[15]

Koeppen's choice of Rome as the setting of his novel has a similarly metonymical effect, for he is interested primarily in its implications for twentieth-century *German* history in the wake of the Nazi regime which had driven Benjamin to suicide in 1940. If the constellation of German characters who gather there reflects the contradictions of Rome, marked by a classical heritage, by cultural and religious strengths, but also by its recurrent flirtations with dictators, then it reflects even more strongly the paradoxes of their own country: Germany's historical dominance built on military strength, its musical and literary heritage effaced by its shameful recent history, and its tentative search for new cultural values in the aftermath of war. Siegfried Pfaffrath, a young avant-garde composer of twelve-tone music who has come to Rome for the première of his prize-winning experimental symphony, and his cousin Adolf Judejahn, a Roman Catholic priest who has travelled there in order to be ordained, both represent a post-war generation horrified by their fathers' involvement in the Nazi party. Adolf's father, Gottlieb Judejahn, is a former SS general who escaped trial in Germany. He is now military advisor to an Arab sheikh, on whose behalf he too has come to Rome, to buy illegal weapons. Siegfried's father, Friedrich Wilhelm Pfaffrath, once a high-ranking official under the Nazis and now mayor of his home town, has arrived in Rome with his family to try to bring his brother-in-law

Gottlieb Judejahn home to a Germany in which he hopes the former Nazi may now live in safety.

Siegfried's music has distinctly political implications which are given an ironic touch by the Wagnerian connotations of his name.[16] His atonal composition is a deliberate subversion of German nationalism, a concept mortally contaminated by the Nazis:

> [The septet] represented Siegfried's rebellion against his surroundings, against the prisoner-of-war camp, against the barbed-wire fences, against his comrades with their boring conversations, against the war, for which he held his parents responsible, against his whole hellish and hellbent Fatherland.[17]

Indeed, when all the principal characters attend the performance of his symphony, the gamut of different responses his music provokes in them, from excitement to incomprehension to disgust and even fear, illustrates their own political and ethical diversity (*TiR* 144-150).

Like Butor, Koeppen was keen to exploit the creative analogies to be made between musical and narrative structures.[18] That Siegfried should be the composer of atonal music is an appropriate means of mirroring the book's own formal experimentation. The frequent shifts from the omniscient, anonymous third person narrator to free indirect speech, and to Siegfried's and his uncle Judejahn's inner monologues, are announced only by paragraph breaks which often occur in mid-sentence. The effect of this polyphonic narrative structure is multifold: on one level, it foregrounds the non-mimetic, formal characteristics of the text, emphasising its contrasting tonalities and thereby underscoring the musical paradigm that underpins its very conception. At the same time, Koeppen harnesses this subversive narrative structure as an indirect vehicle for his own criticism of Nazi Germany. This he achieves by aligning the anonymous narrator to Siegfried in direct opposition to Judejahn: whereas the latter's free indirect speech consists of short sentences with heavy repetition and frequent anaphora, both Siegfried and the anonymous narrator share a fondness for lengthy, serpentine sentences rich in asyndeton. In this collusion between narrator and main protagonist, the novel may be seen as deliberately departing from the narrative strategy of *Der Tod in Venedig*, whereby a gap emerges between Aschenbach's free indirect speech and the observations of the anonymous narrator. Like Siegfried's musical compositions, the proliferation of discourses and the liberation of syntax in Koeppen's novel could be interpreted as a protest against the tyranny of pseudo-logic which Hitler had put to such malevolent use.

The plurality implicit in such musical analogies also characterises the treatment of space and time in both novels, which set modern Rome alongside another location and other historical periods. In *Der Tod in Rom* the notion of place, and of displacement, is closely related both to Koeppen's experimental narrative technique and to his critical engagement with Germany's political and historical development in the twentieth century. While the entire plot of the novel unfolds exclusively in Rome, the chance meeting of the Pfaffrath and Judejahn families in that setting is a convenient, if rather schematic, device allowing Koeppen to portray a microcosmic 'virtual' Germany. The Roman setting also accentuates the allegorical function of the various characters, whose political and ethical differences serve as a microcosm of Germany's moral clefts in the immediate post-war years. Thus, Judejahn senior bemoans the desecration of the *Duce's* monuments and feels threatened by the present-day city, in stark contrast to Kürenberg, the internationally famous conductor who will conduct the première of Siegfried's symphony. Both Kürenberg and his wife Ilse are highly cultured and cosmopolitan Jews accustomed to a nomadic lifestyle as 'excursionists who had made themselves at home in a possibly inhospitable planet' (p.45), and they seem to belong to all ages and none: perfectly at ease in Rome, they love its vestiges of antiquity, whose beauty they both absorb and reflect, and they quote from Horace and Virgil. Siegfried, on the other hand, is too suspicious of his father's generation to be comfortable with the past, and proclaims his love for all that present-day Rome can offer (*TiR* 48 / *DiR* 50).

The problematisation of the physical locus is equally crucial to *La Modification*, whose very plot centres on a train journey: Butor's protagonist, the successful middle-aged businessman Léon Delmont, visits Rome ostensibly on business, but his real purpose is to escape the monotony of family life with his wife, Henriette and their two children, by visiting his lover, Cécile, whom he intends to bring back to live with him in Paris. The time he spends in the train allows him to consider his marriage, his relationship with Cécile and their projected future together: his ultimate realisation that his love for her is inextricably linked to the 'mythe romain' prompts the modification of his plan to divorce Henriette for her. Delmont realises that his relationship with Cécile could not survive in Paris because his feelings for her are inextricably bound to the city in which their affair blossomed, and which has become an extension of her very identity: 'the Roman light she reflects and concentrates is extinguished as soon as she is in Paris'.[19]

As even this brief summary suggests, *La Modification* derives much thematic and structural import from the act of travelling from Paris *to* Rome; indeed, Butor's fiction repeatedly explores the literary work as a journey, a parallel which he defines as 'the fundamental theme of all novelistic literature'.[20] He maintains that his conception of *La Modification* sprang initially not from any specific interest in Paris or Rome *per se*, but from the formal interest of a work focusing on two distinct cities:

> while working on *L'Emploi du temps*, whose principal character was a city, I asked the question: how might one create a novel with two cities? It was not yet a question of Paris and Rome. But as I thought it through a little more, these capitals inevitably made their presence felt.[21]

Elsewhere in his theoretical writings, Butor reiterates the central importance of spatial metaphors in his fiction, especially as a means of portraying the passage of time: 'In fact to be able to study time in its continuity, and therefore to be able to make gaps apparent, it is necessary to apply it to a space, to consider it like a route, a journey'.[22]

The metaphor of the train journey also generates and reflects the book's multi-layered structure. The narrated time spans the twenty-two hours taken by the journey from Paris to Rome, which unfolds in a continuous present. Different time levels are generated by Delmont's various proleptic and analeptic reflexions, all of which are related to his different visits to Rome or his life in Paris. These are regularly interspersed, and kept in check, by reminders of his present journey in the form of microscopic observations of the train, his fellow travellers and the view from the window. Just as Siegfried's experimental symphony generates a *mise en abyme*, the repeated references to the book of railway timetables on Delmont's lap remind us of the network of signs and interconnected narrative threads which compose *La Modification*.

A particularly revealing point of convergence in the two novels is the way in which their protagonists internalise Rome and attempt to appropriate it. In *La Modification*, Delmont progresses towards the realisation that his love of the eternal city is inseparable from its mythological associations and his own affective baggage (pp.73-80). On his return to Paris, he tries to prolong vicariously the feelings Rome instills in him by indulging in some aimless *flânerie*, 'letting your mood be your guide, without any clear idea in mind of any specific direction' (p.64). Ironically, however, he ends up following a 'Roman itinerary' (p.76), which, like his conception of Rome itself, is a composite construction, and as much a product of popular myth as it is a reflection of the real city. This ambivalent status is evoked metatextually by means of a reference to Pannini's paintings, in which 'there is no appreciable material difference between the objects represented as real and those represented as painted' (p.64). As the train takes him towards the very different modern-day Rome, Delmont begins to suspect that his relationship to that city would be hollow without Cécile's presence: 'You are afraid that the 'Eternal City' will seem quite empty from now on' (p.86).

In a similar way, but with somewhat different narrative aims, Koeppen too portrays Rome not as a harmonious whole, but as a series of disparate fragments, each one defined by the subjectivity of his various characters. The one common feature, noted both by the anonymous narrator and by the different protagonists, is decay: once inhabited by the gods, the city is now plagued by sickness and decadence (*TiR* 7 / *DiR* 9). Some of the book's most powerful tensions stem from the different ways in which its characters react to Rome, its people and its institutions, not least its religious ones. While the young priest Adolf hopes to cleanse his and his nation's guilty conscience in the home of the Roman Catholic Church, his father enjoys recollecting the shadier aspects of the Vatican's recent history, a fact which adds an extra note of irony to his first name, Gottlieb (connoting 'love of God'):

> At school little Gottlieb had learned that even popes allied themselves with death, and there was a time, not so very long ago, when popes engaged the services of executioners, of people like Judejahn.[23]

The architecture of Rome, too, is a vehicle for Koeppen's subjectivising narrative, and, like Siegfried's symphony, it reflects the spectrum of political and moral perspectives embodied by the various characters. On visiting the labyrinthine dungeons beneath the Papal Burg, Adolf prays for Rome's tortured prisoners of old; to his horror, he then glimpses his father, Judejahn, strolling impassively through the dungeons 'like someone returning to his house after a long absence',[24] and expressing his contempt for the dead by urinating through a crack in the stone onto the ancient graves of the city's poorest prisoners. These scenes are presented in a cinematic montage sequence alongside Siegfried's descent into the 'Underworld' – a tiny cell in a bathing ship on the Tiber – where he has sex with a boy prostitute before swimming in the polluted river. Siegfried's encounter with this 'Ganymede' is narrated with a frankness which does nothing to conceal the sexual nature of Siegfried's desire, in direct contrast to Thomas Mann's euphemistic treatment of homoerotic desire.[25]

As the above scenes suggest, the most resonant manifestations of Rome in Koeppen's novel are to be found not in the public sites of the city's tourist guides, but rather in its hidden spaces, in the network of passages and narrow lanes which cover the city. In *Der Tod in Rom*, a significant gap opens up between the different generations of characters in terms of how they react to the unfamiliar milieu. As Gottlieb Judejahn wanders around the city, he hears the sound of workers restoring a mosaic floor, and with all the trained responsiveness of Pavlov's dog he immediately adopts a warring posture: 'it made a sound like the whetting of long knives'.[26] The very opposite of the *flâneur*, this former Nazi feels not uplifted but disorientated in this unfamiliar city, and angered by its refusal to comply with his orders: 'Rome sleeping was sabotage, it sabotaged a war that was far from over, or that hadn't properly begun yet, Judejahn's war'.[27] Just as his brother-in-law, Pfaffrath senior, becomes 'bare naked powerless', we are told 'Judejahn was disempowered'. This feeling of powerlessness is compounded by Judejahn's linguistic disorientation: in a restaurant he orders 'fritto scelto', which he thinks is fried liver, only to be enraged when he is served mixed seafood (*TiR* 42 / *DiR* 43).

Siegfried is equally foreign in Rome, but unlike his father's generation, he *enjoys* the estrangement this entails: while Judejahn is drawn by the familiar, such as the illuminated sign advertising Pilsener outside a bar, Siegfried forces himself to drink Grappa because his reading of

Hemingway has taught him that it is *de rigueur* to do so. And in sharp contrast to Judejahn's fear of the unknown, Siegfried is attracted in equal measure by the conversation of the wine drinker in the working-class bar and the Latin spoken by the priests, precisely *because* he understands neither. This feeling of alterity and classlessness, of being an outside observer, makes Siegfried the archetypal *flâneur*, an identity he willingly bestows upon himself: 'I love Rome because I'm a foreigner in Rome and perhaps I always want to remain an outsider, an agitated observer'.[28] This kind of wilful *disponibilité* is intolerable for Judejahn, who clings to his German nationality as fiercely as he grasps his map of Rome. When he accepts a lift to the railway station from two Viennese tourists, he is thrown into a blind panic by the circuitous route it takes:

> Judejahn sensed that they weren't going to the station at all, that their progress was rambling, they were driving around in circles, searching no doubt for dead ends and quiet alleyways, or alternatively for the roar and confusion of traffic where a gunshot might go unnoticed.[29]

In resisting assimilation in this way, the topography of the city itself contributes to the seizure which kills Judejahn, although not before he has shot and killed Ilse Kürenberg in a final, belated attempt to fulfil the Führer's orders (*TiR* 183 / *DiR* 201). The ironic relationship between this novel and Mann's novella is seen most clearly in the closing sentence of Koeppen's novel, which Michael Hofmann has described as 'a dirty, tawdry version of the last sentence of *Death in Venice*',[30] an intertextual connection which Koeppen stresses further by re-employing Mann's closing sentence as an epigraph: 'And before nightfall a shocked and respectful world received the news of his decease'.[31] In response, Koeppen's low-key ending enacts textual revenge on Judejahn, ensuring that he is denied a glorious death: 'That same evening, Judejahn's death was reported in the press; its circumstances had made it world news, though the fact of it can have shocked no one'.[32] This Pyrrhic defeat of Judejahn has ethical as well as political implications: it represents the victory of Germany's present over its recent past, of *flânerie* over fascism.

As we have seen, the heavy impact of architechtonic space on the subjective consciousness is apparent in Aragon's and Benjamin's textual explorations of Paris. In a similar fashion, Koeppen's and Butor's main protagonists appear to gain a greater insight into their own subconscious impulses by voluntarily submitting themselves to whichever random encounters the topography of Rome might cast their way. As already mentioned, the most revelatory discoveries in this regard often appear to have been prompted by the protagonist's interaction with the angular alleyways and narrow passageways which beckon the curious wanderer. On one of his visits to Rome, Delmont looks forward to the prospect of a couple of hours of aimless strolling 'with nothing to hold you back, with nothing to prevent you from exploring the detours, however long, however angular, however unpredictable they may be, which will seduce you'.[33] The serpentine syntax of the extended sentence from which this is cited, with its accumulation of appositions and its proliferation of embedded clauses, imitates the labyrinthine space it describes, and foregrounds the importance of the passage as a metatextual metaphor of the book's narrative structure. But this is not the only level on which the portayal of space functions in the novel; shortly after the proleptic imaginings cited above, Butor's narrative produces a series of spatial observations, as if to suggest that the topography of Rome has surreptitiously infiltrated Delmont's conscience and sensitised him subliminally to the entrancing power of spaces. One page further on from the passage cited above, Delmont's attention is drawn to the cover of his book of railway timetables depicting a 'network of tiny cracks', which the narrator likens to 'the lead frame of a stained-glass window whose subject is missing'.[34] Shortly thereafter, he notes how a fellow passenger leans out of the train's window to observe 'that white enamelled iron sign stained with rust around the bolt attaching it to its post [...], and the grey sky striped with black catenaries, the black earth striped with shiny rails'.[35] The striated patterns of white, grey and black seem to be imbued with an occult meaning.[36]

It is only later in his journey that Delmont realises the implications of such topographic portents for his personal situation. Significantly, this illumination occurs as the train passes through a series of long tunnels; as his inner monologue reveals, he is only too aware of the power of this enclosed space to bring him squarely face-to-face with his conscience:

> All of a sudden another, slightly longer, tunnel goes by.
> You need to focus your attention on the objects your eyes see [...] in

order to put an end to this inner turmoil, this dangerous intermingling and rumination of memories.[37]

Despite his efforts to resist such thoughts, it is shortly after this passage, as the train enters another tunnel, that Delmont comes face-to-face with the truth of his relationship with Cécile. To bring her with him to Paris, he now realises, would be just as misplaced as his attempts to reconstruct mentally the Rome of antiquity from its ruins:

> the train enters a tunnel and its noise has become muffled once more. [...]
> when you strolled on the Forum, you did so not only amongst its few meagre stones, its broken capitals, and its impressive walls or brick bases, but in the midst of an enormous shared dream which became more and more solid, precise and justified every time you passed through it.[38]

With its own inexorable and obscure logic, the movement of the train through the enclosed space of the tunnel prompts this revelation and enables Delmont to reconcile the 'Rome' of his private mythology with the Rome of historical reality.

A similar conjunction of inner space and a state of enhanced self-awareness is to be found in the *Passagen-Werk*: at one point Benjamin likens the arcades to houses or tunnels which have no exterior – in which respect, he remarks, they are like dreams;[39] in another instance he sketches out an itinerary which leads from the enclosure of the arcades, via the dream, to a pre-natal, uterine state – a route to which the activity of the *flâneur* can offer access:

> And in no other way can one deal with the arcades – structures in which we relive, as in a dream, the life of our parents and grandparents, as the embryo in the womb relives the life of animals. Existence in these spaces flows then without accent, like the events in dreams. Flânerie is the rhythmics of this slumber.[40]

This image has unmistakable overtones of Freudian interpretation, according to which subterranean regions in dream imagery represent the womb.[41] And yet, for Benjamin, the unconscious mind is clearly less a point of arrival than a port of call on an itinerary that leads ultimately from the personal to the collective, from mythology to history. Similarly,

Butor has made it clear that *La Modification* cannot be interpreted satisfactorily by means of Freudian analysis alone: 'A Freudian interpretation in the strict sense, a psychoanalytical interpretation in the narrow sense of the word, is clearly inadequate. [...] All of that only takes on meaning in the sense of a historical analysis, in the relationship with universal history.'[42]

In similar fashion, Koeppen's Siegfried finds a higher level of self-awareness; and for him, too, contact with an enclosed space seems to be the catalyst:

> I went into the espresso bar in the passage, went up to the counter and stood among the men, polished, shaved, combed, brushed, clean-shirted, crisply ironed, after-shaved men, and like them I drank hot, strong steam-machine-made coffee, I drank it *à la cappuccino* with sugar and a froth of milk. I liked standing there, I was happy there [...] (*DiR* 98)[43]

Here too, the parataxis and the insistent repetition might suggest the physical characteristics of the elongated, labyrinthine arcade to which it alludes. But, just as Delmont appears to be affected by enclosed spaces, this site of transit and ephemerality appears to penetrate into Siegfried's consciousness, leading him towards greater lucidity and self-awareness. At this moment, in the 'Espressobar der Passage', he spots his own photograph in a newspaper and, in a reversal of Aschenbach's striving for immortality, Siegfried realises that his existence is just as ephemeral as the image on newsprint. This revelation occasions not despair, but a renewed strength of purpose:

> and then the picture would become waste paper, food-wrapping, or fulfil some other function, and that was fine by me, it had my full consent, because I don't want to remain for ever as I am today, I want to live in continual change, and I'm afraid of not existing.[44]

By now it is evident that the two novels employ the spatial paradigm not only as a metatextual reflector of their own labyrinthine narrative complexity, but also as a means to explore the psyche and its receptivity to external stimuli. Indeed, in both novels, the arcade or passage is a privileged point of contact between the external world and the human psyche, and it is above all in this respect that analogies with Aragon's and Benjamin's narratives become meaningful.

For all that Benjamin, as late as 1935, rated Aragon's narrative 'the best book about Paris',[45] he acknowledges the important divergence in the respective conclusions they draw from the identification of a modern urban mythology. For Benjamin the way ahead lies not in the extensive exploration of the subconscious, but in socio-historical engagement. And so he situates his own approach in explicit opposition to that of Aragon, stating instead his intention to bring the thematics of his own project out of the penumbra of dreams and into the waking daylight of History.[46] A similar process of awakening, and the reconciliation of private mythology with history, might be seen as the central characteristics of Delmont's change of plan, the importance of which is signalled at a textual level by the shift from second to first-person narration. If the present emptiness of his life may be avoided, Delmont reasons, then this will be achieved by creative means alone, 'for example by means of a book', which he now recognises to be the sole means of constructing 'that future freedom beyond our reach' (p.276). The unattainability of this realm, Delmont realises, stems from the 'gaping fissure within me', a gap which he now knows he will never bridge, 'for it opens onto a cavern which is its reason, which has been inside me for a long time, and which I cannot expect to fill because it is the means of communication with an immense historical fissure' (p.276).

This last term prompts us to consider the particular status the motif of fissure commands in both Butor's and Koeppen's novels. In *La Terre et les rêveries du repos*, Gaston Bachelard explores the central importance of the fissure in the labyrinth dream, where it serves as a starting point for the creative imagination.[47] The thematic importance of the fissure in *La Modification* is prefigured, as we have seen, by a series of references throughout the text, including the 'network of tiny cracks' formed by the web of lines depicted on the cover of Delmont's railway timetable (p.45), or the crack in the door handle of his railway carriage. For all that he may never gain the entry key to his ideal world of illumination, he hopes he may 'at least enjoy its reflection'; and yet, he is aware of the impossibility of explaining the mystical enchantment that the idea of Rome radiates, as this would be to attempt to rationalise and quantify a phenomenon which transcends such terms of reference. He resigns himself to the fact that he cannot hope to 'produce an answer to this enigma which the name of Rome etches on our consciousness or our unconscious, to account even crudely for this source of marvels and obscurities' (p.276). As the final clause of this quotation confirms, Butor's metaphysical topography appears to situate him squarely alongside Aragon, discovering a modern mythology in the dark underbelly of the city. Delmont's emphasis on the toponym ('the *name* of Rome'), rather than the city itself, reminds us that it is the Rome of his personal mythology and not the actual physical locus that dominates his interaction with it and his relationship to Cécile.

Like Butor's protagonist, Siegfried too conceptualises the elusive force governing our existence not only in spatial terms, but in terms of fissure. In this visualisation of the human mind in terms of a gap, Koeppen too appears to borrow from Bachelard, who wrote in 1948: 'the fissure is the start of the labyrinth dream. The fissure is narrow, but the dreamer slips into it [...] the labyrinth dream is, all in all, a series of doors left ajar'.[48] Koeppen communicates a strikingly similar image through Siegfried, who argues with the newly ordained priest, Adolf, about the existence of a higher spirit. While Adolf imagines this in terms of a humanised divinity, Siegfried can only conceive of a far more abstract, elusive force. Significantly, however, he defines this presence not only in spatial terms, but in terms of fissure. We might, he argues, gain greater insight into our lives if we could find an opening, a fissure in the wall which normally bars our way to the unknown: 'if we could find a door to this other domain, a crack in the wall, then we would have a completely different view of ourselves and our lives'.[49]

Butor's Delmont, for his part, renounces his hope of bridging the physical distance between his two cities; and yet he does suggest that the mind *can* achieve this goal, can transcend the conceptual space that lies between them, by means of a passage of the imagination:

> Would it not be better to retain the distance between these two cities, all these stations, all these landscapes that separate them? But in addition to the normal channels of communication by which everyone could travel from one to the other whenever he wanted, there would be a certain number of points of contact, instantaneous passages which would open up at certain moments determined by laws with which we would only gradually become acquainted.[50]

This passage towards a conceptual 'Rome' requires Delmont to create, through the act of writing, the effect of displacement he felt in making the physical journey: his finished text, which the reader assumes to have been written after his arrival in Rome, is the product and the proof of his new-found purpose. Analogously, Siegfried's experimental music will lead him to search beyond the 'three-dimensional cage we perceive with our senses' (*DiR* 166), where creativity is impossible, towards the hidden recesses of his mind where the key to the mystery of existence is kept: '"If God exists, He will also live in dead ends", I said'.[51]

In conclusion, the motif of passage, both as an action and as a place of transit, suggests a multitude of levels on which to compare these two post-war novels and to set them alongside Aragon's and Benjamin's evocations of a new urban mythology. In a structural sense, the passage functions as a metaphor of their formal innovation, reflecting their syntactic complexity and their shifting narrative voices; but it clearly exceeds this role, serving additionally as a key to understanding the relationship between the subjective consciousness and the external world. The site of an encounter between inner and outer realms, it reflects the potential of certain places to engage the forces of imagination and propel the individual towards an intensified sense of selfhood. The great extent to which both Butor's and Koeppen's novels are preoccupied with passages, gaps and clefts not only exemplifies their close intertextual connections; more importantly, perhaps, it also reminds us of the interstitial nature of all textual production, which incessantly negotiates the intermediary space between self and other, between present, past and future, between individual and collective consciousness, between *histoire* and *Histoire*.

NOTES TO CHAPTER VI

1. Michel Butor, *La Modification* (Paris: Minuit, 1957). Translated into English as *Second Thoughts* and *Change of Heart*; quotations are my own translations. Wolfgang Koeppen, *Der Tod in Rom* (Stuttgart: Scherz & Goverts, 1954; Frankfurt am Main: Suhrkamp, 1975; page references are to the latter edition). Translated with an introduction by Michael Hofmann as *Death in Rome* (London: Hamish Hamilton, 1992). Quotations are from this edition. The two texts will hereafter be referred to as *TiR* and *DiR*.

2. Genette defines hypertextuality as 'toute relation unissant un texte B (que j'appellerai *hypertexte*) à un texte antérieur A (que j'appellerai, bien sûr, *hypotexte*) sur lequel il se greffe d'une manière qui n'est pas celle du commentaire.' Gérard Genette, *Palimpsestes. La Littérature au second degré* (Paris: Éditions du Seuil, 1982), p.13.

3. See e.g. T. J. Reed's introduction to *Der Tod in Venedig* (Oxford: Oxford University Press, 1971, 1978), pp.32-51. John Pizer, 'From a Death in Venice to a Death in Rome: On Wolfgang Koeppen's Critical Ironization of Thomas Mann', in *The Germanic Review*, vol.LXVIII, no.3 (Summer 1993), pp.98-107. Dana Strand, 'The Role of Dreams in Michel Bùtor's *La Modification*', in *Kentucky Romance Quarterly*, 32, 1 (February 1985), pp.91-100. Virgil's *Æneid* is also present in *Der Tod in Venedig*, although to a lesser extent than the three Greek dialogues cited above.

4. Walter Benjamin, *Das Passagen-Werk*, in Walter Benjamin, *Gesammelte Schriften*, Vol. V, 1 and 2, ed. Rolf Tiedemann (Frankfurt am Main: Suhrkamp, 1982). English translation: *The Arcades Project*, trans. by Howard Eiland and Kevin McLaughlin (Cambridge Mass.: Harvard University Press, 1999). Louis Aragon, *Le Paysan de Paris* (Paris: Gallimard, 1926, 1953). Page references are to the Folio edition. English translation: *Paris Peasant*, trans. by Simon Watson Taylor (Boston: Exact Change, 1994).

5. Michel Butor, *Passage de Milan* (Paris: Éditions de Minuit, 1954). On its intertextual construction, see Jean-Claude Vareille, 'Butor ou l'intertextualité généralisée', in Raimund Theis and Hans T. Siepe (eds), *Le Plaisir de l'intertexte* (Frankfurt am Main: Peter Lang, 1986), pp.277-96.

6. Michel Butor, *Le Génie du lieu* (Paris: Grasset, 'Les cahiers rouges', 1958). Of the Castalia spring, he writes in terms similar to those of *La Modification*: 'à grand plaisir et à longs traits j'y ai bu l'audace d'affronter ce spectre professoral [...], la certitude qui me manquait auparavant du droit absolu qui m'est imparti par l'écho qu'elle éveille en moi, d'appliquer ma propre divination vénérante à cette énigme que propose l'immense bouche d'or rocheux.' (pp.86-87).

7. 'ces sortes de galeries couvertes que l'on nomme d'une façon troublante *des passages*'. Aragon, *Le Paysan de Paris*, p.20.

8. 'les sanctuaires d'un culte de l'éphémère, [...] le paysage fantomatique des plaisirs et

des professions maudites, incompréhensibles hier et que demain ne connaîtra jamais'. ibid., pp.20-21.

9. Amongst the best-known essays on these themes are 'Das Kunstwerk im Zeitalter seiner technischen Reproduzierbarkeit' (1936) and 'Charles Baudelaire. Ein Lyriker im Zeitalter des Hochkapitalismus', both in Walter Benjamin, *Gesammelte Schriften*, Vol. I, 2, ed. Rolf Tiedemann and Hermann Schweppenhäuser (Frankfurt am Main: Suhrkamp, 1974).

10. 'Methode dieser Arbeit: literarische Montage. Ich habe nichts zu sagen. Nur zu zeigen. Ich werde nichts wertvolles entwenden und mir keine geistvollen Formulierungen aneignen. Aber die Lumpen, den Abfall: die will ich nicht inventarisieren sondern sie auf die einzig mögliche Weise zu ihrem Rechte kommen lassen: sie verwenden.' Walter Benjamin, *Das Passagen-Werk*, N 1a 8, in *Gesammelte Schriften*, Vol. V, 1, p.574. English translation from *The Arcades Project*, trans. by Howard Eiland and Kevin McLaughlin (Cambridge Mass.: Harvard University Press, 1999), p.460.

11. 'Diese Tore – die Eingänge der Passagen – sind Schwellen. Keine steinerne Stufe markiert sie. Aber das tut die wartende Haltung der wenigen Personen. Sparsam abgemessene Schritte spiegeln, ohne daß die selbst davon wissen, es ab, daß man vor einem Entschluß steht.' Walter Benjamin, *Das Passagen-Werk*, C 3, 6, in *Gesammelte Schriften*, Vol. V, 1, p.142. *The Arcades Project*, p. 89.

12. *Das Passagen-Werk*, p.140.

13. The text is from Amédée Kermel, *Les Passages de Paris*, in *Le Livre des Cent-et-un*, X (Paris: 1833), p.71. ibid., p.512.

14. ibid., pp.140 and 141.

15. See the section entitled 'Traumhaus, Museum, Brunnenhalle', ibid., pp.511-23, esp.511 and 513.

16. Mann's principal protagonist, Gustav von Aschenbach, was inspired by Mahler, whose first name he shares, and by Wagner, about whom Mann wrote a short piece in 1911 while staying in Venice. See T.J. Reed, op.cit. p.172, n.131. The name of Butor's protagonist, Léon Delmont, harks back ironically to a series of popes and to the hill on which the Vatican is situated. See Jennifer Waelti-Walters, *Michel Butor: A Study of his View of the World and a Panorama of his Work 1954-1974* (Victoria: Sono Nis Press, 1977), pp.7-8.

17. '[das Septett] war Siegfrieds Auflehnung gegen seine Umgebung, gegen das Kriegsgefangenencamp, den Stacheldrahtzaun, die Kameraden, deren Gespräche ihn anödeten, den Krieg, den er seinen Eltern zuschrieb, und das ganze vom Teufel besessene und geholte Vaterland' (*TiR* 9 / *DiR* 7).

18. On this dimension in Butor's work, see 'La Musique, art réaliste', in *Répertoire II*

(Paris: Minuit, 1964), pp.27–41.

19. 'la lumière romaine qu'elle réfléchit et concentre s'éteint dès qu'elle se trouve à Paris.' *La Modification*, p.279.

20. 'tout roman qui nous raconte un voyage est donc plus clair, plus explicite que celui qui n'est pas capable d'exprimer métaphoriquement cette distance entre le lieu et celui où nous emmène le récit'. Michel Butor, *Essais sur le roman* (Paris: Minuit, 1969), p.50.

21. 'en travaillant sur *L'Emploi du temps*, dont le principal personnage était une ville, je me suis posé la question: comment faire un roman avec deux villes? Il ne s'agissait pas encore de Paris et de Rome. Mais en fouillant, un peu plus, ces capitales se sont imposées inéluctablement'. Entretien avec Jean-Louis Rambures, *Le Monde*, 6 Nov 1971, cited in Dana Strand, op.cit. p.93.

22. 'En fait pour pouvoir étudier le temps dans sa continuité, donc pouvoir mettre en évidence des lacunes, il est nécessaire de l'appliquer sur un espace, de le considérer comme un parcours, un trajet.' Michel Butor, 'Recherches sur la technique du roman', in *Répertoire II*, pp.88–99 (95).

23. 'Der kleine Gottlieb hatte in der Schule gelernt, es gab eine Zeit, daß auch die Päpste sich dem Tod verbündeten, und es gab eine Zeit, sie war noch nicht so lange her, da beschäftigten die Päpste sogar Henker, Menschen wie Judejahn [...]' (*TiR* 77 / *DiR* 81).

24. 'wie einer, der nach langer Abwesenheit sein altes Haus besichtigt' (*TiR* 119 / *DiR* 126).

25. In *Der Tod in Venedig* [*TiV*], Aschenbach's elevation of Tadzio's beauty into spiritual terms is likened to Ganymede's literal elevation as cupbearer of the gods, carried up to Olympus by Zeus's eagle. Mann, *Der Tod in Venedig*, p.118.

26. 'Es hörte sich wie das Wetzen langer Messer an' (*TiR* 82-83 / *DiR* 87).

27. 'Es war Sabotage, daß Rom schlief, es war Sabotage eines Krieges, der noch lange nicht zu Ende war oder der noch gar nicht recht begonnen hatte und der in jedem Fall Judejahns Krieg war' (*TiR* 83 / *DiR* 87).

28. 'Ich liebe Rom, weil ich ein Ausländer in Rom bin, und vielleicht möchte ich immer ein Ausländer sein, ein bewegter Zuschauer' (*TiR* 128 / *DiR* 136).

29. 'Judejahn merkte, daß die Fahrt nicht zum Bahnhof ging, daß sie schweifend war, weiter, planlos, suchend in Bogen fuhren sie, forschten wohl nach Winkeln und Sackgassen, nach stillen Mordplätzen oder auch nach Lärm und Verkehrsgewühl, wo ein Schuß nicht zu hören war' (*TiR* 75 / *DiR* 78).

30. Michael Hofmann, 'Introduction', in Wolfgang Koeppen, *DiR* p.x.

31. 'Und noch desselben Tages empfing eine respektvoll erschütterte Welt die Nachricht von seinem Tode.' *TiV* p.157.

32. 'Die Zeitungen meldeten noch am Abend Judejahns Tod, der durch die Umstände eine Weltnachticht geworden war, die aber niemand erschütterte.' (*TiR* 187 / *DiR* 202).

33. 'sans rien vous contraignant, sans rien vous empêchant d'explorer les détours, si longs, si anguleux, si fantasques soient-ils, qui vous séduiront'. *La Modification*, p.43.

34. 'l'armature d'un vitrail dont le sujet est perdu'. ibid., pp.45-46.

35. 'cet écriteau de fer émaillé blanc taché de rouille autour de la vis qui l'attache à son poteau [...], et ce ciel gris rayé de caténaires noires, le sol noir rayé de rails luisants'. ibid., pp.46-47.

36. This extract recalls the equivalence of physical locus, colour and mental states elaborated by André Breton in *La Clé des champs*: 'Une carte sans doute très significative demanderait pour chacun à être dressée, faisant apparaître en blanc les lieux qu'il hante et en noir ceux qu'il évite, le reste en fonction de l'attraction ou de la répulsion moindre se répartissant la gamme des gris'. André Breton, 'Pont-Neuf', in *La Clé des champs* (Paris: Gallimard, 1967), p.280. See Michael Sheringham's illuminating analysis of this and other narratives inspired by Paris in 'City Space, Mental Space, Poetic Space: Paris in Breton, Benjamin and Réda', in Michael Sheringham (ed.), *Parisian Fields* (London: Reaktion Books, 1996), pp.85-114.

37. 'Voici que passe un autre tunnel un peu plus long. Il faut fixer votre attention sur les objets que voient vos yeux [...] afin de mettre un terme à ce remuement intérieur, à ce dangereux brassage et remâchage de souvenirs.' *La Modification*, p.156.

38. 'le train entre dans un tunnel et son bruit est redevenu sourd. [...] quand vous vous promeniez sur le Forum, n'était-ce pas seulement parmi les quelques pauvres pierres, les chapiteaux brisés, et les impressionnants murs ou soubassements de briques, mais au milieu d'un énorme rêve qui vous était commun, de plus en plus solide, précis et justifié à chaque passage'. ibid., pp.166-67.

39. Walter Benjamin, *Das Passagen-Werk*, in Walter Benjamin, *Gesammelte Schriften*, Vol. V, 1, p.513.

40. 'Und nicht anders kann man von den Passagen handeln, Architekturen, in denen wir traumhaft das Leben unserer Eltern, Großeltern nochmals leben wie der Embryo in der Mutter das Leben der Tiere. Das Dasein in diesen Räumen verfließt denn auch akzentlos wie das Geschehen in Träumen. Flanieren ist die Rhythmik dieses Schlummers.' ibid., pp.161-62. *The Arcades Project*, p.106.

41. According to Freud: 'If the 'unconscious', as an element in the subject's waking thoughts, has to be represented in a dream, it may be replaced very appropriately by subterranean regions. – These, where they occur *without* any reference to analytic treatment, stand for the female body or the womb.' In Sigmund Freud, *The Interpretation of Dreams*, trans. James Strachey (London: Penguin, 'The Penguin Freud

Library', 1991), p.536.

42 'Une interprétation freudienne au sens strict, une interprétation psychanalytique au sens étroit du mot, est évidemment insuffisante. [...] Tout cela ne prend son sens que dans le sens d'une analyse historique, que dans les relations de tout cela avec l'histoire universelle.' F.C. St Aubyn, 'Entretien avec Michel Butor', in *French Review* (October 1962), p.19, cited in Dana Strand, op.cit. pp.91-100.

43. 'Ich ging in die Espressobar der Passage, stellte mich an die Theke, stellte mich zwischen die Männer, die wohlgewichsten, wohlrasierten, wohlgekämmten, wohlgebürsteten, die sauber-gehemdeten, steifgeplätteten, streng parfümierten Männer, und ich trank, wie sie, den heißen starken Dampfmaschinenkaffee, ich trank ihn *à la cappuccino* mit Zucker und Rahm gequirlt, hier stand ich gern, hier war ich froh [...]' (*TiR* 93 / *DiR* 98).

44. 'und dann würde das Bild Makulatur werden, Einwickelpapier oder von anderer Nützlichkeit, und es war mir recht, es war gut so, ich stimmte zu, denn ich will nicht bleiben, wie ich heute bin, ich will nicht dauern, ich will in ewiger Verwandlung leben, und ich fürchte das Nichtsein' (*TiR* 94 / *DiR* 99).

45. This is the title given by Benjamin to a manuscript note forming part of the *Hauptplan* (main plan) of his book which he began to compile in March 1934. In Benjamin, *Gesammelte Schriften*, Vol. V, 2, p.1207.

46. Walter Benjamin, *Das Passagen-Werk*, N 1, 9, in Walter Benjamin, ibid., Vol. V, 1, pp.571-72.

47. Gaston Bachelard, *La Terre et les rêveries du repos* (Paris, 1948).

48. 'la fissure est le début du rêve de labyrinthe. La fissure est étroite, mais le rêveur s'y glisse [...] le rêve de labyrinthe est en somme une suite de portes entrouvertes.' ibid., p.216.

49. 'würden wir eine Pforte zu diesem Bereich finden, einen Spalt in der Wand, sähen wir uns und unser Leben anders.' (*TiR* 154-155 / *DiR* 166). This image recalls the scene, cited above, in which Adolf, in the nethermost dungeons beneath the Papal burg, catches sight of his father Judejahn. This traumatic confrontation, both with his family history and with world history, occurs through a narrow gap in the wall. (*TiR* 116-119 / *DiR* 123-127).

50. 'Ne vaudrait-il pas mieux conserver entre ces deux villes leur distance, toutes ces gares, tous ces paysages qui les séparent? Mais en plus des communications normales par lesquelles chacun pourrait se rendre de l'une à l'autre quand il voudrait, il y aurait un certain nombre de points de contact, de passages instantanés qui s'ouvriraient à certains moments déterminés par des lois que l'on ne parviendrait à connaître que peu à peu.' *La Modification*, p.282.

51. '"Wenn er ist, wohnt Gott auch in Sackgassen."' (*TiR* 155 / *DiR* 166).

Woolf   Nietzsche   Wilde
                Butor   André Gide   Marinetti   Woolf
E. M. Forster   Kavafy   Augustine
        Derek Walcott
            Aragon   Charles Baudelaire
Mc Almon   Edgar Allan Poe   **Michael Aflaq**
                                Malraux
netti   Butor   **Kafka**   Woolf   Baroja
            Lorca   John Dewey   **Joyce**
                            T.S. Eliot
Kafka   Benjamin   Kavafy   Nietzsche   Beckett
        Malraux   Woolf   Proust
William Carlos Williams   John Dos Passos   Koeppen
                            E. M. Forster   Thomas Mann   E
ayres   Benjamin   Baroja   John Dos Passos   Kafka
    Ezra Pound   Koeppen   **Michael Aflaq**   Becke
alcott   Butor
        Nietzsche   Robert Mc Almon   Marinetti   Aragon
ett   **Proust**
arinetti   Joyce

PART II

MODERNISM AND THE ENCOUNTER WITH THE FOREIGN OR EXOTIC OTHER

CHAPTER VII

Staging Sinbad's Return
The 'Ithaca' chapter of *Ulysses* and
'The Death of Sindbad: A Narrative in One Act',
by Michael Aflaq

Fiona Richards

Fiona Richards is a doctoral student at Leeds University. Her special interest is in the subversive potential of modernist and postmodernist writing, particulary in works by James Joyce and Salman Rushdie. She has contributed to academic and popular journals, including a report on the cultural phenomenon of Bloomsday.

In her introduction to a recent collection of essays the critic Ellen Carol Jones defines Joyce's relation to modernism as inherently ambiguous, asserting that

> Joyce constructs a contra-modernity bordering on – contingent to, discontinuous with, in contention with – the modernity of Western European imperial powers. He does not posit the postcolonial as other to modernity in an absolute binary. His works use the cultural hybridity of Irish borderline conditions to translate – reinscribe and thus reclaim – the social imaginary of both metropolis and modernity.[1]

Such a formulation depends upon an equation of modernism with imperialism, and indeed Jones subsequently describes 'the totalising narratives of modernity' as 'narratives whose concealed but central logic is imperialism'.[2] Fredric Jameson, also with reference to Joyce, has linked modernism with imperialism through a similar notion of lack and a consequent drive towards totalising narrative, concluding that Joyce's writing portrays simultaneously 'the two incommensurable realities... of the metropolis and the colony'.[3] The argument is not that Joyce's work occupies a liminal position on the fringes of modernist writing, but rather that it occupies two different, incommensurable positions simultaneously, having a kind of dual perspective.

Ireland's ambiguous political status and geographical position in relation to the British Isles made it formerly at once a colony and a part of the United Kingdom. I want to consider the idea that Joyce's writing opens up a space which is neither entirely within a metropolitan discourse, nor entirely outside it, through an examination of his use of the Sinbad theme. I will then consider this usage alongside that made by the Syrian writer and politician Michael Aflaq in his short story 'The Death of Sindbad: A Narrative in One Act', published fourteen years after *Ulysses*, in 1936.[4]

The colonised nation is caught physically between being the centre of its own world, and feeling itself to be defined and regulated by a centre that is elsewhere, by whose standards it is defined, and with which it can never fully integrate. In Jones's words, it is a location where 'the shadow of the Other falls upon the Self'.[5] The paradox of a binaristic logic in which self and other are mutually defining and necessarily mutually exclusive has been rehearsed at length. The idea informs many critical readings of the dynamics of Imperialism, including the relationship between Britain and its colonies. In the early twentieth century Ireland and large expanses of the Middle East were subject to rule by the British Empire, and if the Orient offered Britain a strange and exotic Other against which to define itself, so too did Ireland, its oldest colony.

Edward Said's formulation that 'European culture gained in strength and identity by setting itself off against the Orient as a sort of surrogate and even underground self'[6] has lately been echoed in several critical descriptions of the relationship between Britain and Ireland, notably that of Declan Kiberd in his *Inventing Ireland*. Kiberd asserts that 'through many centuries Ireland was pressed into service as a foil to set off English virtues, [...] and as a fantasy land in which to meet fairies and monsters'. He concludes: 'If England had never existed, the Irish would have been rather lonely. Each nation badly needed the other; for the purpose of defining itself'.[7]

Both of these critics go further and point to the similarity in the positions of both the Irish and the Arabs as colonised peoples, a similarity utilised both by the Imperial centre which sought to homogenise both races into an amalgam of inferior traits which justified their government from London, and by the peoples themselves. Though accepting the status of Other implies accepting definition on someone else's terms, it also offers a space from which to challenge the claims to authority and meaning of the centre.

The Sinbad story, taken from *The Arabian Nights,* offers both Joyce and Aflaq the possibility of a different subject position from which to tell a story. Jameson has suggested that Joyce's use of the *Odyssey* as a source text for *Ulysses* is subversive in 'appropriating the great imperial space of the Mediterranean', but Homer is a cornerstone of the English literary canon.[8] How much more subversive to juxtapose the classic Greek text with a Persian tale preserved for hundreds of years only in oral form, and only translated into English in the nineteenth century! Originating in Persia in the tenth century, *The Arabian Nights* offers a vivid picture of a different cosmopolis and another empire, far preceding that of the British, and affording a different cultural capital on which to trade.⁹

But the Tales are also steeped in the trappings of Orientalist fantasy, and their popularity in Europe was in no small part due to their exotic and erotic appeal. As such they only reflect what the stereotyping gaze of the Imperial centre wished to see. The problems accruing to their adoption by either writer are complicated still further in the case of Joyce by Ireland's ambiguous position within the Empire. Being in such proximity to the centre, the Irish could not avoid absorbing the hegemonic culture's fantasies of Imperial domination. After all, Queen Victoria's last State visit was to Dublin, where she congratulated the Dublin Fusiliers for their valour in the *Tugela*.[10] Joyce's use of the Sinbad story provides a model for how far his work repeats fantasies of the Orient as commodified and sensual Other, and how far it manages to exceed them.

The pantomime of *Sinbad the Sailor* seems to have been indissolubly linked in Joyce's mind with ideas of colonial exploitation, including a specific link between Ireland's position and that of Britain's other colonies. In *Finnegans Wake* there is a passage which runs:

> Proudpurse Alby with his pooraroon Eireen, they'll. Pride, comfytousness, enevy! You make me think of a wonderdecker I once. Or somebalt thet sailder, the man me-gallant, with the bangled ears. Or an earl was he, at Lucan? Or, no, it's the Iren duke's I mean. Or somebrey erse from the Dark Countries.[11]

Sinbad has become 'somebalt thet sailder', and we can also discern the presence of Perfidious Albion and his poor Ireland in 'Proudpurse Alby and his pooraroon Eireen', accompanied by pride, covetousness and envy, though whose these are is left unclear. Sinbad follows the captain of the Flying Dutchman, and these two mythical mariners are succeeded by Magellan ('me-gallant'), the first explorer to circumnavigate the globe in an attempt to find a western trade route to Indonesia. He appears like a pirate, with bangled ears. After them comes the Earl of Lucan, Patrick Sarsfield, one of the Wild Geese (a term applied to Irish rebels who chose exile rather than English rule following the defeat of the Jacobite revolt in 1691). Ending this list of wanderers is the Iron Duke, Wellington, who was born in Dublin but famously dismissed his Irish nationality, saying 'If a gentleman happens to be born in a stable, it does not follow

199

that he should be called a horse'.[12] Previously a military commander in India, as well as Commander in Chief of the British army which defeated Napoleon at Waterloo, he became synonymous with British Imperial power; which perhaps explains why between the reference to him and the Dark Countries the phrase 'or somebrey erse' occurs. McHugh glosses this as a compact of 'somebody else' and 'ass', which following on from the sin of covetousness two lines earlier conceivably passes a very moral judgement on the activities of Empire.[13] There is no space here to consider possible readings of the above passage, but the occurrence of the name of Sinbad amongst a cluster of references to Empire certainly suggests that Joyce is using the theme with political issues in mind.[14]

In the 'Ithaca' chapter of *Ulysses*, Leopold Bloom reflects on a comic song he had been commissioned to write for the pantomime of *Sinbad the Sailor* which was to be performed at Dublin's Gaiety Theatre. He never succeeded in composing this song, primarily, I will argue, because of the difficulty of positioning himself within it; a difficulty linked to his ambiguous position as a citizen of Dublin, and a subject of the British Empire.

The song was to be about topical Dublin events and was to be inserted into the valley of diamonds episode of the pantomime. This episode has a particularly exotic setting, containing both the undreamable riches of a valley full of huge and precious diamonds and the unimaginable horrors of the enormous and numerous snakes which guard them. Judging by the programme for the pantomime – which was actually performed at the Gaiety in December 1892 – the scene was the highpoint of the first act, and offered the spectacle of a 'grand ballet of the diamonds' and a 'serpentine dance'. There is some evidence to suggest that Joyce saw this production, and the spectacle impressed him sufficiently to mention the principal dancer by name.[15] Bloom's song would have had the unenviable task of situating the day-to-day affairs of Dublin within this opulent and strange setting. Small wonder that he cites the first reason for his not composing it as a problem of positioning, or as he more precisely puts it, of 'oscillation between events of Imperial and local interest'. The nature of the problem is the ambiguous position of the Irish colonial subject in relation to the Orientalist fantasies of Empire.

Throughout the preceding chapters of *Ulysses*, Bloom has indulged in fantasies about the Orient, even managing to squeeze in two before breakfast. His long-unsatisfied desire for his Gibraltar-born wife, which has been on his mind all day, frequently elides her Spanish ancestry with stereotypical Orientalist sensuality.[16] Bloom's Orientalising desire for Molly culminates in his fantasised vision of her in the 'Circe' chapter, where she represents the apotheosis of Oriental splendour, cruelty and sensuality.[17] She appears to him amid date palms in a Turkish costume worthy of a pantomime, complete with cummerbund, yashmak and toe-rings, and plays the cruel mistress superbly, mocking his desire for her, and scolding her camel in Moorish with her 'goldcurb wristbangles angriling'.[18]

Bloom, we are told, is 'spellbound' by this fantasy, so what grounds are there to see him as not wholly absorbed by it, but rather ambivalent in his relation? It is not enough merely to observe that he does not get to possess Molly, either in his fantasy or in the book itself. Vincent Cheng's argument that throughout the day many of Bloom's fantasies of the exotic East have been checked and modified by his realisation of their partiality and probable falsity is more convincing. For instance, after the first of Bloom's Oriental imaginings he is able to recognise his make-believe as just that, and, furthermore, to pinpoint its source to a book he owns; a travel memoir of the East called *In the Track of the Sun*. All his ideas derive from cultural constructions, but he simultaneously absorbs them and realises their artificiality. Cheng suggests that

> [i]t is inevitable that Bloom is both a consumer and a product/propagator of the dominant (and racist) cultural discourse about otherness; but – perhaps because he is himself repeatedly being typed by his fellow Irish as just such a reified Other – he is repeatedly sceptical of such images and sensitive to the cultural processes by which they are erected.[19]

Bloom's position as a Jew in predominantly Catholic Ireland underwrites his status as an outsider both in race and creed. His double exclusion, both from the Imperial centre and from the colony within which he lives, serves as an illustration of the situation of the Irish themselves in relation to the Orientalist fantasies of Empire. Their proximity to England and position within Europe allow them to dream of the same exotic conquests as their English counterparts, but their own colonised status in relation to the metropolis complicates the pairing of self and other.

Ranjana Khanna, writing about Joyce's short story 'Araby', notices just such a phenomenon of displacement occurring in the young narrator's trip to the bazaar from which the story takes its name. He has been looking forward to this trip for some time, and has fantasised about bringing home some exotic present for the sister of his friend, upon whom he has a schoolboy crush. The name of the bazaar takes on a magical significance for him: 'The syllables of the word *Araby* were called to me through the silence in which my soul luxuriated and cast an Eastern glow over me'.[20] It is clear that his romantic desire for his friend's sister has merged with the idea of the exotic East available to him for purchase in the form of goods from the bazaar. But when he finally arrives there the bazaar is closing, and his journey ends in disillusionment, encapsulated in the tawdry flirtations of the stallholders, and the clinking of coins. These are the same exploitative conditions of trade which England has long imposed on her Irish colony. Khanna describes the duality of position exposed by the boy's trip to the bazaar, as a figure of his dreams of an Araby which is both within his – and Ireland's – grasp, and not. As she observes:

> What the narrator experiences here is the journey into the other, into Araby and woman, only to realise that the other is not his. Araby becomes the colony within Ireland, just as Ireland was a colony of Britain. Here there is a kind of inversion, where the metropolitan colony – the colony close to home – confronts itself in the other.[21]

I would suggest that this is precisely the reason that Bloom is unable to compose his song for the pantomime of Sinbad.

Bloom ruminates on this failure as the last of several youthful attempts at poetic composition, and in all of them it is clear that for him literary construction and personal identity are linked. The first poem he remembers writing closes with his own name incorporated into the final line almost as a punchline. One later creation is simply a collection of anagrams of his name, and another is a love poem to his wife structured acrostically around her nickname for him. When Bloom writes he emphatically places himself within the text, frequently in fragmented or rearranged form. His inability to compose this song reflects his failed attempt to take up a single position between the competing claims of metropolis and colony. The pantomime represents that same staging of the Oriental for vicarious consumption which was figured by the Araby bazaar and runs the same risk of a journey into the other – an other which may turn out not to be one's own.

Pantomimes at the Gaiety generally suffered from no such qualms about mentioning local people and events; topical allusions and Dublin gossip all served as grist to the mill.[22] But the key to pantomime is its transformation of the everyday into the fantastic. Kitchens which become ballrooms, streets enchanted islands and shops magician's caves were the staple of the spectacle.[23] The 1892 production of *Sinbad* ended with a 'Grand Transformation entitled Winter and Summer'. In Widow Twankey's descriptions local dignitaries are transfigured into larger than life versions of themselves. They step through a fairground mirror into another world. But this transformation works on the inversion of the binary of self and other: Cinderella's rags become riches, Widow Twankey is played by a man, and the principal boy is a girl. There is no place in this fantasy of a revealed 'underground self' for a third term.

The programme for the pantomime of 1892 is bordered by Dublin's everyday business, and advertisements for hats, furs and furniture represent an eminently respectable middle-class reality within whose frame the pantomime is staged as absolute Other.[24] There is no trace of a different Imperial centre to offset Dublin, which plays the role of metropolis consummately. The make-believe of absolute opposition is precisely what Bloom, with his checks and considerations – 'Probably not a bit like it really' – can't manage.[25] The pantomime world is one of myth, and as such it offers escape into an-other world. Once reality is represented within the fantasy world of the play, the question of whose fantasy is being depicted arises.

One of Bloom's chief concerns in the writing of his song is over the clashing myths of British royalty and Irish nationalism. His song was to have been entitled 'If Brian Boru could but come back and see old Dublin now'. He equates the imaginary visit of Boru with the real visit of the Duke and Duchess of York, and worries about 'opposition from extreme circles'. Brian Boru was the tenth century King of Southern Ireland who famously defeated the Danes at Clontarf in 1014, and therefore represented the successful repulse by the Irish of foreign invaders. The Duke and Duchess of York were members of that same British royalty which is mentioned in the form of Queen Victoria's diamond jubilee. The implication is that both extremes of opinion, Royalist and Nationalist, would object to the juxtaposition, and although the reasons for this are unclarified we may suppose that the cause was both their total antipathy and their representation within a fantastic setting for comic purposes.

Bloom had some grounds for his concerns. In 1887 the celebrations for the Jubilee were so successful that they were repeated ten years later, to the great consternation of W.B. Yeats, Maude Gonne and James Connolly, who mounted a counter-commemoration of the rebellion of 1798, in its centenary the following year. Yeats declared: 'This year the Irish people will not celebrate, as England did last year, the establishment of an empire that has been built on the rapine of the world'.[26] Both celebrations demonstrate myth-making enterprises dependent upon spectacle, which may be too close for comfort to the theatricalised myth of the Orient which functions for both the Imperial centre and the Occidental Irish as constructed Other, and yet which, in Bloom's song, was to provide their setting. The bringing together of Monarchist, Rebel and Orientalist myths threatens to deflate the illusion, as Joyce has Bloom comically deflating the grandeur of specific allusions throughout this section.

Bloom's immediate quandary seems to have been how to choose between the diamond jubilee of Queen Victoria and the opening of the new municipal fish market, both of which occurred in the summer of 1897.[27] The effect is a satirical deflation of the pomp of Royal occasion through its juxtaposition with the fish market and all its associated features of coarseness and stink. But the equivalence of Victoria, the Sea's Empress, with a Dublin fishwife is a more pointed political jibe at the myth of majesty, which is as removed from reality as the fantastic valley of diamonds. The implication is that the sixty diamond years of Victoria's reign have been based on a trade and practice no less ignoble than that which takes place in the fish market. Khanna describes a similar juxtaposition in 'Araby' as 'the shock of sordidness beneath the colonial venture'.[28] The juxtaposition is echoed in the professional rivalry of the two theatres between which Bloom finds himself torn: the Lyric and the Royal. The Royal stands on Hawkins Street, imaginatively associating Royalty once more with fantasy and piracy through the cabin boy of Treasure Island, while the Grand Lyric Hall more soberly stands upon the municipal sounding Burgh Quay.[29]

The tension in the short section of the text which deals with the pantomime is set up between the Imperial, with its attendant pomp and grandeur, and the colony; the mythic and the local, the everyday, the profane. In a paragraph telling us about the pantomime, details of its story are scant while those about the realities of cast, setting and production are laboured over to excess. All that we are told of the plot of *Sinbad* is that it has a scene known as 'the valley of the diamonds'. What we are told about its production, however, is not only the date, author, edition, and exact address of the theatre, but also the names of the lessee, the scenery and costume makers, the producer, the choreographers and the singer. This Sinbad is not populated by princes and peris, but by Dublin townspeople.

The critic Jeri Johnson terms the language of 'Ithaca' 'scientific'; in the spirit of precision we could go even further and term it empirical, with all the implications of knowledge and dominance, even to the point of exclusion, which that implies. Said's observation seems appropriate:

> knowledge of subject races or Orientals is what makes their management easy and profitable; knowledge gives power, more power requires more knowledge, and so on in an increasingly profitable dialectic of information and control.[30]

This is one explanation for the 'Ithaca' chapter's obsession with naming, its repetitive formula of 'whats'. What are catalogued, as though in a census, are Dublin buildings and people. What is excluded is both the story of Sinbad and Bloom's own artistic creation. Johnson has remarked of this chapter that it 'appears formally to have taken leave of literature altogether', and so it seems pertinent to ask why it is here, of all places, that we are told of Bloom's own literary leanings.[31] Although the text presents, almost as if they were scientific specimens or evidence in a courtroom, the three early examples of composition, Bloom's adult attempt at literary creation for a public audience never gets written, and the facts and figures with which the chapter as a whole is so obsessed stand in its place. Earlier Joyce has mapped the entire Dublin waterworks system from reservoir to tap as part of a description of filling a kettle to make tea.[32] In short, the local is privileged over the mythic, both in the concrete geographical sense and in the sense of detail over abstraction.

Such prolific detail dupes us into believing in the accuracy of the data with which we are presented, but many of these details are random, erroneous, or anachronistically yoked together. Bloom was to have included in his song allusions to the Lord Mayor, High Sheriff, and solicitor-general, all of whom are named, as he remembers the difficulty of finding rhymes for them. (Incidentally, their inclusion ought to dispel any notion that the local is being unproblematically valorised at the expense of the Imperial.) But none of these officials were elected until the autumn, and Bloom was supposedly composing his song over the summer, between the opening of the fish market and the Jubilee celebrations.[33] This was the summer of 1897, and as we have seen, Bloom was professionally torn between the Lyric theatre and the Theatre Royal, even though the Lyric did not open until the December of the following year. Furthermore, as Adams notes, the Gaiety's pantomime for 1897 was not even *Sinbad*, but *Aladdin*.[34]

The inclusion of so many details and references to existing people and places positions *Ulysses* at a slight angle to Dublin reality. Its effect in this instance is to trap Bloom in an indeterminate moment, not real or meaningful to the events of metropolis or colony, but taking what meaning it has from its elliptical position between them. As if to verify this, Bloom is presented as being pinned in a moment both out of time and defined by it, paralysed by his inescapable 'oscillation' between 'the anticipated diamond jubilee [...] and the posticipated opening of the new municipal fish market'.[35] Bloom's temporal position is legitimated only by those events it lies between (and is further dislocated by the inversion of the order of those events).

The most revealing reason for Bloom's songwriting failure is his distraction by the principal girl Nellie Bouverist's 'non-intellectual, non-political, non-topical underclothing'.[36] There is obviously an instruction here to the reader that what has gone before is precisely to be read as intellectual, political and topical. Jones asserts that 'Joyce stages the female at significant moments in his work as the extra-textual, extra-linguistic'.[37] Nellie Bouverist's apolitical underwear is revealed beneath the Oriental costume as the absolute difference which the Orient itself, for Bloom, is not. Jones asserts that

> the sexual other remains in Joyce's work the fantasy of a certain cultural space or knowledge that is in Joyce forever the horizon, the unfolding, the boundary of difference. If Joyce's political project to write the incommensurable differences of colonial subjectivity founders in his

writing [...] it would founder precisely because that writing retains traces of the fantasy of the ontological other imagined as pure difference.[38]

But Bloom is not merely overcome with a masculinist 'concupiscence' which would align him damnably with both municipal and metropolitan fantasies of the absolute Other that is woman (even though Nellie's entrance into the text is immediately preceded by reference to those 'recent erections', the Grand Lyric Hall and the Theatre Royal). Once again his paralysis is the result of being in two opposing positions at once, his lust held in check by his compassion for the 'non-intellectual, non-political, non-topical expression' (presumably of embarrassment) on Nellie's face, which perfectly counterbalances the effect of her underwear.

In the 'Ithaca' chapter of *Ulysses*, Joyce uses the Sinbad theme to several ends. In Bloom's hands it becomes the focus for a representation of the paralysed energy of the individual under colonialism – Bloom cannot create – as well as the means of satirising those forces which suspend the individual in such a state. But Joyce also presents Bloom himself as Sinbad. The chapter's many references to wandering, water and navigation apply as much to Sinbad as to Odysseus. Above all, the myth of Sinbad as the triumphantly returned traveller is upheld, on however burlesque a level, by Bloom's return to the marital bed and the hint that things may now begin to change.

Bloom/Sinbad triumphs through what critics have traditionally called his humanism, but those qualities of generosity, tolerance and optimism about life and his countrymen could easily be applied to the Sinbad of tradition.[39] In staging Sinbad's return, Joyce does not change anything of the spirit or values of the original; Sinbad, as a representative of the East, partakes of an eternal essence, his character is unchanged even though he has been transposed into modern Dublin.

To appreciate the full force of this it is necessary to turn to Aflaq's story of 'The Death of Sindbad', which depicts Sindbad's return in stark contrast to both the original and its Joycean counterpart.[40] I am not attempting to argue that Aflaq read and was influenced by *Ulysses*, although copies were certainly available in Baghdad from as early as 1922.[41] I do feel, however, that Aflaq's story presents such a sharp contrast to Joyce's use of the Sinbad material, even while it displays some strikingly similar features, that it is worth comparing the two.

Aflaq's story was published in 1936, the year in which the Arab rising in Palestine began, as the culmination of tension between Arabs and the massive influx of Jews from Europe, following Balfour's declaration of 1917. The Arab Nationalist Party had been launched in Beirut the previous year, defining Arabs as 'those who spoke Arabic, lived in Arabic lands and had no group affiliations preventing them from being integrated within an Arab nation'.[42] The political background was one of tumult, with a desperate sense of the fragmentation of society leading to a countervailing move for Arabic unity.

In his introduction to Aflaq's story, Mohammad Shaheen talks about the use of the Sinbad theme as a register for the disjunction between traditional and modern societies, and the breakdown of the community:

> The modern Sindbad is, then, a man of sorrows who suffers from alienation [...] If the old Sindbad stands for a celebration of individual freedom, communal spirit, sympathy, courage, goodwill and the like, the modern Sindbad is the lamentation of the absence of these things.[43]

In the original story Sinbad has retired, having amassed enough wealth to live in comfort himself and give generously to the poor and those he chooses to entertain. In the 'Ithaca' chapter of *Ulysses* Bloom's modest means are sufficient to allow him to offer the dispossessed Stephen a bed for the night, and possibly for longer. In Aflaq's story, Sindbad returns empty handed, to discover that his wife and children are dead and his house and goods have been sold.

Both the original tales and *Ulysses*, while showing the returned traveller at rest, hold out the promise of other voyages. In the *Arabian Nights*, Sinbad tells his audience that he has now given himself up to his family and friends, and intends to enjoy the leisure which he has earned, but this is undermined by similar resolutions at the close of the first and sixth voyages. In *Ulysses*, Bloom's wandering and return will clearly be repeated the following day, and so on, as he roams the city canvassing for advertisements. But there is no doubt in Aflaq's tale that this is the last of Sindbad's voyages. The title is uncompromising, and the story ends with the confirmation of his death.

Chapter VII

Ulysses takes elements from the Sinbad theme and utilises them within its own plot, affirming that their value persists and is open to change. Aflaq's story seems to be asserting in the most emphatic manner that the fantasy of Sindbad is over and done with. If we consider that in Aflaq's story both Sindbad and the tale are returning to their place of origin, Baghdad, this suggests the most profound ramifications for the culture which produced the *Arabian Nights*. Such a view of Arabic culture is at odds with the idea of it which is presented in *Ulysses*, where the Orient is largely imagined as unchanged in its predominant features from the times of the tales themselves.

The dialogue form of 'Ithaca', both in the catechistic question and answer formula of the chapter as a whole and in the juxtaposition of conflicting detail, problematised the position of the individual and suggested a split consciousness or view of the world. The objectivity it pretended to was exceeded by the details and their implications, which frequently revealed its random, flawed, or incomplete nature. In Aflaq's story, the dialogue form dramatises the confrontation between Sindbad and the citizens of Baghdad, and serves to heighten the distance between them. His Sindbad, who returns from his travels blinded and lame, seems to come from an older time, with a different set of values to the community to which he is supposed to belong.

Confronted by the loss of his home and family, he climbs onto a stone in front of the house which used to be his. The stone represents an old order which is gone, and it will become the altar on which Sindbad is sacrificed. The solidity of this old order has fragmented and fallen away; and the children symbolically pelt the dying Sindbad with stones. The voices which assail him are likewise fragmented; questions never come singly, but from four or five voices one after another, each succeeding voice changing the nature of the question. For each of the questioners Sindbad represents something different, in each case a distortion of what he feels himself to be.

The children who crowd around him see him as a figure of mockery. Between the youths and the old men there is a competition to see him as either a romantic adventurer, similar to the fantasised figure of the West, or as the embodiment of the necessary failure of such fantasies. While the youths implore him to tell them stories of far off lands, the riches he has amassed, and how he has held the world in his hands, the old men urge him to admit that he is an example of the folly of such dreams; an avaricious man who has ended up bankrupt, an egotist abandoned by all. Sindbad denies their accusations and refuses to validate the romantic fabrications, but no-one is capable of listening to what he really has to say, so the questions become increasingly mocking, even from those who are sympathetic to him, because they do not understand him.

Sinbad represents the old values of generosity and community. In the *Arabian Nights* each of his voyages ends with him returning to his friends and family and giving plentifully to the poor out of his newly acquired wealth. The Sindbad of Aflaq's story still represents these values. His hands, he says, are not worn with the riches he has accumulated, but with giving. His quest was to find a new world, not as a merchant but in order to restore hope. His account of his quest is reminiscent of a spiritual journey. Not only has he been blinded by the truth, but he has discovered in himself the nearest and furthest points of existence. His vision of the world is an holistic one, and the aim of his journeying was to become one with that unified vision; he says 'I took and gave till my hands had touched everything and my heart held every living thing'.[44] It is this idea of the world as mutually dependent which he represents, and it is this which has fragmented. Its disintegration is figured in the multiple voices of his interrogators and the stones which the children throw at him.

He speaks like a prophet, but his audience can understand him only in terms of profit of a different kind. It is the apparently religious old men who have introduced the notion of profit, urging him to speak 'one profitable word' to the young before he dies.[45] Sindbad strips their assumed piety of its religious mask and reduces it to a wholly capitalist spirit which is antipathetic to everything he believes: 'You seek profit even from one whom you hate and slight; you think of profit even in the hour of my death…'.[46] It is a measure of his distance from them that they appear not to comprehend him, still accusing him of spending his life accumulating wealth, even though he has already described himself as having continually mocked profit, and squandered everything he has gained.

The story closes with Sindbad about to reveal the secret that he has discovered. This secret takes the form of a word, but before he can utter it he falls to the ground and dies, and a black snake emerges from his mouth instead.[47] The meaning of this sinister apparition is held in the balance. Shaheen concurs with the old men, who see Sindbad's muted death as having given them life, and asserts that it is that of a prophet who 'bears the sins of his people alone'.[48] He makes much of the fact that 'Aflaq himself left Beirut in 1966, but where the writer merely chose silence and exile, Sindbad's story does not actually end in muteness, but in the birth of the serpent from his mouth.[49] The macabre quality of this final image problematises a positive reading, and adds weight to the voices of the youths who seem to be warning against the dangers of censorship; 'silence has killed him', they say.

The principal message of the story's conclusion may simply be that Sindbad's death has resolved nothing, since the old men and the youths are still able to interpret the figure of the Sailor, though dead, in directly antagonistic ways. The ending throws the focus outward to the reader as an accusation; it is not only the crowd who are unable to read Sindbad faithfully, but we, since we too have no idea what his final unspoken word might have been.

This foregrounding of the unreadability of Sindbad is finally what differentiates Aflaq's use of the Sinbad figure most sharply from Joyce's. Where Aflaq's Sindbad registers the absolute rupture between a traditional community and the modern colony, and between that colony and the world beyond, Joyce's Sinbad is translatable, not only between continents but between myths; he can be equally equivalent to Odysseus and the captain of the *Flying Dutchman*. Joyce's Sinbad is endlessly translatable, Aflaq's emphatically refuses translation.

The Sinbad Joyce inherits from the *Arabian Nights* has, of course, already been translated many times. The translation is a cultural as well as a linguistic one. Sinbad, rendered in English, represents the commodification of the East into an Orient of exotic locations, fabulous beasts, barbaric customs and fantastic fortune, not only in the badlands of the travels, but in Baghdad itself. In the *Arabian Nights* Baghdad is the home to which Sinbad strives to return; a place of safety and rest. The foreign is located beyond it: every time Sinbad leaves Baghdad he encounters strange and potentially threatening situations which are beyond the economy of the domestic space which he has left. The riches which he brings home are out of the blue, and the profits of casting himself adrift at the mercy of fortune exceed all expectations, all attempts to calculate and map. In translation, Baghdad itself functions as an Other space of adventure and excess, and Sinbad is an exotic figure, not simply because of his wonderful voyages, but because of his Oriental origin. The translation depends upon estrangement.

In 'The Task of the Translator', Walter Benjamin argues that translation is emphatically not a case of transliteration, the substitution of words in one language for their perceived equivalent in another, because words depend for their meaning not upon themselves but on the system of which they are a part. The relationships and gaps between words are as important to meaning as the words themselves. These relationships and gaps operate differently in different languages. Benjamin states that: '[i]n all language and linguistic creations there remains in addition to what can be conveyed something that cannot be communicated'.[50] The incommunicable has a distinct relationship to the communicable, which changes between different linguistic systems. Benjamin argues that the task of the translator is not to attempt to cover up or fill in the gaps in what can be communicated, but to foreground them, since it is here that true meaning takes place.

Tejaswini Niranjana sees the attempt to occlude these gaps as a covering up of the process by which meaning is constructed, not innocently, but with a politically charged agenda of fixing the identity of that which the translation represents. Such a fixing (in the sense of freezing into a permanent definition, but also with the implication that such a definition is itself a 'fix', a frame-up) presents itself as innocent, covering the methods and assumptions of its own production. Niranjana asserts that

> In creating coherent and transparent texts and subjects, translation participates – across a range of discourses – in the fixing of colonized cultures, making them seem static and unchanging rather than historically constructed. Translation functions as a transparent presentation of something that already exists, although the 'original' is actually brought into being through translation.[51]

The cultural translation of the *Arabian Nights* presents Sinbad as an exotic traveller in an unchangingly fantastical Orient: he is always the stranger in a strange land. His return is always staged, as it is never to the Baghdad he originally left, but to a 'fixed' representation of it which is changed, and unchanging. His ahistorical nature is the reason Joyce is able to transpose his story onto other myths so effortlessly. But this fixing estranges him from his original context, and it is this estrangement which Aflaq's account of his final return registers.

In the *Arabian Nights* the gap, the unknown, is beyond Baghdad in uncharted, fantastic territory, and what is brought home is plenitude. In the Sinbad Joyce inherited the unknown or strange has been displaced to Baghdad itself, and to Sinbad, not as fabulous traveller, but as representative of the foreign East. Joyce's Sinbad is translated and infinitely translatable, but it is a translation which depends upon the covering up of the incommunicable familiarity of Baghdad by its representation as exotic and fantastic, and of Sinbad as representative of the Orient as strange. The kind of translation which pretends an easy equivalence of terms covers up the way it merely constructs meaning in its own terms. The incommunicable ellipses of the original text are replaced by a cultural overcoding which endlessly stages Sinbad's return to unfamiliar places which he never left.

Sinbad's easy translatability is due to his representation in the language of an Imperial power which sees itself as centre and all else as 'other'. His transposition to Ireland is both endlessly possible and absolutely impossible, because he represents the eternal foreign, and because he represents it in terms that designate the Irish too as 'other'. Those terms are part of the language of the Imperial centre which Ireland shares, but shares through the erosion of its own language and culture, and through the occlusion of the untranslatability of its own situation.

On his return in the 'Ithaca' chapter, Bloom has uttered nothing but an incoherent string of names which are variations on Sinbad the Sailor: Tinbad the Tailor and Jinbad the Jailer and Whinbad the Whaler and so on. His drunken litany ends with 'Sinbad the Sailor roc's auk's eggin the night of the bed of all the auks of the rocs of Darkinbad the Brightdayler'.[52] It is left to Molly at the beginning of 'Penelope' to translate this mumbo-jumbo into a request for breakfast in bed with a couple of eggs. Her interpretation is no more accurate than the assertions of the crowd at the end of Aflaq's story. It offers an example of the kind of wilful occlusion of incommunicability which is necessary to the representation of a version of the Sinbad story which can domesticate it, transform it and keep it endlessly translatable into other tales.

In Aflaq's tale Baghdad is culturally and morally, as Sindbad is financially, bankrupt. The home itself has become strange. The story depends upon our familiarity with Sindbad, but who is he: the original Sinbad or the translated Oriental with his trappings of wealth and indulgence? As readers we ultimately know him no better than the crowd. Estranged from his homeland, he is readable not even to those whose language and culture he supposedly shares. The unknown, the ellipsis in the text, has been finally brought home, and insisting on its inclusion, it absolutely refuses translation.

NOTES TO CHAPTER VII

Notes to Chapter VII

1. Ellen Carol Jones, 'Borderlines', in *Joyce: Feminism/Post/Colonialism*, ed. Ellen Carol Jones (Amsterdam: Rodopi, 1998), pp.7-22, p.7.

2. ibid., p.8.

3. Fredric Jameson, 'Modernism and Imperialism', in *Nationalism, Colonialism and Literature*, ed. Seamus Deane (Minneapolis: University of Minnesota Press, 1990), pp.43-66, p.60. Jameson argues that modernist form results from the dislocating effects of imperialism. Since 'colonialism means that a significant structural segment of the economic system as a whole is now located elsewhere, beyond the metropolis', the 'daily life and existential experience in the metropolis – which is necessarily the very content of the national literature itself, can now no longer be grasped immanently; it no longer has its meaning, its deeper reason for being, within itself', pp.50-51.

4. Reproduced from a journal publication in Mohammad Shaheen, *The Modern Arabic Short Story: Shahrazad Returns* (London: Macmillan, 1989), pp.95-98.

5. Jones, op.cit. p.12.

6. Edward Said, *Orientalism: Western Conceptions of the Orient* (London: Penguin, 1995), p.3.

7. Declan Kiberd, *Inventing Ireland: The Literature of the Modern Nation* (London: Vintage, 1996), pp.1-2.

8. Jameson, op.cit. p.64.

9. This was not the more famous Ottoman empire, but the Abbasid caliphate (750-1258AD), although the tales continued to develop in transmission over several hundred years. The first manuscript dates from the fourteenth century AD.

10. The Marquis of Lorne K.T., *VRI: Her Life and Empire* (London: Harmondsworth, 1901), p.363.

11. James Joyce, *Finnegans Wake* (London: Faber, 1971), p.620.

12. Roland McHugh, *Annotations to Finnegans Wake* (London: Routledge, 1980), p.10.

13. ibid., p.620.

14. There is a similar cluster of associations around the old sailor, specifically referred to as Sinbad, in the Eumaeus chapter. See James Joyce, *Ulysses*, ed. by Jeri Johnson (Oxford: OUP, 1993), p.591.

15. I have been unable to discover the script of the pantomime. The usual source for information on the production is an advertisement in the Freeman's Journal; see Robert Martin Adams, *Surface and Symbol: The Consistency of James Joyce's Ulysses* (Oxford: Oxford University Press, 1962), p.77. However, thanks to Tony Carey, librarian at Trinity College Dublin, to whom I am extremely grateful, I have been able to locate an original programme for the performance which could equally well have been Joyce's source, and would support Adams' contention that Joyce had watched the pantomime.

16. Gibraltar had a history of occupation, not only by the British and the Spanish, but by the Moors, from whom it was captured by Castile in 1462. Its situation on the southernmost tip of Spain puts it in sight of Morocco.

17. Said cites these traits as part of a 'complex array of 'Oriental' ideas', op.cit. p.4.

18. *Ulysses*, p.418.

19. Vincent J. Cheng, *Joyce, Race and Empire* (Cambridge: Cambridge University Press, 1995), p.176.

20. James Joyce, *Dubliners* (London: Penguin, 1992), p.24.

21. Ranjana Khanna, '*Araby*: Women's Time and the Time of the Nation', in Jones, op.cit. pp.81-101, p.100.

22. J.S. Atherton, '*Finnegans Wake*: 'The Gist of the Pantomime'', *Accent*, 1955 (Winter) v 15-16, 14-26, p.19.

23. ibid., p.20.

24. It is possible that Joyce was attracted to this pantomime by an advertisement for a firm at 62 Grafton St which borders the title page of the programme. The establishment was called 'Joyce, Furrier'.

25. *Ulysses*, p.55.

26. Quoted in Kiberd, op.cit. p.140. W.B. Yeats, postscript, *Ideals in Ireland*, ed. Lady Gregory (London, 1901).

27. Adams, op.cit. p.80.

28. Khanna, op.cit. p.98.

29. Adams, op.cit. p.80.

30. Said, op.cit. p.36.

31. *Ulysses*, notes, p.958.

32. *Ulysses*, pp.623-24.

33. Adams, op.cit. p.80.

34. ibid., p.80.

35. *Ulysses*, p.631.

36. *Ulysses*, p.632.

37. Jones, op.cit. p.13.

38. ibid., p.15.

39. See, for example, Richard Ellmann, *James Joyce* (Oxford: Oxford University Press, 1983), p.5, where Ellmann sees Bloom as representative of 'Joyce's discovery, so humanistic that he would have been embarrassed to disclose it out of context, [...] that the ordinary is the extraordinary'; also, Frank Budgen, *James Joyce and the Making of Ulysses* (Oxford: Oxford University Press, 1972), p.284, where Bloom is described

as 'the most reasonable and humane of all the Dubliners in *Ulysses*', and especially S.L. Goldberg, *James Joyce* (London: Oliver & Boyd), pp.92-94, where Goldberg describes Bloom as 'a man [...] able to accept the 'necessary evils' of life with human grace', and sees his 'justifying [...] spirit' escaping the 'assault of the cold, 'scientifically' objective intellect' which seeks to reduce him to its terms, in the catechismic 'Ithaca'.

40. Since Michael Aflaq is not known primarily for his literary output a brief introduction may be helpful. Born in Damascus in 1905 into a Greek Orthodox family of grain merchants, he studied at the Sorbonne, and later taught Humanities at the Tajhiz school in Damascus. In 1940 he founded Ba'th as a small discussion group which eventually became a major political party in Syria and also Iraq. Ba'th was Pan-Arabic and hostile to Imperialism and Zionism. Arrested and imprisoned on numerous occasions by various government factions, Aflaq served as Minister of Education in the all-party government of August 1949, but failed to win a seat in Damascus in the November elections of the same year. In 1965 he was instrumental in the moderate stand against in-fighting within Ba'th, which was the party in power. A counter-coup forced him to flee to Beirut. In 1971 he launched an appeal from Baghdad for union between Syria, Egypt and Iraq, and in the same year was accused of plotting against Syria and sentenced to death *in absentia*. See David Roberts, *The Ba'th and the Creation of Modern Syria* (London: Croom Helm, 1987).

41. Alec Craig, *The Banned Books of England and Other Countries: A Study of the Conception of Literary Obscenity* (London: Unwin, 1962), p.79.

42. Raghid Solh, 'The Attitude of the Arab Nationalists towards a Greater Lebanon during the 1930s', in Nadim Shehach and Dana Haffar Mills (eds), *Lebanon: A History of Conflict and Consensus* (London: I.B. Tauris, 1988), pp.149-65, p.155. Aflaq himself saw Pan-Arabism as 'add[ing] to the sects of Arabs a new sect and lay[ing] on the soul of the Arabs a coating over all the trivialities which cover it'. Roberts, op.cit. p.19, n.1.

43. Shaheen, op.cit. p.33.

44. Michael Aflaq, 'The Death of Sindbad: A Narrative in One Act', in ibid., pp.95-98, p.97.

45. ibid., p.95.

46. ibid., p.95

47. Contrast this with Molly's affirmative 'yes' which ends Bloom's participation in *Ulysses* and opens the 'Penelope' chapter. It also begs comparison with Stephen's invocation to his mother's ghost in 'Circe': 'Tell me the word, mother, if you know now. The word known to all men'. Stephen, like the crowd at Sindbad's death, does not get an answer. *Ulysses*, p.540.

48. Shaheen, op.cit. p.34.

49. Aflaq, in fact, did not choose to remain silent rather than denounce his party, as Shaheen maintains. In a speech two days before the counter-coup which exiled him he denounced the ruthless perversion of the form and membership of the party by certain of its leaders, and in a speech in Beirut in July 1974 he criticised the Ba'th leadership of Syria at this time as having been preoccupied with internal problems, and as not being in control of the government of the country. Roberts, op.cit. p.87, p.94.

50. Walter Banjamin, 'The Task of the Translator', in *Illuminations*, trans. Harry Zohn (London: Jonathan Cape, 1970), p.79.

51. Tejaswini Niranjana, *Siting Translation: History, Post-Structuralism, and the Colonial Context* (Oxford: University of California Press, 1992), p.3.

52. *Ulysses*, p.689.

CHAPTER VIII

Closets with a View: Sodom, Hellas and Homosexual Myth in Modernist Writing

Alberto Mira

Alberto Mira is Reader in Languages at Oxford Brookes University. He has published extensively in the field of Gay and Lesbian Studies. A specific area of interest is the representation of Mediterranean homosexuality and Mediterranean homosexual identities. His book *Para entendernos* is an encyclopaedia of gay culture with a special focus on Spain and Latin America. Other research includes homosexual writing in pre-civil war Spain, including some work on Lorca's *El publico*. Other interests include Spanish Cinema and theatre, especially during the Franco years, and translation. His publications include a critical edition and translation in Spanish of Albee's *Who's Afraid of Virginia Woolf?* and a volume on Spanish theatre under Francoism, as well as a number of articles on translation, cinema and homosexuality.

Whole countries lay behind creaky closet doors in Modernist writing. One of the most appropriate metaphors to describe the situation of the homosexual in the century between 1870 and 1970, bridging the gap between inner feelings and outer experience, is that of exile. 'Being' a homosexual always meant being an outcast, away from one's own homeland, inhabiting some sort of foreign country which was also an inner landscape. Homosexuality was constructed as something which simply didn't belong with a conventional experience of the world. Therefore, in order to achieve any identity as a homosexual, the individual had to travel. In other words, identification with homosexuality meant a chain of *dis-locations*: when 'transgressive' desires were identified and accepted as part of the self, the self had to re-shape its connections to the world. Sometimes this was achieved through 'physical' dislocation – the individual could find a sense of belonging in different lands; more often, such dislocations took place on a discursive level, and travelling and the notion of exile into distant lands was used as a metaphor. Through these changes in location, it was possible to find a space where a homosexual selfhood made sense in terms of discourse, whether inside the closet or in the 'outer' world, but the process would make the homosexual into an exile: in terms of social expression, homosexuality had to be bounded by secrecy and crossing that boundary meant falling victim, in the best of cases, to scandal, or, worse, to jail. The rhetorical strategies that forced homosexuality into the discourse of otherness and shrouded it in secrecy in turn-of-the-century writing have been discussed by Eve Kosofsky Sedgwick in her masterly *Epistemology of the Closet*,[1] a work informed by Michel Foucault's reflections on the medicalisation of sexuality (and especially of same-sex desire) as dealt with in works such as, respectively, *The Birth of the Clinic* and *History of Sexuality*.[2]

In the following pages I concentrate specifically on metaphors used by Modernist writers to bridge the rhetorical dislocation produced by homosexuality. I would like to argue that these tropes and images are used as intertexts that strengthen positive values in the presentation of homosexual experience, thus challenging institutional discourse on the topic. Modernism as an artistic ideology is relevant in this process as a framework where these strategies of resistance could take place: after all, if something can sum up the whole Modernist impulse, it is precisely this notion of discontinuity with the past which is expressed through mistrust of and challenge to the classical style of writing favoured by nineteenth century realism as well as to a worldview based exclusively on scientific discoveries. The general feeling among intellectuals at the turn of the century that realism could no longer account for the problem of artistic expression will be mirrored by the way in which homosexual discourse had to find strategies for expression against the prevalence of pathological ('classical') accounts of same-sex desire.

The way in which landscapes, whether real or mythical, are activated in reference to a homosexual tradition is relevant for the study of the works of such canonical early and high modernist European authors as André Gide, Oscar Wilde, Marcel Proust, Thomas Mann, Stefan George, Federico García Lorca, Luis Cernuda, Antonio Botto and Constantin Cavafy among many others. In some of them (most notably Proust and García Lorca), the difficulties of homosexual self-expression were parallel to the general problem of writing. In all of them, the metaphor of exile into faraway countries (and, more generally, of dislocation) is often a node of homosexual signification.

In one very concrete way, homosexual exile was a reality for those who could afford it: there were actual places (e.g. Capri, Taormina, Tangiers) where homosexuals traditionally took refuge from the harshness of the law and social disapproval, a practice that has endured until very recently for northern European homosexuals (the opposition north/south is relevant in this discussion: we shall see how homosexuality becomes 'a problem' in society precisely as medical discourse makes same-sex desire into one, and medical discourse was central to the British, French and German cultures to a larger extent than in Mediterranean ones). In terms of writing, this search for the foreign was expressed in the use of literary landscapes in the south (or to the east) chosen for their value as homosexual myths, in order to explore homoerotic desire or the outcast state of homosexuals.

Often, the real and the fictional were two sides of the same coin. In his insightful *The Seduction of the Mediterranean*,³ Robert Aldrich shows how homosexuals from northern European countries could avoid scandal (stricter laws against homosexuality applied in Britain (1885) and Germany (1871) from the second half of the nineteenth century) and still be able to find expression for their desires by going abroad, preferably to such sun-drenched destinations as some northern African countries, southern Italy or the Greek islands. On the one hand there were practical reasons for this: not being recognised and not being subjected to homophobic laws, for instance (the diaspora of British homosexuals following the Wilde trials has been well documented by Aldrich and others); also, as was often the case, being wealthy among poorer people tended to stretch the limits of sexual tolerance in these cultures. In this sense, the closet could be quite a cosy place to be as long as scandal could be avoided.⁴ One did not need to be alone in his/her closet either: Aldrich describes how some of these locations became something like 'gay Meccas', where homosexuals gathered, met and shared thoughts and pursuits.

This is not a new trend started by late nineteenth century writers: we have evidence of 'sexual tourism' since as early as the late eighteenth century (Byron seems to have made use of his southern exile to explore homosexual desire; later, Flaubert's correspondence seems to suggest homosexual as well as heterosexual experiences in northern Africa) that can be linked to the growing conception of homosexuality as a guilty secret. Still, the notion of travelling in search of the 'homosexual self' has a specific centrality in Modernist homosexual writing that deserves attention: this is the moment when truths based on tradition were being revised by exploring the gap between experience and the conventions of literary discourse; also, a strand in Modernist ideology challenges ideas on gender roles which were deeply imbeded in nineteenth century bourgeois culture.⁵ This often resulted in new ways of codifying experience risking solipsism. True, the works discussed here are seldom solipsistic (with the possible exception of García Lorca's work on homosexual rhetoric in *El público*), but the expression of a homosexual selfhood in them is often difficult to read (being often ignored by critics as a result), given that it is wrapped up in codes with no explicit signifiers in this direction.

It is easy to see how actual travels could be the inspiration for writing set in those lands, much of which is an account of actual experiences. But the relation between text and experience worked also in the opposite direction: destinations were chosen because they were already inserted in a tradition of homosexual culture: a matter of 'life imitating art'. Homosexuals were not only *running away from* intolerance, but also travelled *in search of* some legendary Arcadia. Northern Africa, southern Italy and Greece were, indeed, 'promised' lands, the 'promise' being made in legends on the availability of sexual partners in those cultures as well as the possibility of a homosexual social identity that didn't make the individual into an outcast. Sometimes a whole culture became part of homosexual mythology through a series of misreadings: the south and the orient first became representations of otherness that in time would metonymically include *sexual* otherness.[6]

The key defining move in the process of association of certain cultures to homosexual tradition, as it will be manifested in Modernist writing, can be found in the writings of Johann Joachim Winckelmann on Hellenic art: aesthetic appreciation and homoeroticism become inextricably united; his reflections seem to have provided the perfect alibi and fix the relationship between high-art and homosexual discourse, although, explicitly, it is a version of manhood which is being proposed.

Literary representation of such destinations and mythical lands as appropriated by the homosexual tradition was double-edged, both a product of the culture of the closet (it was necessarily codified) and of mainstream high culture. Research shows that this active use of intertexts to convey homosexuality in a way that was both indirect and clear has a long tradition: John Boswell discusses, for instance, the use of the Ganymede legend in mediæval texts;[7] the story of Achilles and Patroclus in the *Iliad* has a strong tradition as a homosexual intertext; and even biblical passages such as King David's grief after the death of his beloved Jonathan were occasionally used as apologies, as were, especially from the late eighteenth century, the lists of famous homosexuals.[8]

The use of such 'authoritative' intertexts placed artistic works in the realm of legitimate cultural expression, but on the other hand it was used to frame homoerotic desire and homosexual experience in codified ways that would only be deciphered by those personally acquainted with it. In this way, the nineteenth century saw the consolidation of a 'homosexual tradition' that was a sign of increasing awareness of a 'homosexual self'. There were many such codes, on different levels of communication, that ranged from homosexual slang to key characters from classic literature; sometimes they came close to being common knowledge, but often they bordered the solipsistic and are therefore practically lost to readers of later generations. But the reference to certain lands well established in the homosexual tradition is consistent and highly visible in apologetic writing.[9] It was something, as we have seen, symbolically central to homosexual experience, and therefore constituted an appropriate system of metaphors to deal with the topic. In particular, the use of the biblical legend of Sodom, to represent the depravity of the homosexual, and of Hellas (the word used by Symonds and other nineteenth century apologists to refer to Classical Greece) as an idealised world that welcomed homoerotic desire, has been central to homosexual discourse in the past two centuries. Medicalisation was an obstacle to the development of this growing sense of homosexual awareness by placing 'homosexuality' in the realm of pathology, as an individual flaw, rather than as a cultural identity rooted in tradition and history.

Several authors have,[10] following Foucault's example, pointed out how, during the last quarter of the nineteenth century, delimitations of same-sex desire go through a 'paradigm shift'. It it questionable how literally we should take this account,[11] and indeed some research suggests that continuities may have been stronger than ruptures; also, at any one point in time, several paradigms of knowledge coexist, and the centrality of medicalisation to dealing with homosexualiy did not mean the end of religious or moralistic accounts. Still, it is safe to admit, as evidence seems to point out, that homosexuality was increasingly discussed and framed in legal and other institutional texts, and also that authoritative discourse on same-sex desire became articulated by science. Maybe one of the more problematic aspects of this new discourse is the way in which homoeroticism and sexual identity (which so far could easily be kept as different concepts) are inevitably conflated in a new type: 'the homosexual'. These changes in public discourse on homosexuality (sodomy, the previous concept attached to same-sex love, as a transgression defined in different terms, had been displaced but not completely superseded) had to affect the way writers dealt with their homosexual experiences. They could no longer subtly introduce homoeroticism in their work without being forced into the new category of sexual identity (and therefore marginalised). Pressures around homosexual definition will be influential in homosexual representation especially from the beginning of the twentieth century.

Other elements are to be taken into account. First, psychoanalysis was becoming the epistemological tool for achieving knowledge of 'human nature' and it encouraged (but not necessarily determined) a pathological view of homosexuality; at the same time, homosexual visibility was increasing in the great European metropoles (especially Paris and Berlin; London seems to have been the exception in the aftermath of the Wilde scandal). There were signs that homosexual societies were being articulated and shy attempts at homosexual self-definition (including pro-homosexual fiction), which challenged scientific discourse, could be perceived (leading this movement was the German scientist Magnus Hirschfield) and regarded as a threat by 'normal' society.

It is no coincidence that early Modernism has received a fair share of attention from critics working in gay studies. Same-sex desire, as experienced and textualised by authors central to the European modernist canon such as Marcel Proust, André Gide, Federico García Lorca, Thomas Mann, E.M. Forster and Constantin Cavafy, has strong if often conflicting undercurrents of, on the one hand, a rich homoerotic tradition, but also, on the other, a pressure to adopt a minoritising homosexual 'identity' and the punishment that could afflict those who did so. Modernist writers were responding to the pressures of scientific discourse by resorting to intertextuality as a principle to generate meaning, rather than accepting that signifiers can accurately and univocally account for experience. This general principle will be reflected in the new ways of dealing with homosexuality in discourse. When homoeroticism appears in Shakespeare, Michelangelo, Marlowe, Byron and other canonical authors it is never under the sign of illness or framed in scientific discourse; at worst, it could be expressed in terms of morality, but it didn't need to be so. In fact homoeroticism did not even need to be associated with the public concept of 'sodomy'. Now medical discourse was presenting a vision of homosexuality which limited the expression of the homoerotic as a life-affirming force.

It is my contention that tension between both paradigms, the homoerotic tradition on the one hand and the medical account on the other, was keenly felt by authors as an obstacle to giving literary expression to homosexual selfhood or to their own (homoerotic) desire. Travelling and mythical landscapes were the specific intertextual tools often used to deal with the problem of homosexual self-expression. The conditions in which homosexuality can be expressed in 'normal' literary discourse are highly dependent on the changes mentioned above. Responses to this situation varied: even if the tension between new institutional (i.e. medical or legal) discourses and homoerotic desire framed in a homosexual tradition is common to a number of authors, it is not expressed in the same terms in their works. Still, in all of them we become aware of a dislocation, a sense of being split between two different paradigms. The following list of prominent examples only attempts to outline the ways this might affect their writing: I suggest a series of different signifiers in which the tensions I have been referring to can be observed and the ways in which these authors set about resolving such tensions.

The work of André Gide makes use of the rhetoric of confession; in his autobiographical writings (especially *L'Immoraliste* and *Si le grain ne meurt*) we witness his struggle to come to terms with his own sexuality in the face of disapproving society: elements of an assertive homosexual tradition are set against the new 'homosexual' paradigm. Oscar Wilde's texts, as well as his lifestyle, were brutally re-read during his trials and legal discourse took up the authority to fix the 'hidden' meaning of his aesthetics. This harsh de-codification is a clear illustration of how homosexuality can be understood as a problem of writing.

Some works by Federico García Lorca, most notably his avant-garde play *El público*, reflect the poet's personal struggle to reconcile public and private identities, guilt-inducing paradigms and homoerotic desire; his *Oda a Walt Whitman* acknowledges homoerotic tradition while rejecting contemporary articulations of 'the homosexual'. In Marcel Proust's *A la recherche du temps perdu*, Eve Kosofsky Sedgwick has pointed out a similar tension between the author's own desire, as articulated in the narrator's relationship with Albertine and what she terms *the spectacle of the closet*,[12] in which 'the homosexual', Baron Charlus, is constructed in terms of minoritising definitions. In the case of E.M. Forster, reflecting the situation in England at the time, the tension between paradigms is reflected in the opposition between the unpublished apology of homosexuality *Maurice* (written in 1914 but not in print until after the author's death in 1971) and the published narratives in which homosexuality is not even present. Finally, in the works of Constantin Cavafy there is a shift in the way same-sex desire is articulated: the early poems, set in legendary lands, often in a mythical Hellas, offer implicit homoeroticism which seems to be marginal or accidental to the text, while in later works, set in contemporary Alexandria, homosexual experiences are explicitly presented but the context is that of prohibition and secretiveness.

In all these instances there is a 'positive' term of acceptance, i.e. an attempt to deal with homoerotic desire, which is always counterbalanced with a 'negative' pressure toward minoritising definitions that restrict the value of such desire in the real world; each writer has to acknowledge negative stereotypes imposed on him, but their own desire eventually appears elsewhere in their work. From the examples suggested, it seems difficult for these authors to reconcile the demands of homoerotic desire with those of a positive view of a homosexual selfhood in their writing as long as they worked within the limits of classical (pre-Modernist) aesthetics. At best, such selfhood is bound to be displaced, i.e. located outside prevailing contemporary cultural discourses and presented through avant-garde artistic forms which acknowledge such displacement.

Institutional discourse demanded that homosexual representation be framed into minoritising paradigms. Any explicitly apologetic discourse on homosexual desire which was devoid of guilt, morality or pathology, or even any discourse in which homosexuality was present but went unexplained or unremarked, would certainly make these writers into outcasts (both social and literary), condemning their writings to the category of literary curiosities and even risking turning the author into a marginal figure. In this situation, unproblematised expression of homosexual pleasure (when acknowledged at all) had to be inserted into a framework which legitimised representation and made it compatible with the rules of authoritative discourse.

This is the function fulfilled, for instance, by the strategy of the 'confessional' in Gide's writing: the rhetoric of confession acknowledges difficulties in expression even before this expression takes place. In this way, the structure of *The Immoralist* (1902), which presents the character's experience as a confession to a group of close friends (one of whom relays it to the reader in the framing narrative), is not a simple literary convention: it is a strategy that allows representation of homosexual desire through the metaphor of self-realisation and growth into 'new' manhood.

Still, in this work Gide also felt the need to insert personal narrative into a 'public' narrative: the rhetoric of confession was a perfect alibi, but on its own still would not make the experience narrated 'credible' enough. Tunisia appears in the novel as a healing landscape: the protagonist Michel starts his journey as a sick man, but this physical weakness is overcome under the African sun, finding also healing for his numbed soul, buried under layers of history. Explicitly, the narrative turns around the emergence of the 'new' man out of the wrappings of dead convention; but the key stages in this evolution always involve the narrator's encounter with a youth (Moktir, Charles).

The narrative motive of the journey is, as we have seen, inspired by individual experience of homosexuals in the period. But, more interestingly, it made homosexuality credible in literary terms: by presenting same-sex love as something that happens abroad or as something that is learnt abroad, its 'otherness' is acknowledged. The rhetorical tension between individual expression and institutional definitions can be formalised in terms of an acknowledged distance between home and abroad, the latter standing for this otherness. Something, in this case homosexual identity, is to be found beyond the boundaries of conventional everyday experience: at the end of the narrative, Michel has to take his wife Marceline back to Tunisia in order to complete the cycle (she has to die, as old morality must be overcome) and start his new life. Michel's confession is ostensibly about loving life more than Marceline, but the real cause of Michel's neglect is clearly (although not too explicitly) articulated in the narrative. This new self is, it is suggested, a homosexual self, free from the conventions of bourgeois marriage. As Robert Aldrich points out,[13] this reading of travelling as searching for a homosexual identity can also lead, for instance, to a richer interpretation of the symbolic structure of Thomas Mann's *Death in Venice* (1914) (another text in which acknowledgement of homosexual desire is expressed through references to a spiritual awakening): the intensity of desire experienced by Aschenbach is manifested in the south; it is the symbolism of Italy as a homosexual landscape that Mann is using to deal with desire. As is the case with *The Immoralist*, the choice of destination is far from coincidental. Venice is in the story's title and the narrative would have a different meaning if it was set farther north: a novella with much of the same plot called, for instance, *Death in Blackpool* would be about a set of different things and would belong to a different genre. The balance between intellectual search and eroticism is achieved through the charged meaning of the destination chosen. 'Venice' is a signifier that carries through intertextuality connotations of a certain aesthetics of decadence (therefore contributing to the philosophical theme of this work), as critics have pointed out, but it also has a place in homosexual tradition and this tradition is relevant to the meaning of the text as a whole by introducing homoeroticism in the framework of intellectual reflection.

Both Gide and Mann have their alter-egos Michel and Gustav Von Aschenbach travel south in order to stage the drama of their desire; both use this journey to justify their artistic or biographical explorations of homoerotic desire. And both make use of and inject new life into locations and motives that have a long history in the homosexual tradition. Readings of their works take into account different strands in these texts, but consistently ignore the fact that the places are used as tropes to explore the difficulties of homoerotic desire.

In most cases, however, this trope is re-worked in more explicit terms and its anchoring in the homosexual tradition is made even stronger, although it is still easy to miss. 'Abroad', as I suggested above, did not need to be an actual country where characters went, but it could be represented as the imaginary country inside one's closet: an imaginary place activated to attach oppositional value to the expression of homosexual experience. Imaginary countries are used as tropes to explore homoeroticism in the context of a homophobic culture. This exploration is not necessarily idealised. The pressure for representation to be framed in minoritising delimitations of homosexuality results in the use of myths belonging to the homophobic tradition as well as others that provide a space for less strained homoeroticism.

Hellas and Sodom came to represent these two attitudes and, I would argue, the homosexual tradition in Modernist writing from Wilde to Cavafy can be framed in terms of these two myths and the way they are tackled by homosexual writers and activated as conduits for individual expressions of homoeroticism. As we have seen, there were other real locations associated with homosexual discourse and narratives could be set in a variety of settings. What is distinctive about Hellas and Sodom is their continuity in the homosexual tradition and the fact that the realities such myths refer to are set in the distant past; Hellas and Sodom do not articulate the actual experience of a journey but emphasise the symbolic aspects of discussions of homosexuality. In using Hellas and Sodom, the artist could stay safely within his (or, more seldom, her) closet. Rather than using real life as a reference, through Hellas and Sodom it is fiction and cultural discourse that become prominent. It is also important to realise how they complement each other and how they can coexist in a different text to explore the contradictions within minoritising definitions of homosexuality.

The story of Sodom can be found in Genesis, chapters 18 and 19. Yaveh had in mind to punish the Sodomites because they were wicked, but Abraham talks Him into giving them one last chance: He will send two angels to investigate whether there are enough just people in Sodom to justify saving the city from destruction. The Sodomites notice the strangers' arrival and demand to 'know' them. But they are staying with Lot, who offers his daughters instead to be thus 'known'. The Sodomites' insistence becomes violent and this means they haven't passed Yaveh's test. The city will be destroyed. Not much is said about how the Sodomites were wicked, and recent research suggest that homosexuality had nothing to do with the story originally: if the narrative had to be taken literally, we would find too many contradictions, too many things no one could account for.[14] Whatever the original intention was, what concerns us here is how the narrative has been activated in order to be used as a specific condemnation of homosexuality. As such, it has been used in the pulpit and in literature as the justification for homophobic actions: the Lord rained brimstone and fire on Sodom, and so 'Sodomites' should thereafter be punished, if not in such a drastic manner, certainly in more subtle ways, such as social disgrace. Sodom becomes a symbolic country for men who prefer to have sex with other men,[15] the place for their exile. Still, as the central myth about homosexuality, the Sodom story provided an alibi to at least make homosexuality visible. It has to be emphasised that the biblical story provides us with very little information, and retellings of the Sodom passages, as well as descriptions of the Sodomites' vices, are introduced apocryphally throughout a long tradition, in ways which are not even consistent among themselves.

The anthology of texts collected in Paul Hallam's *Book of Sodom*[16] gives a comprehensive idea of how this myth is constructed and what its meanings are. In Hallam's view, Sodom also had its pleasures:[17] once individuals resigned themselves to go into that particular place there was a possibility of happiness and/or self-realisation, even if this took place within shared closets. Some of the literature about Sodom is damning rather than praising, but that does not mean that the place could not be enjoyable, as evidenced in John Wilmot's play *Sodom*.[18] This text indicates that the myth could still be appropriated in the seventeenth century. Later, descriptions become grimmer following the sexually conservative trends gaining ground throughout the nineteenth century.

John Addington Symonds' poem *The Valley of Vain Desires* (1880)[19] is an excellent example of how the landscape of Sodom took a new life in the homosexual tradition. This is neither the mock-heroic setting of Wilmot's play, nor the symbolic space construed in religious discourse. Pathology and myth are inscribed in Symonds' dark valley where the stench of rotten fruit fills the air. This is a nightmarish Sodom as the place where those with certain desires go. There is no attempt at appropriation, but still a certain kind of sad pleasure is conveyed. Hallam goes on to suggest that Sodom becomes the filter through which homosexuals will filter their own experiences living in a homophobic society: Sodom, especially (but not exclusively) until the 1970s, is a notional country that exists simultaneously with the modern city; its institutions and its locations can be seen by everybody but not everybody can recognise them; these are made up of dark alleys, parks and other meeting points for those who feel pursued by the law. This is also the implication in one of the most influential accounts of Sodom in literary history.

Marcel Proust's use of the Sodom tradition is articulated in the third volume of *Remembrance of Things Past* and has been discussed by Eve Kosofsky Sedgwick in terms of its relation to Proust's own closet. The tropes through which Sodom is presented in his introduction are very similar to those used by Symonds and further summarised by Hallam: homosexuals are lonely outcasts, prone to betrayal, their love sterile and sad, their desires trap them into unhappy, fearful lives. What concerns us here is the writer's attitude to the Sodom legend: in order to represent his fascinating homosexual Baron Charlus, Proust needs to call upon the myth of Sodom as the point of origin of all homosexuals, a myth that is activated as an alibi for representation. The Sodomites are seen as a wretched race, incapable of faithfulness, incapable of ever finding a home. In one particular passage included in the first section of *The Cities of the Plain*, Proust establishes some links and differences with the Jewish diaspora:

> [...] but I have thought it as well to utter here a provisional warning against the lamentable error of proposing (just as people have encouraged a Zionist movement) to create a Sodomist movement and to rebuild Sodom. For, no sooner had they arrived there than the Sodomites would leave the town so as not to have the appearance of belonging to it, would take wives, keep mistresses in other cities where they would find, incidentally, every diversion that appealed to them. They would repair to Sodom only on days of supreme necessity, when their own town was empty, at those seasons when hunger drives the wolf from the woods; in other words, everything would go on very much as it does today in London, Berlin, Rome, Petrograd or Paris.

Homosexuality becomes thus framed as an otherness. Like the jews, homosexuals become, as described in Proust's introduction, strangers in the midst of 'normal' society. A symbolic diaspora is presented: not all sodomites died under the fire and brimstone, and those who escaped came to constitute some kind of secret society of the damned. At the same time, it has to be remarked that Proust eschews the pathological paradigm: Sodomites are not to be trusted because rejection turns them into fearful, unreliable creatures; there is nothing wrong in their nature. As Proust pointed out, when homosexuality was the norm, there was nothing exceptional about what is now regarded as a sin. It is striking that Proust felt he needed to root Charlus in myth and, as Sedgwick emphasises,[20] the detailed introduction on Sodom becomes a shrewd cover to the writer's own closet. Sodom is presented as extreme depravation and it justifies presenting homosexuality as spectacle, rather than as a point of view. In other words, it is this recycling of a myth of otherness that allows presentation of the writer's experience through the Albertine plot.

As presented by Proust, Sodom is a negative presentation of

homosexuality which nevertheless carries some oppositional value to minoritising delimitations. The Hellenic world had been used throughout literary history in most European cultures to express homoeroticism in a positive way: Classic Rome and Renaissance England, for instance, took settings and motives from Hellenic literature for the expression of homoeroticism in the work of Ovid and Christopher Marlowe, for instance. The work of Johann Joachim Winckelmann constitutes a turning point in this tradition as it reassesses Hellenic art and culture placing the homoerotic in its centre: it is the beauty of the masculine body that seems to be the sole aesthetic concern for the Greek artist, and there is an emphasis on the physical that creates a problem when set against contemporary paradigms of desire. Winckelmann's aesthetic writings would be the main point of reference for nineteenth century apologists of homosexual desire. For over a century a fascinating story of attempts at appropriations of classical Greek culture unfolded. Conservatives as well as aesthetes claimed that Greece had represented the highest expression of civilisation and art. Of course this meant that efforts had to be made to conceal the uncomfortable presence of same-sex desire, sometimes institutionalised and completely integrated into politics and the army.[21] Sometimes this was done through censorship but often expressions of homoeroticism were explained away as manifestations of idealised (and sexless) friendship.

If the issue of cultural authority had always been relevant in homosexual representation, by the end of the nineteenth century it had become crucial. Until this moment, the Hellenic tradition had mostly been used passively within the homosexual tradition: there was no feeling of transgressiveness, nothing political was attempted, narratives seemed devoid of moral. True, passages dealing too explicitly with same-sex desire were excised from translations of classic texts, even in the case of canonical authors such as Plato, and it was for homosexual writers to point this out; the link between the study of the classics and same-sex desire was anything but a coincidence, as the case of A.E. Housman clearly illustrates. Still, for centuries, the use of Hellenic culture as intertext seemed to be the product of mere inertia. No oppositional value was attached to this, although its homoerotic potential was felt with some nervousness, which was appeased by references to the ideal (and therefore non-erotic) nature of such representations. One of the most influential inter-texts in the homoerotic tradition, maybe the one that has been taken as a point of reference through the centuries in the most systematic way, Virgil's *Corydon* ode, belongs to the Latin tradition, but its inspiration can be traced to Theocritus. Since the Renaissance, themes, characters and even aesthetic framings (genre, narrative motives, backgrounds) in homosexual literature were normally drawn from Hellas: Gide's apology of homosexuality takes its name, *Corydon* (1922), from the shepherd in Virgil's poem.

Until the turn of the century, the opposition between Sodom and Hellas had hardly been active in literature. Given that sodomy and homoeroticism did not quite belong to the same semantic field and were framed into different systems, they hardly appeared together. The late nineteenth-century homosexual, however, is made up of pieces of both Sodom and Hellas under the strain of minoritising definitions.

The opposition is apparent in the work of André Gide. At this point, things changed as a consequence of the late nineteenth-century paradigm shift in the perception of homosexuality, and what had been a 'passive', natural use of Hellenic literature comes under pressure. In Gide's 'Socratic dialogue', Corydon has left the ahistorical world of Hellas and is now a courageous apologist who draws from the natural sciences, anthropology, philosophy and ethics to defend homosexuality. *Corydon* was read by canonical authors in Europe and in America and appeared in France at a moment, 1922, in which discourse on Hellenism had been appropriated by conservative positions. Intellectuals and critics proposed classical Greece as a model for the new France, but of course they avoided dealing with structures in Hellenic life that entailed homosexual bonding. At best, homosexuality was underplayed and treated as the flaw of a great culture.

Gide intervened in these discussions by using the authority of classical Greek culture in order to present homosexuality in a positive way: pederasty (the version of homosexuality he favours) is a high form of affection and, he adds, it has its uses, such as helping to keep the virtue of women intact and preventing them from becoming prostitutes. His arguments were a source of heated discussion among his contemporaries, and voices were raised about what was perceived as an illegitimate use of classic culture. As a Socratic dialogue, *Corydon* approached the subject in intellectual terms, thus making a positive discourse available to the world: the antagonist's arguments were always proved false and the positive proposal finally triumphed. This undeniably bothered Gide's opponents. But it was even more important to homosexual writers who could use Gide's arguments to place their own desires in a normalised frame. In particular, Luis Cernuda tells in the epilogue to his collected poems how *Corydon* actually helped him 'to deal with certain personal problems'.[22] Critics have pointed out how in this book homosexual justification is placed in terms of abstract love rather than in terms of physical desire. But there were limitations to what the Hellenic model could do, and emphasising physical love would have defeated Gide's purpose, as its description had already been colonised by pathologising discourse. On the other hand, Gide is precisely taking advantage of the ways in which classical Greece is being valued from positions of power: the stronger the claims of the conservatives for classical Greek culture, the greater the force of the text.[23] The triumph of a homoerotic Hellas is the vehicle for making homosexual experience more visible.

But one text in particular illustrates the tension between the 'Hellenic' and the 'sodomitic' traditions of homosexual writing. Wilde's *The Picture of Dorian Gray* (1890) can be read as a novel about duplicity which articulates the opposition we have described exactly at the threshold of the Modernist period. The title subtly hints towards the opposition between both models in the protagonist's name: Hellenic 'Dorian' is juxtaposed to gloomy, sodomitic Gray/'grey'. Both worlds gesture toward the exotic, reflecting the conflict between both sides of the character's sexual identity: if the homosexual is always an outsider he can be 'outside' in two different ways, as was also suggested in Proust's literary creation. On the one hand, Dorian Gray is the creature of the high world of classic culture in which he is admired and respected. He can collect beautiful things and handle homoerotic codes that remain unreadable by his acquaintances. But he also inhabits a world of shadows, a landscape that could be linked to the twilight world of Sodom as outlined by Hallam and in which his lifestyle is represented as vice, his artistic leanings as perversion. It is tempting to see the changing picture as a translation of his public identity. In other words, the novel presents Sodom and Hellas as different sides to the same coin: each Hellas is also a Sodom, each Dorian is also 'grey'. Both metaphors are acknowledged to be extreme ways of representing the two directions of homosexual representation in the period. In Wilde's novel, Sodom eventually prevails, Hellenic Dorian is reduced literally to a handful of ashes. This can be read as a convention within decadent writing, but also as a reflection of Wilde's experience: eventually it is not the world of idealised desire, but the world of minoritising definitions that wins. In the light of his subsequent experience with justice, there is a chilling element to this closure.

In decadent narratives the gloom of Sodom is necessarily more attractive than the considerably more luminous landscapes of classic Greece. But as we move into the twentieth century homosexual discourse will adopt more positive positions that go beyond the fascination of looking at depravation. It is then that Hellas acquires additional values. Being a faraway, mythic land sanctioned by tradition, it authorises the expression of homoeroticism as something that belongs to cultural discourse and not to individual pathology. The use of Hellenic imagery in the poetry of Luis Cernuda or in the early work of Cavafy does place homoerotic desire away from the real world. But this is not done passively: both poets will acknowledge in their work the difficulties for their desires to find expression. This new framing, given the new situation, actively resists literary pathological constructions and provides a space where the homoerotic can be valued, denying the stigma of social convention. If Cavafy's characters tend to find fleeting pleasure in a world of dirty hotel rooms and dark alleys, there is no doubt that this pleasure is valid and that its evanescent quality does not make it unworthy. In the poetry of Cernuda, there is pain in that such pleasure is never fully achieved and remains distant often because of social intolerance, but again this does not make it less desirable.

For Modernist writers, the presentation of homosexuality through strategies which made use of intertextuality and the appropriation of cultural traditions had a clear oppositional use that pointedly challenged prevailing scientific discourses. By presenting intertextuality as an unavoidable feature of writing (i.e. writing cannot but be intertextual), postmodern cultural theory risks losing sight of its specific uses. On the one hand, intertextuality is regarded as a process that strengthens literary traditions and gives literary history continuity by linking text into a complex web of references. On the other, intertextuality constantly recycles and reframes texts, images and traditions. In this re-framing, some elements from the intertext are always preserved, but the overall meaning is different. In the case of the homosexual tradition we have seen how the use of images of mythical lands undergoes a change at the end of the nineteenth century that can be directly linked with the way conceptions of homosexuality have been altered and discourses of same-sex love are appropriated by the scientific institution. If Modernism can be regarded as a trend in art, its main thrust would be to challenge a stable, classical view of the world; art for the Moderns could not 'fix' meanings; reality was conveyed through means which emphasised ambiguity, precariousness and forms of 'knowing' which went beyond scientific research. Gide, Wilde, Cavafy and Forster among others were reacting to minoritising discourses and actively inserting homosexual experience in new frameworks that, on the one hand, challenged institutional discourse and, on the other, somehow placed homosexuality on a higher level as something desirable. In real life, authors sought refuge abroad or in the loneliness of their closets. But in their writing, their journey acquires a more durable value. In the end, their forays in search of mythical lands end at home.

NOTES TO CHAPTER VIII

1. Eve Kosofsky Sedgwick, *Epistemology of the Closet* (Berkeley: University of California Press, 1990).

2. Michel Foucault, *The Birth of the Clinic* (New York: Random House, 1975), Michel Foucault, *History of Sexuality* (New York: Pantheon, 1978).

3. Robert Aldrich, *The Seduction of the Mediterranean* (London: Routledge, 1995).

4. It might be useful to emphasise that 'scandal' is a concept charged with a particular rhetoric which is not always equivalent to the mere revealing of one's sexuality. Oscar Wilde's outing constituted a noisy scandal, whereas André Gide's coming out and transforming his homosexuality in literature was hardly scandalous.

5. As described by George L. Mosse in *The Image of Man. The Creation of Modern Masculinity* (New York: Oxford University Press, 1996). See especially chapters 3 and 5 dealing with the construction of the masculine stereotypes and the concept of 'Decadence' respectively.

6. The implication here is that it was the north that wrote about the south and therefore could attribute this 'exotic' character to its peoples and lifestyle. The history and the strategies that make up this process have been discussed by Edward W. Said in *Orientalism* (London: Routledge, 1978). One consequence of this 'invention of the exotic' is relevant for this contribution: as the north produces a culture of sexual repression, the south, its 'other', increasingly becomes the place where sexual morality can be circumvented.

7. See John Boswell, *Christianity, Social Tolerance and Homosexuality: Gay People in Western Europe from the Beginning of the Christian Era to the Fourteenth Century* (Chicago and London: University of Chicago Press, 1980).

8. Rictor Norton has explored the importance of such lists to strengthening the 'gay' tradition; these continue to be compiled throughout the nineteenth and the twentieth centuries. See *The Myth of the Modern Homosexual* (London: Cassell, 1997).

9. The most central example is John Addington Symonds' essay 'A Problem in Greek Ethics' (1883), included in Chris White (ed.), *Nineteenth Century Writings on Homosexuality* (London: Routledge, 1999), pp.165-72.

10. Following Michel Foucault's work; see especially *History of Sexuality* (New York: Pantheon, 1978).

11. For the argument against a complete paradigm shift see Rictor Norton, op.cit.

12. Sedgwick, op.cit. pp.231-33.

13. Aldrich, op.cit. pp.10-12.

14. For instance, if the point of the story is to punish sodomy why are they given another chance? And particularly, why is Lot's wife punished as well? The answer to the latter question would suggest that the moral of the story was to make a point about obedience to God in general, not necessarily on the matter of homosexuality, about which Yaveh did not say much.

15. Delimitations were not so neat until the eighteenth century. Alan Bray reminds us that 'sodomy' tended to be rather a loose concept that sometimes referred exclusively to anal penetration (no matter the biological sex of the people engaged in the act) and sometimes included by extension any 'non procreative' sexual relationship (e.g. zoophilia). In some cases the term was used in connection to heresy and had no precise sexual meaning. See Alan Bray, *Homosexuality in Renaissance England* (London: Gay Men's Press, 1982).

16. Paul Hallam, *The Book of Sodom* (London: Verso, 1995).

17. ibid., pp.70-74.

18. ibid., pp.229-36.

19. Included in Chris White, op.cit. pp.251-59.

20. Sedgwick, op.cit. p.231.

21. For an account of the uneasy balance between ideal manliness and homoeroticism in the representation of the male body following Hellenic standards since the eighteenth century see Mosse, op.cit.

22. *La realidad y el deseo*, p.384.

23. See Martha Hanna, 'Natalism, Homosexuality and the Controversy over *Corydon*', in Jeffrey Merrick and Bryant T. Ragan (eds), *Homosexuality in Modern France* (Oxford: Oxford University Press, 1996).

CHAPTER IX

The Processed Landscape:
Italy in Pío Baroja's *El laberinto de las sirenas* and
E.M. Forster's *Where Angels Fear to Tread*

Katharine Murphy

Katharine Murphy lectures in Spanish at the University of Exeter. Her doctoral thesis, *Pío Baroja and English Literature: A Comparative Approach to the Novels* (University of Exeter, 1998), presents new readings of Baroja and English authors including E. M. Forster, Thomas Hardy, Joseph Conrad, James Joyce and Virginia Woolf. Her research interests include comparative literature, particularly early twentieth-century Spanish and English literature, Pío Baroja and the so-called 'Generation of 1898', and European Modernism.

In *César o nada* (1910), *El mundo es ansí* (1912) and *El laberinto de las sirenas* (1923), Pío Baroja departs from his native Basque country and transports his fiction to Italy. Despite the Italian origins of some of his maternal ancestors, Baroja's sense of identity centred strongly on his Northern roots, a quality which leads to the portrayal of the Mediterranean in many of his novels as an alien location. Likewise, the contrast between Northern and Southern Europe is an essential component of E.M. Forster's *Where Angels Fear to Tread* (1905) and *A Room with a View* (1908). This dichotomy forms the basis of the two-part structure of *Where Angels Fear to Tread* in which the protagonists are observed in their suburban English environment before they are sent to Italy to be transformed by an alien and vitalistic culture. The collision of different values engenders the ensuing battle between North and South. In *El laberinto de las sirenas* and *Where Angels Fear to Tread* Baroja and Forster thus develop an idea often present in the turn of the century novel, transplanting Basque and English characters to Southern Europe and observing their reactions to a foreign culture. This transplantation provides the basis of the 'internalised' landscape created by Forster and Baroja in their Italian novels. While Forster's Italy may appear to be portrayed in a more naturalistic fashion, the location is carefully manipulated by both authors to reveal a close relationship between mental and physical landscapes. My comparative approach thus focuses on the encounter with the foreign, or Other, in each novel. This comparison of Baroja's and Forster's representations of Italy seeks not just to identify *El laberinto de las sirenas* and *Where Anges Fear to Tread* as literary intertexts which reveal structural similarities and therefore unconsciously echo one another, but seeks also to suggest the presence in each novel of a range of painterly and musical intertexts, as we shall see.

Baroja visited Italy twice between 1906 and 1909, spending time in Rome where he became interested in Cesare Borgia, the inspiration behind *César o nada*. Forster also based his Italian novels on his own experience of the country, having visited Italy in October 1901.[1] Both authors allowed some time to elapse before writing about their impressions of the Mediterranean. Yet this type of distancing rendered through a retrospective vision modified by time and memory does not signify a higher degree of objectivity in the portrayal of Italy. Although Baroja criticised Galdós for describing places he had not visited, it is clear that in writing about personal experiences from memory he creates an even more subjective portrait of the locations presented. The novelistic location, like the entire novel itself, is the product of the author's subjective vision.

Baroja's characteristic interest in the pagan history of the Basque country is replaced in *El laberinto de las sirenas* by an exposition of the mythology and folklore of the classical world.[2] He invents a highly stylised and 'enclosed' landscape in which the action and characters of the novel converge on one confined location: the elaborate house and gardens which overlook the strange labyrinth of rocks at Roccanera. The sensuous depiction of the South suggests intertextual relationships with romantic and impressionist artists, in particular the Swiss painter Arnold Böcklin, whom Baroja praises in *Desde la última vuelta del camino: Galería de tipos de la época*.[3] Moreover, the *conversación preliminar* indicates that this unusual novel is written in the style of a fantasy or a 'melody' rather than a realist novel.[4] It is significant that this 'melodic' work is created by an author who expressed a constant and acute mistrust of language throughout his life. Yet, the repetition of the phrase 'Galardi era un vasco decidido y valiente' ('Galardi was a decisive and brave Basque'),[5] the inclusion of O'Neil's poems and Baroja's lyrical descriptions of landscape compose the poetic evocation of Italy produced in *El laberinto de las sirenas*, revealing an interest in exploring the possibilities of different forms of language on the part of the author.

The evocation of setting is a pivotal element of Baroja's novelistic art. In *El laberinto de las sirenas*, Italy is highly dependent upon the senses, particularly sight; the striking use of colour in Galardi's descriptions of Italy allows Baroja to create pictorial and stylised landscapes which dominate the novel. Although he denied the resemblance, Baroja was likened to painters such as Zuloaga.[6] Indeed the Spanish author took a particular interest in landscapes, but in their power to evoke moods rather than in their physical appearance. 'A mí, en la pintura, lo que más me interesa es el ambiente' (*OC*, VII, 891)

('What interests me most in painting is the setting'), Baroja states. In *Desde la última vuelta del camino: El escritor según él y según los críticos*, he quotes an article by Gaziel, published in *La Vanguardia*, entitled 'Error de Pío Baroja'. In this article, Gaziel expresses his view that the subject-matter and characters of Baroja's novels are unmemorable, while his settings are etched on the reader's mind.[7] Baroja's landscapes dominate the novels, he argues, while the characters appear as 'sombras fugaces, casi imperceptibles, en la lejanía' (*OC*, VII, 437) ('fleeting, almost imperceptible shadows in the distance'). Baroja comments that this is characteristic of all impressionists, comparing his own novels to modern art: 'Los únicos cuadros interesantes de nuestro tiempo son los impresionistas. [...] El hombre ante la Naturaleza va bajando de importancia: el ambiente se agranda y el hombre se achica' (*OC*, VII, 437) ('The only interesting paintings of our time are impressionist. In the presence of Nature man decreases in importance: the setting grows larger while man grows smaller'). Indeed Baroja categorically identifies himself as an impressionist:

> Gaziel no comprende, sin duda, que yo soy un impresionista, y que para un impresionista lo trascendental es el ambiente y el paisaje. Eso, un mediterráneo de gustos clásicos y académicos, no lo puede entender.
>
> Nosotros no buscamos el delinear la figura, grande y destacada, con una línea fuerte que la separe del medio en que vive, sino que queremos hacerla vivir en su ambiente.
>
> Yo, si hubiera sido pintor, hubiera sido un discípulo de los impresionistas desde Turner hasta Sisley, y de los antiguos pintores holandeses, sobre todo, de Vermeer de Delft. (*OC*, VII, 438)

(Gaziel certainly does not understand that I am an impressionist, and that for an impressionist setting and landscape are of overriding importance. A Southern European of classical and academic tastes is unable to understand this.

We do not seek to depict a character who stands out in the foreground, clearly delineated and separated from the environment in which he lives; rather we want to show him living in his setting.

If I had been a painter, I would have been a disciple of the Impressionists from Turner to Sisley, and of the old school of Dutch painters, above all, of Vermeer de Delft.)

Baroja therefore drew an analogy between his novels and painting. In *El laberinto de las sirenas* Baroja subordinates character to landscape, but as in the majority of his novels, it is not the depiction of humankind as a product of environment, but the interaction between psychology and setting that interests him. Baroja appears to be involved in an attempt to transfer a different form of art to the novel in *El laberinto de las sirenas*. Nevertheless, the stylised depiction of landscape as a work of art is to some extent less successful than the 'artistic' environment that reflects the protagonist's artistic neurosis in *Camino de perfección*.[8] In the novel of 1902, setting is quite clearly the product of Ossorio's mind, and landscape is thus dependent upon the development of the central character. Baroja's identification of his art as essentially impressionistic is of extreme importance, suggesting that he breaks away from realist art in favour of the importance of personal impression and sensation.

In *Mis mejores páginas* (originally published in 1928) Baroja declares that the first part of *La ruta del aventurero* (1916)[9] originated as an attempt to evoke the paintings of Arnold Böcklin:

> *El convento de Monsant* es una novela del Mediterráneo. Me hubiera gustado hacer un libro romántico, así como una pintura de Arnoldo Böcklin. A pesar de que algunos críticos judíos alemanes han resuelto que el pintor suizo no vale gran cosa, a mí me gusta. Al intentar la novela de aire böckliniano vi que en nuestras costas no había elementos para ello. Hubiera habido que ir al Mediterráneo oriental y poner la acción en edades pasadas.[10]

> (*El convento de Monsant* is a Mediterranean novel. I would like to have created a romantic novel, as if it were a painting by Arnold Böcklin. Despite the fact that some German Jewish critics have decided that the Swiss painter can be easily dismissed, I like him. When I tried to write a novel in the style of Böcklin, I realised that our coasts did not contain the right elements for that. I would have had to go to the Eastern Mediterranean and set the action in past ages.)

Given the highly visual quality of the setting it is just possible that Baroja tried again in *El laberinto de las sirenas* to create a novel in the style of Böcklin. Although the transposition of medium produced by the novelistic evocation of painting is not entirely successful,[11] the innovative concept is typical of the growing awareness of authors at the turn of the century that they no longer had to adapt to the limited number of novel forms which already existed.

It is therefore plausible that in *El laberinto de las sirenas* Baroja evokes the Swiss Romantic, Arnold Böcklin, of whom the author writes: 'Yo no creo que en la pintura romántica del siglo XIX haya nadie superior a él. Naturalmente era un epígono' (*OC*, VII, 884) ('I do not believe that in nineteenth-century romantic painting there is anyone superior to him. Naturally he was an inspiration'). Described by critics as 'heightened Romanticism and poeticism',[12] the sensuousness of Böcklin's paintings and the unrestrained expression of emotion are recalled by the Italian landscapes of *El laberinto de las sirenas*. Baroja's use of colour may also have been inspired by the 'harsh, often shrill colour-chords' and 'liberated' local colours'[13] of much of Böcklin's art, particularly in his early years. The depiction of intense colours, particularly in relation to the strange labyrinth of rocks off the coast of Roccanera in *El laberinto de las sirenas*, underlines the author's vitalistic and sensuous portrayal of Italy, allowing Baroja to describe landscape as if it were a scene in a painting. The portrayal of winter scenes in the Apennines conforms to this technique:

> Aquellos mares azules del cielo, con sus nubes blancas, y los bloques, más blancos aún, de los picos nevados, tan pronto plata, tan pronto mármol sonrosado, producían una embriaguez de aire y de espacio. (162)

> (Those skies that are seas of blue, with their white clouds, and even stronger blocks of white of the snow-capped peaks, changing from silver to marbled pink, gave rise to an intoxicating sensation of air and of space.)

Baroja is concerned with more than just a visual depiction of landscape. Just as a painting may conjure up sounds or textures in the imagination, Baroja evokes all the senses in his depiction of setting. The portrayal of Toscanelli's garden, for example, encompasses the scents as well as the colours of the plants and flowers:

> Los cerros secos mostraban sus retamas y sus jaras, que perfumaban el aire. Los días de siroco, estos perfumes eran más fuertes que de ordinario, y la exhalación de las plantas y la humedad del mar dejaban

un ambiente de invernadero, tibio, perfumado, a veces turbador como un vino generoso. (113)

(The dry hills were dressed in broom and cistus, which scented the air. On days when the sirocco blew, these scents were stronger than usual, and the emanations from the plants and the moisture from the sea created the atmosphere of a hothouse, warm, scented, and stirring at times like a heady wine.)

These descriptions contribute to Baroja's sensuous evocation of the South, revealing an emphasis on sense-impressions fundamental to impressionist artists.[14]

Like the evocation of Italy in *El laberinto de las sirenas*, the portrayal of the Mediterranean in *Where Angels Fear to Tread* is linked to perception. In his letter to R.C. Trevelyan in October 1905, Forster states: 'The object of the book is the improvement of Philip, and I did really want the improvement to be a surprise'.[15] The motif of transfiguration is very closely connected to perceptions of Italy, a country which acts as the catalyst for psychological development in Philip and Caroline. In Monteriano, 'Philip found a certain grace and lightness in his companion which he had never noticed in England. She was appallingly narrow, but her consciousness of wider things gave to her narrowness a pathetic charm. He did not suspect that he was more graceful too' (104). It is significant that Forster carefully places the observation of this development in both characters immediately after a description of Caroline and Philip leaning out of the Gothic window of the hotel dining-room to look at the view of the town. Their comments on the tower visible from the window present location as the product of the observing mind:

'It reaches up to heaven,' said Philip, 'and down to the other place.' The summit of the tower was radiant in the sun, while its base was in shadow and pasted over with advertisements. 'Is it to be a symbol of the town?' (104)

Both characters recognise the coexistence of good and evil in Italy. Likewise, although Forster was committed to philosophical liberalism, particularly in his belief in individualism, reason, and the importance of personal relations,[16] he 'saw through the liberal tradition's naïve faith in progress: its simple oppositions of good and evil, its failure to recognise 'good-and-evil' in man'.[17] 'If [Forster] defends Mediterranean instinct against British cant or phlegm, he knows the limits of its value', writes Trilling. 'The invigoration of the book comes from two ideas meeting and one of them being modified'.[18] Thus, while Forster exposes the deficiencies of middle-class suburban England, he is not blind to the limitations and corresponding restrictions of life in Monteriano. Lilia becomes aware of the confining conventions of a society dominated by *machismo*, and while Gino may represent the vitalism of the natural world, he is also exposed as vulgar, conceited and brutal.

The tower is also used as a symbol for the disastrous consequences triggered by the 'rescue-party'. The next night when Philip waits for Harriet at the hotel, unaware that she has gone to steal the baby, only the base of the tower is visible. The dream-like quality of the narrative (which is common to both *El laberinto de las sirenas* and parts of *Where Angels Fear to Tread*) is heightened at this point in the novel with a passage reminiscent of a nightmare. The apparition of the 'ghastly creature' (140) sent by Harriet as a messenger gives Philip the sense that 'the whole of life had become unreal' (141). This is one of several scenes in the novel which constitute the 'fairy tale' descriptions of Italy. Forster's description of the approach to Monteriano when Philip arrives to 'save' Lilia portrays an oneiric city built like a ship with towers for masts, and establishes the dream motif that is to modulate into the nightmarish episodes preceding the tragic death of the baby: 'The hazy green of the olives rose up to its walls, and it seemed to float in isolation between trees and sky, like some fantastic ship city of a dream' (38). The location's magical quality, the 'solid enchantment' (91) of Italy detected by Philip, is continued with a reversal of association later in the novel. Lilia's death alters Caroline's perceptions of Monteriano, making her regard the place as a 'magic city of vice, beneath whose towers no person could grow up happy or pure' (85). Philip's and Caroline's views of Italy are disproportionate in their perception of both romance and evil. Thus, the oneiric portrayal of Italy is connected to the unreality of characters' views of the physical world: the values imposed by the mind on the external environment. In *Where Angels Fear to Tread*, Italy is quite clearly a setting processed by the mind of the English characters.

Baroja's Italy, too, displays 'magical' characteristics, suggested by the intensity of the colours described. Andía, for example, contemplates the bay of Naples and the Isle of Capri at sunset:

> El crepúsculo fue admirable. El gris perla del mar se obscureció y se convirtió en un color de mica; el horizonte más claro, pasó del amarillo pálido al rosa, y en el momento de ponerse el sol brillaron un momento las olas con reflejos sangrientos, como las escamas de un dragón fabuloso. Luego, el cielo quedó verde y azul y comenzaron a aparecer las estrellas. (28)

> (The sunset was magnificent. The pearly grey of the sea grew darker and became the colour of mica; the lightest part of the horizon changed from pale yellow to pink, and at the moment the sun set, the waves shone for a moment with a blood-like glimmer, resembling the scales of a mythical dragon. Then the sky became green and blue and the stars began to appear.)

The view of the mountains from Belvedere also adds to the pictorial and enchanted presentation of setting. The appearance of immobility suggests that the landscape is evoked as if it were a painting:

> En los días de viento Sur, el aire enrarecido daba al paisaje un aspecto de inmovilidad, de alucinación, y acercaba de tal manera los objetos, que en las cumbres de los montes se dibujaban los árboles y las piedras, como si se les pudiera tocar con la mano; en cambio, en los días de bruma todo se alejaba y parecía nadar en un mar insondable y remoto. (186)

> (On the days when there was a southerly wind, the rarefied air gave the landscape an appearance of immobility, of unreality, and brought objects so close that the outline of the trees and stones was traced on the summits of the mountains, as if one could touch them with one's hand; however, on misty days, everything grew distant and seemed to float in a remote and bottomless sea.)

Although Baroja's novels often contain phantasmagorical scenes, the oneiric settings of *El laberinto de las sirenas* may be attributed to the author's possible simulation of Böcklin's landscapes. Indeed, the artist's most famous painting, *The Island of the Dead*, exhibits a haunted quality; Böcklin, referring to the first version, stated that this was a picture for dreaming about.[19]

In Forster's novel, too, the importance of personal impression is paramount. Indeed, Italy is the product of a projection of the inner world onto setting. The exhilarating atmosphere of the opera inspires Caroline and forms an important stage of her transformation in Monteriano. While Harriet tries in vain to stifle the joyful participation of the audience, Caroline and Philip are transported by the music. Again psychology and location are intimately connected. Just as Philip's resolve to forbid Lilia's marriage is diminished as soon as he sets foot in Italy, his view of Gino as the 'enemy' is weakened first by the effect inspired by the 'really purple sky and really silver stars' (112) and then by the unexpected and charming welcome he receives from his adversary at the opera.

In *Where Angels Fear to Tread*, Italy signifies something different for each character. The music at the opera renders Philip and Caroline defenceless against Italy; indeed it has the continuing effect that Forster describes in *Aspects of the Novel*.[20] After the performance is over, Caroline continues to hear the music in her head, and her transformation reveals that her view of life has expanded. She is ashamed of the happiness which she perceives as sinful, but she finds herself unable to fight against the place which is the antithesis of the 'joyless' Sawston: "Help me!' she cried, and shut the window as if there was magic in the encircling air. But the tunes would not go out of her head, and all night long she was troubled by torrents of music' (113). While Philip and Caroline appear to undergo a process of vivification when transplanted to Mediterranean climes, by contrast Harriet remains 'acrid, indissoluble, large; the same in Italy as in England – changing her disposition never, and her atmosphere under protest' (105). Unmalleable and narrow in the extreme, she finds no charm in the idiosyncrasies of the country nor in the demonstrative nature of its inhabitants.

El laberinto de las sirenas also explores the interaction between the internal and external worlds. Baroja's presentation of the Italian landscape culminates in the fantastical depiction of the mysterious *laberinto de las sirenas*. Indeed, the landscape, which reflects Baroja's sense-impressions filtered through memory, is processed by the mind of the characters and the author himself. A natural formation of rocks jutting above sea level, the labyrinth is reminiscent of art or fantasy. Nature and the alterations carried out by Toscanelli and *el Inglés* combine to lend the rocks a magical atmosphere. Toscanelli's gardens also conform to Baroja's descriptions of landscape as art: '– Quiero darles un carácter mixto – dijo el italiano –; algo que recuerde a Salvator Rosa, con detalles a lo Bosco y a lo Patinir' (103) ('I want to give them a varied character', said the Italian; 'something reminiscent of Salvator Rosa, with elements of Bosch and Patinir'). His aim to create gardens in the exuberant style of fantastical paintings parallels Baroja's attempt to evoke art in the novel. The art motif reappears in Baroja's description of the unity of all the contrasting parts of the countryside visible from the gardens of the 'casa del Laberinto':

> La acumulación de tantos detalles; el aspecto, vario y diverso, de cada parte, daba a todo el paisaje, formado por trozos tan distintos, un aire de cuadro antiguo. (110)

(The accumulation of so many details; the varied and diverse appearance of each part, gave the whole landscape, made up of such different elements, the feel of an old painting.)

Baroja repeatedly employs words and images such as 'dibujo' (drawing) and 'cuadro' (painting) to underline his imitation of another medium.

In *El laberinto de las sirenas* and *Where Angels Fear to Tread* Baroja and Forster focus upon the dichotomy between North and South by transplanting Basque or English characters to Italy.[21] In the prologue to *El laberinto de las sirenas* Pío Baroja sends Shanti Andía and his friend, Recalde, on holiday to Naples. Shanti's self-conscious discussion about the novel indicates that the prologue is not intended as an introduction to a travel book, but as an 'anthropological fantasy' in which he and Recalde investigate the appearance and character of Mediterranean people. The prologue deceptively resembles a tourist guide. However, its theme reflects one of the ideas explored in the novel itself, putting forward the preliminary reflections of two Basque holidaymakers who view Italy as an 'alien' location. Presenting Shanti's and Recalde's observations as those of obvious outsiders, Baroja is able to emphasise the contrasts between Northern and Southern Europe. Soon after their arrival in Naples the sun transforms the city into the antithesis of Baroja's descriptions of the green and misty Basque country:

> Una ciudad sucia, sarnosa, se convierte de pronto en una urbe espléndida en donde todas las casas parecen magníficos palacios. Esto

no ocurre en los pueblos de la costa del Atlántico. Allí el sol es siempre un poco agrio y chillón. (31)

(A dirty, squalid city suddenly becomes a splendid metropolis where all the houses seem to be magnificent palaces. This does not happen in the towns on the Atlantic coast. There the sun is always rather harsh and glaring.)

Once again we find contrast being used by both authors as a technique of characterisation. With the transfer of narrator, *El laberinto de las sirenas* moves from urban Italy to rural Italy. Galardi's arrival in Roccanera, like Shanti's in Naples and the Herritons' in Monteriano, is that of an outsider in Southern Europe. Employing Basque characters to narrate the novel, Baroja presents Italy as a setting which is unfamiliar to them and draws contrasts with his native Spain.

Likewise, the divide between North and South is an important element of *Where Angels Fear to Tread*, not least, as has been seen, in Forster's portrayal of the influence of Italy upon his English characters. Although the collision between English and Italian customs gives rise to much of the comedy of the novel, the juxtaposition of the narrow life of Sawston and the vitalism that Monteriano embodies allows the author to construct a complex relationship between characters and location. The theme of the novel, according to Trilling, 'like that of *The Ambassadors*, is the effect of a foreign country and a strange culture upon insular ideas and provincial personalities. Since the Renaissance, and especially in the eighteenth century, it had been a device of moralists to confront their own culture with the superior habits of foreign lands'.[22] Forster's perception of the 'undeveloped' English heart is embodied in characters such as Caroline Abbott and Philip Herriton who undergo a process of 'transfiguration' in the novel. In contrast, the autocratic Mrs Herriton and her sanctimonious daughter, Harriet, are immune to this development of emotion and self-knowledge. While the rescue-parties represent the shallow attempt to save reputation, true 'salvation' is only achieved by means of an expansion of insight. The pilgrimage towards self-knowledge in *Where Angels Fear to Tread* does not depend on a simple exposure to Italian values and the subsequent assertion of their superiority. Rather, the process of transfiguration entails an admission of the validity of different values. Caroline's, and finally Philip's, recognition of this is occasioned by the collision between English and Italian viewpoints.

As has already been seen, in *El laberinto de las sirenas* and *Where Angels Fear to Tread* both Baroja and Forster create a landscape which is modified by the psychology of the characters. Moreover, Italy is also dependent upon the perceptions of the authors themselves who, as Northern European outsiders and in their need to create a unified novel, modify the Mediterranean to a high degree. Distorted not merely by the perceptions of the characters, but also by the memory of the artist, Italy, like the novel itself, is the product of the subjective consciousness.

Baroja's attempt to evoke painting in *El laberinto de las sirenas* is indicative of a link with impressionism which suggests that he was interested in developing new forms of art.[23] Forster displays a curious mixture of nineteenth- and twentieth-century approaches to the novel, retaining the omniscient voice, while showing a high degree of awareness of developing Modernist concerns. Malcolm Bradbury identifies E.M. Forster as an important author of the transition from the Victorian to the Modern era. 'There is in his work the appeal to art as transcendence, art as the one orderly product, a view that makes for modernism,' he writes, 'and there is the view of art as a responsible power, a force for belief, a means of judgement, an impulse to spiritual control as well as spiritual curiosity'.[24] Indeed, the Forsterian voice adopts the traditional omniscient form and encompasses a degree of moral instruction integral to the Victorian novel. In *A Room with a View* and *Where Angels Fear to Tread*, for example, Forster exposes the 'evil' engendered by rigid middle-class convention and hypocrisy. However, Forster's view of the internal unity of a work of art, 'the one orderly product which our muddling race has produced',[25] is essentially Modernist. In his lecture on 'Art for Art's Sake' he compares the disorder of the temporal world to the consonance of a work of art which is 'the only material object in the universe which may possess internal harmony'.[26] Colmer identifies a connection with Romanticism in Forster's conception of the autotelic nature of the novel. Inspiring his work as a novelist and a critic is 'the ideal of art as an autonomous order, one that achieves a balance and reconciliation of opposite or discordant qualities, a unique order that possesses strict internal coherence'.[27]

Forster's concern with organic unity is expounded in the critical work *Aspects of the Novel*. In the chapter entitled 'Pattern and Rhythm',

Forster establishes an analogy between music and the novel in order to delineate the transcendental possibilities extended by both forms of art. 'Music is the deepest of the arts and deep beneath the arts', claimed Forster in his address before the Harvard Symposium on Music in 1947: music 'more than the other arts postulates a double existence. It exists in time, and also exists outside time, instantaneously'.[28] In his comparison of music and fiction in *Aspects of the Novel*, Forster explains that coherence is provided by 'rhythm' in the form of 'repetition plus variation' (169): the development of an image or expression which corresponds to the musical phrase. However, he also seeks the novelistic equivalent of 'difficult' rhythm: 'Is there any effect in novels comparable to the effect of [Beethoven's] Fifth Symphony as a whole, where, when the orchestra stops, we hear something that has never actually been played?' (169), he asks. The four movements of the symphony comprise the 'common entity' (169) which, like the constituent parts of the novel, expresses something unexpected beyond the reach of everyday life. Forster thus calls for the 'expansion' attained by music to be attempted in the novel:

> Music, though it does not employ human beings, though it is governed by intricate laws, nevertheless does offer in its final expression a type of beauty which fiction might achieve in its own way. Expansion. That is the idea the novelist must cling to. Not completion. Not rounding off but opening out. When the symphony is over we feel that the notes and tunes composing it have been liberated, they have found in the rhythm of the whole their individual freedom. Cannot the novel be like that? (170)

Malcolm Bradbury comments on Forster's attempt in *Aspects of the Novel* 'to place the modes of symbolism and post-impressionism in the context of what might be considered the more 'traditional' story-telling function'. The novel is rooted in the material world, but it has the potential to suggest the 'unseen': 'The problem of whether art can redeem life by transcending it is crucial to modernism'; the encounter between the formally transcendent – the epiphany, the unitary symbol – and the world of history recurs throughout its works. And Forster's view is, like that of most modernism, dualistic: art may reach beyond the world of men and things – the world of 'story' – but it can never leave that world behind, and must 'seek meanings and connections in it'.[29]

While Baroja's and Forster's views on the creation of the 'open' novel are extremely similar, their perceptions of music vary to some degree.[30] Baroja regards music as a 'democratic' art because it does not require an intellectual response. In contrast to Forster, he asserts (in *Juventud, egolatría*) that because music lacks philosophical or political content, it does not have transcendental implications.[31] Yet despite his occasional denigration of music as an art which cannot aspire to the intellectual heights of the novel, the author compares the two arts in the prologue to *Los amores tardíos*: 'Me agrada la novela permeable y porosa, como la llama un amigo nuestro; la melodía larga que sigue y no concluye' (*OC*, I, 1313), says Joe. ('I like permeable and porous novels, as a friend of ours calls them; a long melody which continues and never ends'). Moreover, Baroja's comparison of music and the novel in *La nave de los locos* (1925) is uncannily similar to Forster's call for 'expansion [...] not completion':

> Existe la posibilidad de hacer una novela clara, limpia, serena, de arte puro, sin disquisiciones filosóficas, sin disertaciones ni análisis psicológicos, como una sonata de Mozart; pero es la posibilidad solamente, porque no sabemos de ninguna novela que se acerque a ese ideal. (*OC*, IV, 313)

> (The possibility exists of creating a clean, clear, serene novel of pure art, without philosophical disquisitions, without psychological diversions or analyses, like a Mozart sonata; but it is only a possibility, because we do not know of any novel which approaches that ideal.)

Like Forster, Baroja appears to be striving for new artistic forms which subvert the linear plot and the climactic conclusion of the closed form displayed by the nineteenth-century novel. Indeed, both Baroja and Forster attain the simpler form of rhythm described by the latter with the development of themes and leitmotifs, and Baroja's repetition of 'Galardi era un vasco decidido y valiente' which recurs like a musical phrase.[32] Yet Baroja's novels also reveal interesting examples of *synaesthesia*. In *Camino de perfección*, a novel whose protagonist manifests an artistic vision of the external world, musical notes are described in terms of colour. Of course, Baroja's transference of sense-impressions was not entirely original. The theory of a relationship between sounds and colour is evident in musical terms such as 'chromatic' and 'coloratura', and in the titles of some of Whistler's paintings such as 'Nocturne' and 'Symphony'.[33] Baroja's novelistic evocation of painting in *Camino de perfección* and *El laberinto de las sirenas* reveals a fascination with the association of sense-impressions in different artistic mediums and indicates an interest in exploring new novelistic possibilities.

Despite his reservations about the value of art and the properties of language, Baroja was obviously not merely fascinated, but indeed obsessed with all forms of art, although he commented pragmatically that 'en aquel tiempo se consideraba casi como una obligación del escritor el tener opiniones muy definitivas en cuestiones de arte, sobre todo, en pintura, y yo iba con mucha frecuencia a los museos'.[34] ('At that time it was considered almost an obligation for a writer to have very definite opinions in matters of art, above all, in painting, and I often used to visit museums'). Baroja's circle of friends was dominated primarily by writers, and secondly by painters. He knew many artists including Picasso, Rusiñol, Regoyos, Zuloaga and Sorolla, many of whom made portraits of him (including the well-known charcoal drawing by Picasso);[35] his brother, Ricardo, was also a painter. Indeed his occasional statements about the insignificance of art do not correspond to his well-known attempts with Azorín to revive interest in *El Greco*, and the subsequent creation of *Camino de perfección* and *La voluntad* in which these two authors write about his paintings. Thus Baroja's doubts about the validity of art are contradicted by his intense fascination with art, an interest which indicates not a mere flirtation with the realm his characters so often denigrate, but a recognition (if clouded at times by a fundamental insecurity about his occupation) of the ascendancy of language and the immense potentiality of artistic creation. As I have suggested, it seems that in *El laberinto de las sirenas*, as in *Camino de perfección*, painting is evoked through the language of the novel. In this article, Baroja's interest in painting is analysed principally in terms of its connection to the 'processed landscape' created in the novel of 1923. Nevertheless, much remains to be said about the relationship between Baroja and painting, not least in the field of comparative literature.[36]

There is a strong link between the arts established in both *El laberinto de las sirenas* and *Where Angels Fear to Tread*, most clearly seen in Baroja's evocation of impressionism and perhaps the paintings of Arnold Böcklin. In *Where Angels Fear to Tread*, Forster evokes the visual arts to a lesser extent than Baroja does in *El laberinto de las sirenas*. Yet, the suggestion of this art form is present in Forster's descriptions of characters and their relation to the Italian landscape. For example, when Caroline visits Gino with the intention of persuading him to relinquish the child, he sits 'astride the parapet, with one foot in the loggia and the other dangling into the view. His face was in profile and its beautiful contours drove artfully against the misty green of the opposing hills' (118). Just as Baroja creates a series of painterly landscapes in his depictions of Italy, Forster occasionally 'frames' his characters as if they were part of a painting. Connections with the visual arts are also present in Forster's depiction of Philip, a character whose sensitivity to art deeply affects his perception of his environment. Art is a refuge for Philip Herriton. Finding life somewhat puzzling and unmanageable, Philip retreats into the contemplation of beauty and a cynical observation of others. After her intervention in the combat between Philip and Carella, Caroline acquires the status of a deity in Philip's eyes:

> All through the day Miss Abbott had seemed to Philip like a goddess, and more than ever did she seem so now. [...] Her eyes were open, full of infinite pity and full of majesty, as if they discerned the boundaries of sorrow, and saw unimaginable tracts beyond. Such eyes he had seen in great pictures but never in a mortal. (151-52)

Her vision has expanded beyond recognition, while Philip continues to be hampered by aestheticism. Viewing Caroline as a goddess and comparing her to art, life remains a spectacle to him. He is educated only by the contemplation of others:

> Philip looked away, as he sometimes looked away from the great pictures where visible forms suddenly become inadequate for the things they have shown to us. He was happy; he was assured that there was greatness in the world. There came to him an earnest desire to be good through the example of this good woman. He would try henceforward to be worthy of the things she had revealed. Quietly, without hysterical prayers or banging of drums, he underwent conversion. He was saved. (152)

Finally, life rather than art has brought him insight, and he is saved both physically from Gino's violent revenge, and from his former view of life.[37]

Baroja and Forster also draw connections in their works between the novel and music. As has been mentioned, Baroja suggests the potential for the novel to resemble a sonata by Mozart and concludes that literature has never attained this ideal. Joe's reference in *Los amores tardíos* to a melody which does not end suggests an open type of novel. Likewise, Forster's calls for the novel to aspire to the 'expansion' attained by music refer to the overall effect that music has on the listener. It is clear that there is a strong intertextual dimension in the comparison of Baroja's *El laberinto de las sirenas* and Forster's *Where Angels Fear to Tread*. This is evident both in the connections identified between the novel, the visual arts and music, and the decision of both authors to locate their texts in foreign countries. Transplanting their characters to Southern Europe, Baroja and Forster are able to suggest an encounter with the foreign, or the Other, central to the concept of intertextuality.

Observing their characters' reactions to a foreign country, Baroja and Forster carefully manipulate the setting of their Italian novels, presenting landscape as a product of their characters' perception. In his works Baroja engages with Schopenhauer, who popularised and developed the Kantian philosophy that the world is but a reflection of reality which has been processed by the mind. The processed landscape, intensified in *A Passage to India* and *El mundo es ansí*, is an important element of *Where Angels Fear to Tread* and *El laberinto de las sirenas*. However, the overall perception of art expressed by Baroja and Forster differs in one respect. Forster views the creation of works of art as one of the greatest achievements of the human race, asserting

> not only the existence of art, but its pertinacity. Looking back into the past, it seems to me that that is all there has ever been: vantage grounds for discussion and creation, little vantage grounds in the changing chaos, where bubbles have been blown and webs spun, and the desire to create order has found temporary gratification, [...] and the lighthouses have never ceased sweeping the thankless seas.[38]

Only art can lend a certain coherence to the chaos of the temporal world. For Baroja, art should have a human value if it is to possess a degree of validity. Indeed, he views the exaggerated veneration of culture as absurd. In *Desde la última vuelta del camino: Galería de tipos de la época* he comments that:

> El arte vive en función del hombre, es para el hombre y solamente para él. El hombre no vive sólo en función del arte, sino de otras muchas cosas más. Tiene esa nota en su clave, pero ésta no es la única ni quizá la más importante. (*OC*, VII, 883)

> (The existence of art is dependent on man, it is for man and for him alone. The existence of man is not dependent solely on art, but many other things too. He has that string to his bow, but it is not the only one, nor perhaps the most important one.)

Although he believed that the artist is involved in the pursuit of truth, Baroja also recognised that this search is to some extent impossible: a work of art does not provide truth but the artist's subjective vision.

Indeed, Baroja's statements about his art reveal highly contradictory views. 'He mirado también la literatura como juego' (*OC*, IV, 308) ('I have also regarded literature as a game'), he asserts in the prologue to *La nave de los locos*. Forster's aesthetic statements provided in his theoretical discussions about the novel reveal a degree of confidence entirely lacking in Baroja's suggestive and contradictory statements about the nature of art.[39] Yet the novels of both Forster and Baroja offer clear evidence of an authorial fascination with the nature of the relationship between the artist and his art.

NOTES TO CHAPTER IX

1. Monteriano, the Italian setting of *Where Angels Fear to Tread*, is based on the town of San Gimignano, near Florence, in John Colmer, *E.M. Forster: The Personal Voice* (London: Routledge and Kegan Paul, 1975), p.53.

2. All references to *El laberinto de las sirenas* are from the Espasa-Calpe edition (Buenos Aires: Espasa-Calpe, 1946). All page references in the text are to this edition.

3. *Desde la última vuelta del camino: Galería de tipos de la época*, in *Obras Completas* (hereafter referred to as *OC*), 8 vols (Madrid: Biblioteca Nueva, 1946-51), VII, p.884.

4. Haydée Rivera suggests that the enclosed location of *El laberinto de las sirenas* allows Baroja to create a closed novel. However, it seems clear from the discussion in the prologue that the author-figure wants to produce a novel which resembles a melody, thereby suggesting a more open type of fiction. In Haydée Rivera, *Pío Baroja y las novelas del mar* (New York: Anaya, 1972), pp.163-64.

5. All translations are my own. I am grateful to my colleagues and Dr Mark Gant for their suggestions.

6. *OC*, VII, pp.891-97.

7. ibid., p.437.

8. Pío Baroja, *Camino de perfección (Pasión mística)* (Madrid: Caro Raggio, 1993).

9. Pío Baroja, *La ruta del aventurero*, *OC*, III, pp.645-777.

10. Pío Baroja, *Mis mejores páginas* (Barcelona: Mateu, 1961), p.297.

11. *El laberinto de las sirenas* does not traditionally rank among Baroja's most sophisticated novels, a view reflected by the shortage of critical attention devoted to this work. The technique employed in *Camino de perfección*, in which the countryside is portrayed through Ossorio's artistic vision, reveals a more developed creation of an artistic landscape. However, the presentation of a subjectively-perceived external world is evoked most successfully in the later *El árbol de la ciencia*, ed. Pío Caro Baroja (fourth edition) (Madrid: Caro Raggio / Cátedra, 1989).

12. *The Penguin Dictionary of Art and Artists*, Peter and Linda Murray (eds) (fourth edition) (Harmondsworth: Penguin, 1976; repr. 1980), p.56.

13. Rolf Andree, introduction, *Arnold Böcklin: 1827-1901* (London: Arts Council / Pro Helvetia, 1971), p.8.

14. In *Modern European Art* (London: Thames and Hudson, 1972), Alan Bowness comments that Monet struggled to 'find the pictorial equivalent for his sensations before nature' (p.23), cited by Pamela King, *Joseph Conrad and the Modernist Sensibility: 'Like Painting, Like Music...'* (Brisbane: the author, 1996), p.37.

15. Forster, letter to R.C. Trevelyan on 28 October 1905, *Where Angels Fear to Tread*, ed. Oliver Stallybrass (Harmondsworth: Penguin, 1976), p.161. All references in the text are to this edition.

16. See Lionel Trilling's analysis of Forster's liberalism in *E.M. Forster: A Study* (London: Hogarth Press, 1959), pp.9-23.

17. Colmer, op.cit. p.11.

18. Trilling, op.cit. p.66.

19. Andree, op.cit. p.8.

20. E.M. Forster, *Aspects of the Novel* (Harmondsworth: Penguin, 1962; repr. 1964). This work was originally a course of Clark Lectures delivered at Trinity College, Cambridge, in 1927.

21. In *La aventura de Missolonghi*, one of the five novelettes which make up *Los contrastes de la vida*, for instance, Baroja compares the nature of the Atlantic and the Mediterranean.

22. Trilling, op.cit. p.52.

23. Indeed, a reassessment of the connection between literature and reality is illustrated in Pío Baroja's work by an experimental feature common to both the *conversación preliminar* of *El laberinto de las sirenas* and the prologue of *César o nada*: an encounter between the author and his fictional characters. Baroja steps momentarily into his fiction, not to provide the traditional light-hearted asides of the omniscient authorial voice, but to debate the very nature of his fiction.

24. Malcolm Bradbury, 'Two Passages to India: Forster as Victorian and Modern', in *Aspects of E.M. Forster: Essays and Recollections Written for his Ninetieth Birthday*, ed. Oliver Stallybrass (London: Edward Arnold, 1969), pp.123-42 (p.125).

25. E.M. Forster, *Two Cheers for Democracy* (London: Edward Arnold, 1951), p.101.

26. ibid.

27. Colmer, op.cit. p.13.

28. Cited by James McConkey, *The Novels of E.M. Forster* (Ithaca: Cornell University Press, 1957), p.95.

29. Bradbury, op.cit. pp.128-29.

30. Friedman applies Forster's term 'expansion' (which describes the overall effect that 'rhythm' can produce in the novel) to the treatment of 'the expansion of consciousness: of moral apprehension and emotional grasp' in Alan Friedman, *The Turn of the Novel* (New York: Oxford University Press, 1966), p.115.

31. 'La música, que es el arte más social y el de mayor porvenir, tiene grandes ventajas para los buenos burgueses. En primer término, no hay necesidad de discurrir; con ella no hay necesidad de saber si el vecino es creyente o incrédulo, materialista o espiritualista; no hay, por tanto, discusión posible con él acerca de los conceptos trascendentales de la vida. No hay guerra, hay paz' (*OC*, V, 161) ('Music, which is the most social art and the one with the brightest future, has many benefits for the upstanding citizens of the middle class. Firstly, there is no need for discourse; with

music there is no need to know if one's neighbour is a believer or unbelieving, materialist or spiritualist; there is not, therefore, any possible discussion with him about the transcendental concepts of life. There is no war, there is peace').

32. For an obviously musical analogy see Baroja's use of the *ritornello* in his 'cuentos', e.g. 'La melancolía' and 'La muerte y la sombra'.

33. Percy Alfred Scholes, *The Oxford Companion to Music*, by John Owen Ward (tenth edition) (London: Oxford University Press, 1970; repr. 1978), p.202.

34. Sebastián Juan Arbó, *Pío Baroja y su tiempo* (Barcelona: Editorial Planeta, 1963), pp.377-78.

35. ibid., pp.378, 382 (see chapter on 'Baroja y los pintores', pp.377-85). The author's interest and comments on art are also documented by Gerardo Ebanks, *La España de Baroja* (Madrid: Ediciones Cultura Hispánica, 1974), pp.53-56.

36. There are many connections to be made, for example, between Baroja's *Camino de perfección* and James Joyce's *A Portrait of the Artist as a Young Man*. Likewise, it should not be forgotten that painting is an important theme in Forster's *A Room with a View*.

37. While the absence of the traditional conclusion of marriage makes Philip's redemption appear initially incomplete, he nevertheless achieves spiritual integrity. Harriet and Mrs Herriton are unaware that 'anything was wrong beyond the death of a poor little child' (155), but Philip and Caroline have experienced moments of transfiguration when truth or reality are revealed and their visions have altered for ever.

38. Forster, op.cit. (1951), p.103. W.J.H. Sprott discusses these ideas in 'Forster as a Humanist', in Stallybrass (1969), op.cit. pp.73-80 (p.77).

39. See, for example, Forster's chapters on 'Fantasy' and 'Prophesy' in Forster (1962), op.cit.

CHAPTER X

Derek Walcott's
Epitaph for the Young: A Poem in xii Cantos:
Modernist Texts and the Caribbean Experience

Maria Cristina Fumagalli

Maria Cristina Fumagalli is Lecturer in the Department of Literature at the University of Essex. Her main research interests are Caribbean literature, contemporary poetry and comparative literature. She has written various articles on Seamus Heaney, Derek Walcott, Erna Brodber, Marlene Nourbese Philip, M.P. Shiel, Jean Rhys and Maryse Condé and she is the author of *The Flight of the Vernacular: Seamus Heaney, Derek Walcott and the Impress of Dante* (2001).

In 1949 the Caribbean poet Derek Walcott (then only eighteen) published *Epitaph for the Young: A Poem in xii Cantos*, a long poem that he wrote between 1946 and 1949. The *Epitaph for the Young* depicts a life journey from birth to manhood and the protagonist is a youth/boat sailing through an archipelago of experiences. As Stewart Brown has remarked,[1] from a formal or technical point of view the poem is a pastiche, a conscious and deliberate exercise in imitation: in fact while reading the text we can hear very distinctly the modernist voices of Baudelaire, T.S. Eliot, Ezra Pound, James Joyce and of Dante, an important source of inspiration for all of them. As Walcott himself admits, at the beginning of his career

> [t]he whole course of imitations and adaptations [was] simply a method of apprenticeship. I knew I was copying and imitating and learning […] I knew I had to absorb everything in order to be able to discover what I was eventually trying to sound like.[2]

Walcott, Brown continues, has not chosen his masters arbitrarily: the experimentalism of their works, the fact that they were outsiders (either 'colonials' or, as in the case of Baudelaire, 'social outcasts'), their ambivalent position towards 'Tradition', their being poets of crisis and their search for a language to express this crisis were certainly extremely interesting features for the young Walcott who was looking for poetic models. However, as Simon Gikandi reminds us,[3] the relationship between Caribbean culture and Modernism, especially the 'high' bourgeois variety that developed in Europe after the First World War' (that is, the 'variety' Walcott refers to in the *Epitaph*) has never been an easy one. The reason is very simple: as Simon During has explained, 'the West is modern, the modern is the West. By this logic, other societies can enter history, grasp the future, only at the price of their destruction'.[4] In other words, the concept of the modern is strictly linked to a Eurocentric view of history and culture and can function (as indeed it has functioned) as an excellent tool to promote European (cultural) expansionism. But this is only one side of the coin because, as Gikandi emphasises:

there is a sense in which Caribbean writers cannot escape from modernism and its problematic issues, especially the questions of language, history, and the colonial subject which it raises. Generations of Caribbean writers and intellectuals have had to bear the burden of modern European history and its ideologies as that history was initiated by the 'discovery' and then transformed, shaped, and even distorted by subsequent events and institutions such as the plantation system and the colonial condition.[5]

Consequently, Caribbean writers find themselves in the paradoxical position of not really being able to 'adopt the history and culture of European modernism, especially as defined by the colonizing structure' but also being faced with the impossibility of 'escap[ing] from it because it has overdetermined Caribbean cultures in many ways'.[6] After all, as Gikandi writes, Aimé Césaire's *Cahier d'un retour au pays natal* (published in 1947, two years before Walcott's *Epitaph*), 'one of the most radical gestures in Caribbean literature, is also indebted to, possibly haunted by, the European modernist models it adopts to strike at the foundations of Eurocentrism'.[7] This article will explore how the young Walcott tries to negotiate between European modernism and Caribbean experience at a time (1949) when his native island was still part of the British Empire.[8]

In the *Epitaph for the Young*, the young protagonist is looking for a 'father' and his search appears intertwined with Walcott's search for a 'literary father', a 'guide' to help him through his poetic journey. The epigraph of canto VIII is a statement of Telemachus':

> "...If aught I shall hear of my father's returning alive
> Then may I yet endure this waste for a year."
>
> *Odyssey* [in italics in the text][9]

Telemachus represents the search for the 'natural' father and is a prototype of Stephen Dedalus in Joyce's *Ulysses* who also figures in the poem and with whom Walcott identifies too. It goes without saying that Joyce's Stephen Dedalus' attempt to 'forge the uncreated conscience of [his] race in the smithy of [his] soul' clearly constituted an important aesthetic model for the young Caribbean poet: in Walcott's words,

> You, Stephen, said Buck, armful of traditions in your fumble
> For a voice, you must let us have your poems. (27)

The epigraph of canto IV of the *Epitaph for the Young*, in fact, is 'There is not a West Indian Literature' and the whole poem is an exploration of the possibility of founding/finding one. Walcott has frequently remarked that he has always 'felt some kind of intimacy with the Irish poets because one realized that they were also colonials with the same kind of problems that existed in the Caribbean. They were the niggers of Britain.'[10] In 'Leaving School', this 'intimacy' is more precisely defined: thinking back to his youthful years, Walcott states:

> I had been tormented enough by the priests [...] Like Stephen [Dedalus] I had my nights of two shillings whores, of 'tackling in the Alley' and silently howling remorse. Like him I was a knot of paradoxes: hating the Church and loving her rituals, learning to hate England as I worshipped her language.[11]

It is no surprise, therefore, that when he was writing the *Epitaph*, Walcott's 'hero' was, as he puts it again in 'Leaving School':

> the blasphemous, arrogant Stephen Dedalus.
> 'Help Of the Sick,
> We are sick of Help,
> Towers of Ivory,
> Pay for Us,
> Comforter of the Afflicted
> We are afflicted with Comfort ...'[12]

These lines appear in almost identical form in canto V of the *Epitaph*, where the youth seems to lose his faith and arrogantly refuses every form of help:

> O Mary [...]
> Comforter of the afflicted.
> We are afflicted with comfort.
> Help of the sick
> We are sick of help [...]
> We had enough of the Lady of the promontory,
> *Figlia del tuo figlio*
> The prayer for wanderers, when she herself has made

> Imperfect piety with her perfect pardon. [...]
> Our Lady of Fishermen,
> Protector and Maker of the weak,
> Prevent us the necessity of coming to Thee,
> Or the coming to Thee from necessity. (p.14)

The 'Lady of the Promontory' reminds one of 'The Lady whose shrine stands on the promontory' in Eliot's third part of the *Four Quartets* ('The Dry Salvages').[13] The loss of faith which characterises the young man at this specific moment in the poem is magnified if compared to Eliot's source, Dante's *Paradiso* XXXIII.1. In one of the passages of the *Commedia* where mystic intensity is at its highest, St Bernard pronounces his prayer to the Virgin Mary by starting precisely with the words that Walcott quotes in the *Epitaph*: 'Vergine madre, *figlia del tuo figlio*' ('O Virgin Mother, *Daughter of thy Son*' [my emphasis]). In 'The Dry Salvages', Eliot cites the same line from *Paradiso* in order to emphasise the depth of his faith in the Virgin Mary. However, in canto XII, at the end of his journey, the youth returns to the 'Lady of the Promontory' once again:

> [...] the chapel still kept its ancient place,
> And there, punishing on the promontory,
> The Daughter of her Son,
> symbol of surrender to the will of Heaven. (p.35)

The reference to St Bernard's prayer (and indirectly to Eliot's 'Dry Salvages') here creates a deep contrast between this moment and canto V of the *Epitaph for the Young*, where it was previously mentioned because it sanctions the return of the faith that the youth had previously lost. It seems, therefore, that Stephen Dedalus' 'arrogance' and 'blasphemy' are somewhat counteracted and dismissed at the end of the poem: 'intimacy' or 'affinity' of aspiration are not synonyms of 'identification'.

In canto VIII of the Epitaph, the one signposted by Telemachus' words in the *Odyssey*, the narrator finally finds himself face to face with his father's ghost.[14] This encounter is clearly reminiscent of Eliot's rendition of canto XV of the *Inferno* in 'Little Gidding', the fourth part of the *Four Quartets*. In Eliot's 'Little Gidding', the figure of the 'familiar compound ghost' (probably Yeats) with whom Eliot imagines himself conferring is merged with two different characters of the *Commedia*. One of them is Brunetto Latini, who is in the Seventh Circle of Hell, and the other is Arnaut Daniel, the famous Provençal *troubadour*, who is instead plunged into the 'refining fire' of *Purgatorio* (XXVI).[15] It seems plain that in Walcott's search for what 'he was eventually trying to sound like' Eliot must have been a crucial presence: the very title of the poem contains a distinct echo of the latter's consideration at the end of his meditations both on history and on his personal past in his *Four Quartet*s:

> Every phrase and every sentence is an end and a beginning,
> Every poem an epitaph.[16]

As Keith Alleyne has pointed out in one of the first reviews of the poem (if not the first one), in the *Epitaph*, 'Eliot is not merely an influence but a complete formula'.[17] As a matter of fact, most of the Dantean echoes in the *Epitaph* are to be found 'anthologised' in T.S. Eliot's poems and in his essays about Dante.[18] Eliot's influence on Walcott, besides, can be measured also from a 'linguistic' point of view. It is curious, in fact, that this young West Indian poet in search of a voice and a language adequate to his own predicament does not make more of Dante-the-linguistic-innovator, of his capacity for being intensely local. The reason for this might be precisely Eliot's and Pound's modernist mediation, since, to borrow the words of Seamus Heaney, 'to listen to Eliot one would almost be led to forget that Dante's great literary contribution was to write in vernacular and thereby to give the usual language its head'.[19] Eliot and Pound, Heaney continues, 'at once restored and removed Dante in the English speaking literary mind because they both suggested [...] that Dante's poem was written on official paper.'[20] Actually, Walcott has recently admitted that the impression that 'Dante's poem was written on official paper' accompanied him for a long while:

> I used to think of him [Dante] as a sort of poet on a pedestal, until I think of him, now, as someone writing in jargon, almost.[21]

Moreover, in 'What the Twilight Says: An Overture', Walcott admits that at the time when he wrote the *Epitaph* he was still

> yearning to be adopted, as the bastard longs for his father's household

> [...] I sighed up a continent of envy when I studied English literature, yet, when I tried to talk as I wrote, my voice sounded affected or too raw. The tongue became burdened, like an ass trying to shift its load. I was taught to trim my tongue as a particular tool which could as easily have been ordered from England as an awl or a chisel [...] I was thus proclaimed a prodigy because I insisted on a formality which had nothing to do with [my people's] lives.[22]

Walcott's yearning, therefore, was what, paraphrasing the words of the compound ghost in Eliot's 'Little Gidding', impelled the young West Indian poet 'to purify the dialect of the tribe' in the sense of 'trimming his tongue'. Paradoxically enough, the formality Walcott is insisting upon in the *Epitaph* is the formality of 'informality' that characterised Modernist experimentalism. This can perhaps also explain why, in the *Epitaph*, Walcott never attempts to imitate Dantean *terza rima* despite the fact that the Eliotian rendition of the passage in 'Little Gidding', regarding the encounter of the poet with the 'compound ghost' that Walcott alludes to in canto VIII of the *Epitaph*, has been described as 'influential in interposing itself between *terza rima* as practised by English poets of the past and the practice of the moderns'.[23] Most interestingly, while after the *Epitaph* Eliot's influence on Walcott becomes less and less apparent, in *Omeros* (and again in the first section of *The Bounty*)[24] the propelling force of *terza rima* is what gives the poem its prosodic unity.

At first sight, therefore, it would seem that when Walcott wrote the *Epitaph* he was simply trying to 'ventriloquise' the voices of some of the prominent European Modernists (Eliot, Joyce, Pound, Baudelaire) in order to gain a place for himself in the European 'pantheon'. However, this 'yearning to be adopted' was not as unproblematic as it might seem: as Alleyne has remarked, the *Epitaph* 'betrays an embarrassed self-consciousness [...] the embarrassment of borrowed clothes, no matter how legitimately acquired – the top hat in the tropics'.[25] If we consider the poem more carefully, besides, we realise that it is more complex and intriguing than a mere pastiche. Let us start, as it were, *ab ovo*, from the epigraph, a quotation (in French) from the initial lines of Baudelaire's 'Le Voyage':

> Pour l'enfant, amoureux de cartes et d'estampes,

> L'univers est égal à son vaste appétit.
> Ah! Que le monde est grand à la clarté des lampes!
> Aux yeux du souvenir que le monde est petit!
>
> (For the child, in love with maps and prints,
> the universe is equal to his vast appetite.
> Oh, how big the world is by lamplight!
> In the eyes of memory, how small the world is!) [26]

At first sight, these lines seem to constitute a very good introduction to a poem which witnesses its author's love and appetite for a world literature and for whom the very act of writing the poem is both a way of mapping his own inner world and a voyage of discovery, or in his own words, a way of finding out what he 'was eventually trying to sound like'. Baudelaire – who has arguably been described as the first Modernist if not in terms of style then at least as far as content is concerned[27] – seems to be an important model for the young Walcott since he is repeatedly quoted and referred to in the *Epitaph* and Brown goes as far as saying that 'Le Voyage and Baudelaire emerge as [the *Epitaph*'s] spiritual guides'.[28] Brown focuses mainly on the function of the French poet as an inspiration and an example for Walcott's explorations of the darkest side of the self, as the lines that he selects from canto IX clearly show:

> I kick heels away from the white hairs of remission, am
> Divided between desire and dissolution,
> Between the advice of the red hag and the piety-pilfering sea. (p.27)[29]

Moreover, as Brown underlines, Walcott seems to find Baudelaire's 'sense of himself as being both *outside* the commonweal by virtue of his education and calling, yet crucially attracted to that milieu as the authentic life of his society'[30] clearly resonating with his own colonial condition. Speaking about the colonial writers of his generation Walcott has said:

> We knew the literature of Empires, Greek, Roman, British, through their essential classics; and both the patois of the street and the language of the classroom had the elation of discovery.[31]

This simultaneous presence in Walcott's formation (and in every colonial/ postcolonial writer's) of European (written) and Caribbean (oral) culture is acknowledged at the very beginning of the *Epitaph* where it is clearly indicated that only European culture seems to develop a narrative capable of becoming 'history':

> The past only we can sign; the rest is
> Between the lips of accident. (p.1)

These lines, however, are more subversive than they might seem since they appear to contain in embryo Walcott's desire to devalue history by defining it as 'fiction, subject to a fitful muse, memory' as he does in 'The Muse of History' written in 1974 (twenty-eight years after he wrote the *Epitaph*).[32]

But there is more: the epigraph's reference to 'maps' and 'discovery' reveals the text's concern with colonial discourse. As Bill Ashcroft, Gareth Griffiths and Helen Tiffin point out in *Key Concepts in Post-Colonial Studies*:

> Both literally and metaphorically, maps and mapping are dominant practices of colonial and post-colonial cultures. Colonisation itself is often consequent on a voyage of 'discovery', a bringing into being of 'undiscovered' lands. The process of discovery is reinforced by the construction of maps, whose existence is a means of textualising the spatial reality of the other, naming or, in almost all cases, renaming spaces in a symbolic and literal act of mastery and control [...] Maps can also serve as (allegorical) tools of exploitation [...] of Eurocentrism, defining European latitudes as pivotal reference points for the conception of a world hierarchy, and embodying as geographical fact European attitudes about the nature of the world.[33]

As Simon Gikandi has pointed out:

> Caribbean literature and culture are haunted by the presence of the 'discoverer' and the historical moments he inaugurates. For if Columbus's discovery of the Americas and his initial encounter with the peoples of the New World have paradigmatic value in the European episteme because they usher in a brave new world, a world of modernity and modernist forms [...] these events also trigger a contrary effect on the people who are 'discovered'.[34]

The initial epigraph from Baudelaire, therefore, is not an

unproblematical tribute to the French master but also implies a critical view of the very co-ordinates that organise the 'cartes' and 'estampes' the child in the poem seems to be so fond of. Moreover, as J. Michael Dash has observed:

> The Caribbean archipelago, conceived as an absolute 'elsewhere', as irreducibly different, was from its very inception invented as a blank slate onto which an entire exoticist project could be inscribed. The repercussions of intensive industrialisation in Europe and colonisation's backlash of global culture homogeneity created the need to see in the Tropics an antidote to Europe's sense of loss.[35]

Interestingly enough, as Dash continues in 'Tropes and Tropicality', the

> evocation of a spectacular wilderness that ends with the human spirit soaring over [it] is [...] typical of [the] naturist phase of nineteenth-century exoticism. This ideal is extremely important to early European modernism. Its best-known resonance is perhaps in Charles Baudelaire's lines from *Les Fleurs du Mal*.[36]

It is noteworthy, therefore, that in his own voyage of discovery and in his attempt to draw a map of his own inner self inclusive of both European literature and Caribbean experience, Walcott polemically refuses to refer to (let alone eulogise) the 'spectacular wilderness' of the Caribbean so fondly sung by European writers. Walcott, as we have seen, turns his poem into a highly self-reflexive work that celebrates and/or contests – or simply deals with – textuality and intertextual culture.[37] As a result, by deliberately situating himself and his poem in the literary 'agon', Walcott implicitly counteracts the epigraph to canto IV pessimistically stating 'There is not a West Indian Literature' and also provides some indications concerning the lines along which West Indian literature is actually developing. If we read the *Epitaph* carefully, in fact, we cannot fail to notice that Walcott's 'Dantean/Eliotian' encounter with his late father in canto VIII is strategically placed after two parodies: a parody of Dante's *Inferno* – with Eliot as Virgil/guide and Walcott taking the role of Dante/pilgrim – followed by a parody of Eliot's *Four Quartets*:

> Then I saw one who by the token of my
> Greeting knew me to be alive. I since he

Had been instructed by none other
Than him whose eyes are divided by Cyrano's misery,
'Ah,' said I, restraining him from wrath by guile … 'If
It be not against the will of Him who undid thee
Say why walkest thou with limp so severe that
The right foot is always the lower and in pain?'
'O,' said he with downcast brow. 'Between Dennery
And that fierce village where the ravine breaks sloth
And rages like a mad colt to the sea, I
Came by the grace of the evil stars to a rise in the land,
And there a pebble dislodged itself by ordered chance,
And pricked my heel that go now footless and faithless,
And I for swearing blasphemy at that crumb of pain
As thou seest suffer…'
  And we left him thus unsandalled. (p.22)
At which harsh words my heavy soul tears flooded,
Nor had I near any handkerchief, but that noble shade
Perceiving that my nose run, with natural artifice
Lent me a corner of his gown and I blew gustily…
And as the geese go clanking across an autumn moon
So that the noise they make seems like a fallen chain
So did my nose vibrate through the fiery shades …
Then tugging at my hope my noble guide addressed me.
Whose voice is that of an eagle dying in London,
Revered authority on The Virgil Society, saying …
'What is a classic?
To one has eighty years and no to-morrow?'
And I whom he had instructed paid him heed saying …
'This is the place.
This is the
I say the Word only to those who hear, and who are not here to hear,
Not to those who are afraid of distraction
Of the thrush in the rose garden, not to those who fear the desert
Yet cannot desert, in the desert where there is no water,
In this timeless city where the crowd of spinning faces revolves in the violent air
Sand and sandpaper …
I say this with my mouth, you listen not with these ears,

Because they are mine, but listening with yours …
I say this not out of time, but in time, not timeless
But rhymeless and out of time.
For the
For the wheel turns and the impatient suffer
And the peasant passes distracted by insinuations
Here and now in Castries and Hampstead, burnt nothing,
A Little Giddying,
But where was I?' (p.23)

I have quoted these two parodies in full because I believe that this is a crucial point in the *Epitaph*: this is where the poem is no longer a pastiche – where imitation is an end in itself – but becomes a proper parody – where imitation is a means to mockery – that is something similar, at least in spirit, to a Caribbean calypso. Calypsos are crucial to carnival celebrations and represent both a distinctive verbal art and an important form of social, political and cultural satire. Calypsos (like parodies) are subversive even when they are affectionate, and, although they constitute a model for 'ritualised' forms (therefore contained within the parameters licensed by the establishment) of social and cultural protest and resistance, nonetheless they can function as an anti-authoritarian affirmation of alternative values. Walcott's calypso/parody of Eliot and Dante, therefore, is a somewhat paradoxical activity because it successfully brings together what it ultimately declares cannot be brought together, that is European modernism and Caribbean culture: 'Caribbean genius', as Walcott himself has written, 'is condemned to contradict itself'.[38] In this respect, Walcott's effort is similar to the Caribbean carnival, whose complexity, according to Antonio Benítez-Rojo, 'cannot be reduced to binary concepts […] it serves the purpose of unifying through its performance that which cannot be unified (the impossible desire to reach social and cultural unity – socio-cultural synthesis – that runs within the system).[39]

The *Epitaph for the Young*, therefore, is not simply an apprentice's poem 'blatantly in the style of 'various masters'[40] (although it is *also* this): within the poem, the young Walcott seems to have developed a narrative capable of questioning colonising cultural structures (ironically, in the *Epitaph* the 'colonised' becomes the 'discoverer') and conventional modes of representation of the Caribbean (Baudelaire's exoticism), to dismiss history and the Eurocentric notion of tradition ('A tradition is not made, it evolves / Through those who are not concerned with history.' p.9). By way of conclusion, we can affirm that Walcott's *Epitaph for the Young* gives expression to a form of Modernism that is animated by a deeply transformative spirit since European Modernism can be imported and appreciated by Caribbean writers only if, to conclude borrowing once again Gikandi's words, it is 'fertilised by figures of the 'other' imagination which colonialism has sought to repress. In this sense, Caribbean Modernism is highly revisionary'.[41]

NOTES TO CHAPTER X

Notes to Chapter X

1. See Stewart Brown, 'The Apprentice: *25 Poems, Epitaph for the Young, Poems* and *In a Green Night*', in *The Art of Derek Walcott*, ed. Stewart Brown (Bridgend, Mid Glamorgan: Seren Books, 1991), pp.13-33.
2. Edward Hirsch, 'An Interview with Derek Walcott', *Contemporary Literature* 20 (1979), 279-92, p.282.
3. Simon Gikandi, *Writing in Limbo: Modernism and Caribbean Literature* (Ithaca: Cornell University Press, 1992), p.3.
4. Simon During, 'Waiting for the Post: Modernity, Colonization and Writing', in *Ariel: A Review of International English Literature* 20 (1989), 31-61, p.31.
5. Gikandi, op.cit. p.3.
6. ibid., p.3.
7. ibid., p.21.
8. St Lucia was one of the last of the English-speaking islands to be free of European imperial authority when it became independent in 1979.
9. Derek Walcott, *Epitaph for the Young: A Poem in xii Cantos* (Barbados: Advocate, 1949), p.22. Subsequent page references will be given in parentheses in the text.
10. Hirsch, op.cit. p.288.
11. Derek Walcott, 'Leaving School', *London Magazine*, 5 (1965), 4-14, p.13.
12. ibid., p.13.
13. T.S. Eliot, *Four Quartets* (London: Faber and Faber, 1944), p.36.

In the essay 'Leaving School' (p.12), Walcott himself acknowledges Eliot's influence. Thinking back to the years when he wrote the *Epitaph for the Young*, he says:

> 'What names, what objects do I remember from that time? The brown covered *Penguin Series of Modern Painters*: Stanley Spencer, Frances Hodgkins, Paul Nash, Ben Nicholson: the pocket-sized Dent edition of Thomas's *Deaths And Entrances*, the Eliot recording of *Four Quartets*'.

14. And through the brown smoke with lowered heads
    Against the smoke, I saw a crowd of moving shadows,
    And I know not whether the fierce sand that turned
    In the brown air brought grief into mine eyes when
    I made out as I were dreaming, my father's spirit in arms.
    And when the old mystery had ascertained that it
    Was he whose face I sought through life,
    And whom no filial memory could aid me by I said
    Bending my face to his
            'Are you here, Ser Brunetto?'
    What is thy fault?
    'Towards God I bore only a passive love,

But no mundane judgment can question His will

Who makes me tread this city in the purifying fire.

We do His will least who avoid offending Him, gaining

Only the inertia of an ashen virtue, I lived simply in the other life,

And held fair in esteem, but let it not displease thee.'

I said in tears. 'If I had a voice you had not died so young…'

And he 'If Thou observe the Star that guides the mariner

Beyond the dubious haven of the promontory, you will please your Father …

All things will weary thee,

The stumps of cities thrown up against the sunset,

The wave beat against the ship's tired loins, governments and sharp stars …

But live His will … and live beyond the reefs …'

But now

A great smoke had divided us, and drew me closer to him,

As death has made us closer in the other life …

And it grew darker, and His will ordained division,

And as he turned away he seemed to care

Even less than I who live so helplessly,

And through the ruined city flickering with tortures

That pricked the night like gnat-bewildering lanterns

He seems to run like one who wins not loses… (pp.23-24)

15. T.S. Eliot, op.cit. pp.43-45.

16. ibid., p.47. The sub-title of the *Epitaph, A Poem in xii Cantos* gestures also towards Pound's *Cantos*.

17. Keith Alleyne, '*Epitaph for the Young: A Poem in xii Cantos* by Derek Walcott', BIM 3 (1949), 267-72, p.267.

18. For example, T.S. Eliot, 'Dante', in *Selected Essays* (London: Faber and Faber, 1932), pp.237-77.

19. Seamus Heaney, 'Envies and Identifications: Dante and the Modern Poet', *Irish University Review* 15 (1985), 5-19, p.12.

20. ibid., p.16.

21. Luigi Sampietro, '"An Object Beyond One's Own Life': An Interview with Derek Walcott', *Caribana* 2 (1991), 25-36, p.32.

22. Derek Walcott, 'What the Twilight Says: An Overture', in *Dream on Monkey Mountain and Other Plays* (New York: Farrar, Straus and Giroux, 1970), pp.3-40, pp.31-32.

23. Philip Hobsbaum, *Metre, Rhythm and Verse Form* (London: Routledge, 1996), p.124. The fact that Walcott's quotation from Dante's *Inferno* XXVI comes from the

Temple Classics version, besides, leads us to think that at the time he was probably reading the *Commedia* in a prose version. This certainly contributed to the formulation of his erroneous – or at least 'partial' – idea of Dante. Perusing the *Commedia* in its rhyme-scheme is in fact a radically different and revealing experience.

24. Derek Walcott, *Omeros* (London: Faber and Faber, 1990); *The Bounty* (London: Faber and Faber, 1997).

25. Alleyne, op.cit. p.267.

26. trans. Carol Clark (Harmondsworth: Penguin, 1995), p.136.

27. It is noteworthy that technically speaking, Baudelaire's quatrains in 'Le Voyage' are not the model that Walcott follows in his *Epitaph*, which is mostly in vers libre, like Eliot's *Four Quartets* or Pound's *Cantos*.

28. Brown, op.cit. p.22.

29. ibid., p.22.

30. ibid., p.21.

31. Walcott, op.cit. (1970) p.4.

32. Derek Walcott, 'The Muse of History', in *What the Twilight Says: Essays* (London: Faber and Faber, 1998), 36-64, p.37.

33. Bill Ashcroft, Gareth Griffiths and Helen Tiffin, *Key Concepts in Post-Colonial Studies* (London: Routledge, 1998), pp.31-33.

34. Gikandi, op.cit. p.1.

35. Michael Dash, *The Other America: Caribbean Literature in a New World Context* (Charlottesville: Virginia University Press, 1998), p.17.

36. ibid., p.30.

37. As a matter of fact, also in subsequent poems, Walcott openly challenges this idea of the Tropics. See, for example, 'A Sea-Chantey' in Derek Walcott, *Collected Poems 1948-1984* (London: Faber and Faber, 1984), p.44 and the relationship between the text of the poem and the epigraph from Baudelaire.

38. Derek Walcott, 'The Antilles: Fragments of Epic Memory', in op.cit. (1998), pp.65-84, p.78.

39. Antonio Benítez-Rojo, *The Repeating Island: The Caribbean and the Postmodern Perspective*, trans. James E. Maraniss (Durham: Duke University Press, 1996), p.307.

40. op.cit. p.15.

41. Gikandi, op.cit. p.4.

Woolf Nietzsche Wilde

Butor André Gide Marinetti Woolf Jo
E. M. Forster Derek Walcott Karefy Augustine
  Charles Baudelaire Michael Aflaq Jo
Aragon Edgar Allan Poe Malraux
Mc Almon Kafka Woolf Baroja
netti Butor John Dewey Joyce
  Lorca Nietzsche T.S. Eliot

Kafka Benjamin Woolf Proust Beckett
Malraux John Dos Karefy
William Carlos Williams Passos Koeppen Proust E
      E. M. Forster Thomas Mann
ayce Benjamin Baroja Kafka
Ezra Pound Koeppen Michael Aflaq John Dos Passos Becke
lcott Robert Mc Almon Butor
  Nietzsche Marinetti Aragon Jo
ett Proust Jo
arinetti Jo Ed

PART III

INTERACTIONS WITH OTHER MODERNIST ART FORMS

CHAPTER XI

Modernity and 'Cinematographic Writing' in André Malraux's *Days of Hope* and John Dos Passos' *The Big Money*

Raynalle Udris

Raynalle Udris is a Principal Lecturer in the School of Arts at Middlessex University. She is a specialist in 20th Century French Literature. She has published articles on North African Francophone Literature, French women's writing, and especially on the work of Marguerite Duras. In her book *Welcome Unreason: a Study of 'Madness' in the Work of Marguerite Duras* (1993) she offers a socio-political reading of Marguerite Duras' work. She is also the co-editor of *Marguerite Duras Lectures plurielles* (1997) which includes an article on the reception and the production of meaning in the Duras text, and the co-author of the book *French Discourse Analysis* (2000). She is the co-founder of the international Marguerite Duras Society and one of the two main co-editors of its bi-annual bulletins.

This chapter aims to explore a double comparison, between two major art forms – literature and cinema – and between two novels written by two internationally renowned authors: *Days of Hope* (*L'Espoir*) by the French writer André Malraux and *The Big Money* by the American John Dos Passos. Both were produced virtually at the same time – 1936 and 1937 – at the end of what has often been identified as the modernist period. Though thematically very different – *Days of Hope* is a politically committed war novel set during the Spanish Civil War while *Big Money* is a historical fresco of American society after the First World War –, the two novels were both shaped by the growing importance in the 1930s of the cinematic medium. This intertextual dimension, as the close analysis which follows will endeavour to demonstrate, is indeed central to their textual formation.

The influence of cinema in the two novels is immediately obvious at the thematic level with allusions to film titles, genres or film characters. In *Big Money*, for instance, the narrative refers to the occasion when the main character, Charley Anderson, had gone with his girlfriend to see Griffith's *Birth of a Nation* (*BM* 36).[1] In *Days of Hope*, the description of a war scene includes a reference to the arrival of two Cadillacs, 'wildly zigzagging like cars in gangster films' (*DH* 30), and one of the main characters, Scali, an officer in the International Air Force, is compared to 'an American film comedian' because of his 'Charlie-Chaplin walk' (*DH* 129).

Reference to filmic representation is also striking in various evocations of the world of the cinema. In *Big Money*, one of the main biographical sequences is dedicated to the Hollywood actor Rudolph Valentino (*BM* 169-172); his life and death are evoked and the actress Mary Pickford, described as 'America's sweetheart' (*BM* 172), attends his funeral. Some characters are presented in the narrative as actors, for example the Cuban Tony, who dreams of becoming as famous as Valentino or Margo Dowling, the model who became a star of the silent screen and whose career was ended by the coming of sound. Besides the various thematic allusions to cinema, both narratives also refer to cinematographic techniques: Charley Anderson when in hospital sees 'the pretty pink nurse's face [blooming] above him like a close-up in a movie' (*BM* 333). In *Days of Hope*, referential space is compared to film locations – Madrid is described as a real 'nocturnal studio' – or assimilated to a film set. Thus the movements of the International Brigades, charging 'nation after nation [...] rifle in hand [...] through a mist that was clotted with the smoke of battle' are compared to 'a battle scene in a film' (*DH* 307). The borrowing of notions of cinematographic technique is most obvious in *Big Money* where two of the four recurrent sequences which alternate in the novel draw their names from the world of cinematography. The sequences entitled 'Newsreels' copy a filmic genre, while the 'Camera Eye' sections refer to Dziga Vertov's avant-garde Kino Eye shooting methods. As will be seen later, these two types of sequences articulate a cinematographic treatment of narrative through their specific use of compositional devices. While some of the thematic devices mentioned above contribute to the 'reality effect' for the period depicted (the USA between 1919 and 1929), others, particularly in *Days of Hope*, point to a more definite interest in the cinematic medium.

Apart from using cinema as a recurrent theme and borrowing various film concepts, the two narratives are structurally shaped by the filmic medium; hence the expression 'cinematographic writing' which has often been used to describe these novels. This term constitutes a useful metaphor grounded in the narrative features common to the two arts. The expression 'cinematographic writing' applied to a novel implies a transfer of configurations made possible by the fact that both cinema and literature commonly rely on the same narrative characteristic, that of the unfolding of a story in space and time. The transfer operation from one art to the other also implies that this borrowing of configurations is carried out by the literary work. As Michel Zéraffa suggests in *Personne et personnage*, the transposition of writing configurations appears to take place for reasons of coherence:

> Dos Passos is inspired by cinema techniques because the coherent, conventional forms of language – of discourse – cannot express the fragmented consciousness, itself fascinated by this very fragmentation, of the New York inhabitants.[2]

The expression 'cinematographic writing' can furthermore be understood, according to Christian Metz in *Language and Cinema*,[3] as a reference to the system of codes used to articulate the filmic message. Such reference is made possible by the fact that literature and cinema, which, it can be argued, rely respectively on the word and the image as their basic elements, reveal a similar structure: 'to tell by showing'.

This study of the two novels will focus on two aspects which may be said to constitute the basis of the cinematic process: the framing of a space (in time), and the role of the 'camera-eye' in this process. It will in the first instance concentrate principally on the structure and compositional features of the texts in order to elucidate the cinematic effects of spatial and temporal framing; the importance and characteristic aspects of vision in the two novels will then be examined.

Spatial and temporal framing and related fragmentation effects

Filmic representation relies on compositional and narrative devices which are linked to the nature of the equipment used: the 'camera-eye' which 'selects' fragments of space. Each fragment in turn corresponds to a specific type of framing, and filmic temporality is the result of piecing together these fragments to follow a shooting-script, which breaks up the scenario into scenes and sequences. Fragmentation also constitutes, through a significant number of compositional devices, an important feature of both our two narratives. Such fragmentation takes place through a comparable framing process with regard to fictional 'reality'. Such characteristics can be seen at the level of page layout and in the editing effects of the novels' treatment of time.

The visual layout of the page

The page layout in the 'Newsreels' and 'Camera Eye' sections of *Big Money* creates an effect of spatial framing which can in many respects be compared with display on a screen. The page layout juxtaposes, mixes or alternates various rubrics (newspaper headlines, adverts, extracts from economics reports, sports news…), fragments of sentences highlighted by typographic variations (lower and upper case letters, Roman/italic characters), and inconsistent use of demarcation features such as margins and blank spaces which isolate words or sentence fragments. A visual distinction can however be made between the two types of sequence. The pictorial aspect of the page layout of the

'Newsreels' sequences, which constitute the impersonal inner monologue of a collective conscience, stems from the alternation and variety of the typographic elements used. By their organisation into typographic clusters and by the contrasts thus created, the 'Newsreels' pages acquire a definite visual structure. In the 'Camera Eye' sequences, the visual quality resides in the fragmentation effect created in the text by the cut-up sentences and the regularity of the interspersed breaks, by the arbitrary use of paragraphs and the absence of punctuation. While in the 'Newsreels' the white surface of the page is in the main respected and used as a background for the typography, a different visualisation process seems to be at work in the 'Camera Eye' sections: blanks can intrude into the fabric of the text, imbuing words and sentence elements with a separate existence freed from a logical thought process.

Effect of temporal framing

More significant perhaps is the specificity of the treatment of time in the two novels, which creates a kind of framing effect particularly revealing of this type of writing. As Genette recalls in *Narrative Discourse*,[4] narratives[5] require duration in order to be actualised. Duration can be entirely fictive, divorced from existing or past reality or, as in these two novels, can rely on an historical framework as reference-point for the unfolding of the story.

Big Money evokes the inflationary American period leading to the economic crash of 1929 which brought into question the principles, if not the ideology, of liberal capitalism. In spite of a degree of indeterminacy in the historical chronology, from the novel's beginning with Charley Anderson's return from war in 1919 to its end some years after the Sacco & Vanzetti affair of 1927 (the last precise historical landmark in the book), *Big Money* is nonetheless framed within the historical chronology of Dos Passos' trilogy *USA: The 42nd Parallel*, retracing the period prior to 1917, and 1919 retracing the end of the First World War. Some characters, such as Charley Anderson, Moorehouse and Evelyn Hutchins, reappear from one novel to the next, and a double framing effect takes place whereby *Big Money* carries out a first cut into a limited historical reality but is itself framed within the wider fictional world of USA.

The process of historical framing is more precise in Malraux's *Days of Hope*. The Spanish Civil War provides the background to the novel. Historically the Civil War began in July 1936 after the election victory of the Popular Front in February of that year, and ended with Nationalist victory on 28 March 1939. The novel's narrative, which covers only eight months of the war, starts on 19 July 1936, the day after the uprising of the Barcelona garrison. Malraux ends his novel in March 1937 with the defence of Madrid by the International Brigades; in other words with a Republican victory. The Republicans were, of course, ultimately to be defeated in 1939 by the Nationalists. This narrative interruption is accounted for by the circumstances in which the narrative process was produced, Malraux being involved in the war as an officer of the French Air Force. The novel is therefore contemporary with the historical events that it narrates, hence the title *Days of Hope*. It was a hope justified at that specific moment in the war but finally shattered by later events.

Cinematographic effects of the treatment of time

In addition to the process of historical framing which, especially in the case of *Days of Hope*, gives the texts the value of chronicle, the treatment of *duration* in these novels recalls the features of filmic composition.

Big Money presents the juxtaposition and alternation of four types of sequences which establish in the space of the novel a fragmentation of narrative temporality, and create the effect of cinematic cross-cutting. These sequences can be classified, by their title and in relation to what they represent, as the 'Newsreels', the 'Camera Eye' sequences, the biography sections and the sequences dealing with fictional characters.

The 24 'Newsreels' – from Newsreels 44 to 67 –, characterised by the disparity and the proliferation of the reported events, most often presented as radio bulletins or newspaper headlines, are regularly spread over the novel's 500 or so pages. The nine 'Camera Eye' sections present fragments of discourses which give the text an incoherent and impressionistic character. They are regularly spread at intervals of 100 to 200 pages, often grouped in pairs, with the exception of the last three. Both types of sequences, structurally fragmented and creating a snapshot effect, account for a very limited temporality. Indeed it is practically nil for the non-narrative 'Newsreels'.

As is the case for the 'Camera Eye' sequences, the 10 biography sequences are numerically limited and surrounded by the 'Newsreel' sections. In contrast to the other two types so far mentioned, they are more precisely dated, each one in turn evoking an historical character representative of the United States at the time, whether it be the car magnate Henry Ford, the economist and sociologist, Thorstein Veblen, the newspaper tycoon William Randolph Hearst or the dancer, Isadora Duncan. These biography sequences, with the exception of the final one, provide relatively complete summaries of a character's life from birth to death.

The fourth rubric, dealing with fictional characters and constituting the main part of the narrative, alternates seventeen sequences named according to the main fictional character of that section: Charley Anderson, the war hero who makes a career in aviation design; Margo Dowling, star of the silent screen; Mary French, the political activist, and Richard Ellsworth Savage, the publicist. Charley Anderson dominates the beginning of the novel while other fictional characters such as Richard Savage take more prominence towards the end of the narrative. While the evocation of these characters alternates, their story is also regularly interrupted by a 'Newsreel' section which itself precedes or directly follows a 'Camera Eye' section or a biography. The evocation of the specific fictional character is then resumed, or else the interruption provides the opportunity for a shift to another fictional section.

As Claude-Edmonde Magny stresses in *L'Age du roman américain* (*The Age of the American Novel*),[6] while the reader may be disconcerted by the sections which, 'using the margins of the reader's consciousness', appear external and therefore redundant to the main fictional account, the meaning of *Big Money* nevertheless comes primarily from the alternation of its four sequences, from the cross-cutting montage technique which structures the organisation of the novel. The recurrence and alternation of these sequences gives the narrative a mechanical and stereotypical character, while providing a rhythm for the temporality of the novel. These sequences can also announce a recall or advance notice function in the narrative. In Newsreel LIX (*BM* 256-257) for instance, the evocation of Detroit directly announces Charley Anderson's arrival in Detroit in the next sequence. The Newsreels also tend to provide a model for the fictional characters.

Newsreel LIII (*BM* 142-143), which follows the Isadora Duncan biography section, recalls the latter through an announcement hidden among other disparate facts: 'You too can quickly learn to dance at home without music and without a partner', and as such provides a stereotypical model for the artistic activity of Margo Dowling in the next sequence. Through their regular recurrence in the narrative, the three extradiegetic sections provide a chronological frame to the fictional characters by situating them in a politically inflected America, as in the Sacco and Vanzetti affair in which Mary French is involved, and in an economically dependent America driven by 'the big money' which Charley Anderson and Margo Dowling strive to acquire. Through the repetition of these extradiegetic rubrics and through their linking and explanatory functions, an analogy is established between the various fictional sections; a reality corresponding to 1920s America is thus revealed.

The diegetic significance of *Big Money* is therefore a direct result of its innovative, avant-garde writing. While a linear chronology of events – similar to continuity editing – may be discerned in the 'characters' sequences, the fragmented duration stems directly from the cross-cut 'editing' of these sequences. At the thematic level, this may be aimed at signifying, as Magny shows, 'that the major events of Charley's life are as if prefigured in advance by the evolution of a society which makes them possible and which preconditions them.'[7] At the stylistic level, this technique gives the novel, following in the footsteps of James Joyce's *Ulysses*, a polyphonic value inherent to its very meaning.

Similarly, though executed in a very different fashion, the temporality of *Days of Hope* is essentially marked by fragmentation. If the temporal structure of the novel relies on the linear chronology of the Civil War, it is nonetheless built on a pattern of discontinuity. In this sense, as Christiane Moatti has stressed, *Days of Hope* 'obviously diverges from the model of the nineteenth century novels: from one sequence to the next, the environment, the characters, the nature of the narrative change, breaking up narrative continuity. It is the reader's task to bring the different and often simultaneous actions, reported in fragments, together'.[8]

Fragmentation is indeed present at every level in the novel and is immediately obvious at first sight through the book's unwonted architecture; the 59 chapters of the 500 pages are organised into three parts of decreasing length, corresponding to the three phases of the Spanish Civil War. These parts include sections and subsections of different lengths, from the 27 chapters of the first part (entitled 'Lyrical Illusion') to the six chapters of the unified last part: 'Hope'. This was a pattern no doubt adapted to Malraux's thematic purpose, as Moatti again indicates: 'Malraux wanted to retrace the transformation of the lyrical illusion, that is of the fundamental lack of order and the emotional dimension by which every revolution starts, into an organisation strong enough to carry out the victory of the latter'.[9]

The effect of cinematographic montage in *Days of Hope* stems from the organisation of the text into juxtaposed sequences. The narrative of *Days of Hope* is organised through a series of contrasts inherent in the nature of its sequences: sequences dealing with specific war events or actions alternate with more reflective moments offering a retrospective view or summary of past events or, on the contrary, preparing the terrain for the imminence of another action. This regular narrative movement from the particular to the general establishes a contrastive rhythm in the novel.

As in *Big Money*, a cross-cutting montage can be discerned in the juxtaposition and alternation of the action sequences. This cross-cutting technique involves the juxtaposition of sequences related to the same action in which the fragmentation effect stems from an alternation between the different groups of men involved in that action. In the second part of the novel ('Apocalypse'), for instance, the main action depicts the confrontation between the militia and the fascists in Toledo. Successively and alternately, the left-wing forces are shown in action: the fight carried out by the Republican troops is presented alternately; several attempts are made to free the Alcazar buildings occupied by the fascists and to recover the hostages. In the meantime the squadron intervenes to bomb the Alcazar, and this leads to the fascists' surrender. In parallel, the fighting in the sierra between Talavera and Toledo continues, moving towards the latter, the aim being first to attack the fascist farms, then to organise Toledo's outer defences with the dissemination of groups of bombers and also its internal resistance network. Thus a common action, the organisation of Toledo's defence, is illustrated through a constant movement from one group of men to the next, each group representing a different aspect of the same struggle. This alternating treatment of a single action recalls the cross-cutting technique of other militant actions in parts one and two of the novel, such as the defence of Madrid or the action on the Guadalajarra front.

Use of ellipsis as an editing technique

'By the very essence of its technique, cinema was bound to become an art of ellipsis', points out Claude-Edmonde Magny.[10] Susan Hayward notes in *Key Concepts in Cinema Studies* that the use of cross-cutting and parallel editing implies ellipsis, since ellipsis refers to 'periods of time that have been left out in the narrative.'[11] Both the texts we are considering, where the fragmented temporality remains largely chronological, rely on the use of elliptical devices; hence the regular effect of narrative acceleration in the temporal progression of both novels.

In *Big Money*, the temporal continuity of the fictional sequences is ensured by the evocation of the main stages of the characters' lives. For Charley Anderson, for instance, these are the return from New York, life in Detroit, his marriage and his accident, his meeting Margo Dowling and his return to New York. The narrative retraces only a few key moments of his life, such as the description of his journey to New York (which accounts for one day of his life), a business project with a colleague (of which a few days are evoked), or his liaison with Doris, which accounts for some 4 months. Such episodes are recounted in detail but are surrounded by temporal ellipses. Thus for example an ellipsis of 8 months takes us from Charley Anderson's installation into his New York flat in September 1920 to the start of his business enterprise with Joe in January 1921, and another 7 or 8 month ellipsis can be found between the description of his work on the Askew-Merritt plane engine and his life with his former friend Doris.

The elliptic treatment of temporality accounts for the fact that the narrative discourse for each fictional character covers only a few months, compared with the total story time of several years. The temporal treatment of the fictional sequences furthermore mirrors that of the biography sections. If the narrative time of the latter remains chronological, it is also considerably reduced compared with the story-time, hence the effect of accelerated narrative speed: if we refer to Henry Ford's biography, for instance (*BM* 43-49), 69 years are reported in 7 pages.

Similarly, the narrative of *Days of Hope*, which covers 8 months of the Spanish war in temporal continuity, only evokes certain aspects of the war interspersed – as is frequently the case in film – with temporal ellipses. Between the first and second sections of the first part, for example, we notice a week's ellipsis from 21 July to 'the beginning of August'. Between the second and third sections of the first part, it is more difficult to discern with precision when the actions take place. In the first sequence Manuel, the young Spaniard who has become a lieutenant in the Republican army, visits his old friend Barca, just after a fight in the Sierra which took place at the beginning of August: a week's ellipsis is likely. Between the first and second parts of the novel, another indeterminate ellipsis is likely before or after the Toledo fighting of September 1936 since this lasts only for a few days. Chapter 2 of Part 2, referring to the bombing of Palma, is temporally situated on 6 November 1936, hinting at up to two months' ellipsis in relation to the siege of the Alcazar in September. Another two months' ellipsis takes us from the fighting in Madrid at the end of Part 2 to the beginning of Part 3, on 8 February. The temporal ellipses of the narrative of *Days of Hope* may therefore account for up to 50% of the 8 months of the story-time.

If indeed elliptical treatment of narrative is commonly used in novelistic writing – one thinks perhaps of Camus' *L'Étranger* or of Faulkner's novels – it is also the prerogative and largely unavoidable feature of cinematic narratives, used to great effect to create suspense in thrillers, for example. Such a treatment of time, which reinforces a fragmentary construction of temporality, also constitutes an essential part of the diegetic dimension of the novels under consideration. The elliptical treatment used to evoke Charley Anderson's life signifies that success for the hero is likely to be short-lived since description of the foundations of his growing success is often elided.

As a result of such a technique, as Magny rightly points out, the characters are depicted as 'superficial beings' reduced to the 'most intrinsic (generally economic) determinism', and as such *Big Money*, and Dos Passos' trilogy *USA*, present, albeit implicitly, 'a satire, an accusation of the established order'.[12] In *Days of Hope* the elliptical style, used within a temporal chronology but also in a process similar to that seen in film, transports the reader without transition from land to air battles, from Madrid to Barcelona, from summer to winter and from one character to another. Such treatment contributes to the expression of the various characters' perceptions of the Civil War and the discontinuity of their consciousness.

The importance of vision in the two novels

The eye and its functions is the second essential element of the cinematographic medium, be it at the level of the mechanical camera-eye which 'selects' a frame and the elements of a picture or at the level of the spectator's gaze at the same image. Yet the pre-eminence of the eye and of the look, so crucial to cinema, is also a constitutive feature of novelistic writing. The questions who sees? who is seen? and how? are highly revealing as regards the mode of vision adopted in the various narrative situations which constitute the novel. In the final part of this chapter we shall briefly examine to what extent the importance given to vision in the two novels can contribute to a cinematographic style of writing.

Emphasis on internal focalisation

In both novels the narrative is presented in the third person by an external narrator, but contrary to the classic realist text, the omniscient narrator is practically absent from both these novels. Though there are some instances of external focalisation, especially in *Days of Hope*, these generally operate when one narrator is seen through the eyes of another, and thus support someone else's internal focalisation; as Genette recalls, 'external focalisation with respect to one character could sometimes just as well be defined as internal focalisation through another'.[13] Such is the case when the characters' portraits are described, since these are almost all given through mutual acts of looking or implied looking, as in the passage in which the anarchist leader Puig's biography is evoked:

> Those who had heard of his romantic career were always taken aback when they set eyes on this dwarf-like but sturdy little man, with the predatory face, hook nose and twinkling eyes. The only thing that fitted with his reputation was the black sweater… (*DH* 27)

The type of vision which predominates in the novels, however, is the internal focalisation mode. In *Big Money*, the events of the fictional sequences are shown from a restricted point of view: that of the main character. The narrator appears to be absent inasmuch as the narrative exclusively conveys what the characters feel and perceive. When for instance, at the beginning of the novel, Charley Anderson, on the boat which takes him back to New York, enters the dining room, we read the following:

> The dining saloon smelt of onions and brass polish. The Johnsons were already at the table. Mrs Johnson looked pale and cool. She had on a little grey hat Charley hadn't seen before, all ready to land. Paul gave Charley a sickly kind of smile when he said hello. Charley noticed how Paul's hand was shaking when he lifted the glass of orange juice. His lips were white. (*BM* 5)

It is obvious that what the narrative reveals about the Johnsons is the result of the main character's visual perceptions: Mrs Johnson's small hat, Paul's hands and white lips.

The use of internal focalisation may alternate in the novels. In *Big Money* it can be detected in the progressive passage from an internal to an external mode of vision. In the following example referring to Anderson's mother's funeral, the last sentence, which emphasises Charley's state of mind, reveals the presence of an external vision:

> At the funeral, about half-way through the service, Charley felt the tears coming. He went out and locked himself in the toilet at the garage and sat down on the seat and cried like a child. When they came back from the cemetery, he was in a black mood and wouldn't let anybody speak to him. (*BM* 35)

In *Days of Hope* the various points of view, which account for the famous scene of the pilots' ambulance journey to hospital at the end of the narrative, exemplify constant changes of internal focalisation:

> Through the driver's communicating-window *Scali could see* square patches of the nightbound countryside. Here and there a section of the ramparts of Sagunto showed up, and cypresses, black and massive in the misty moonlight. 'On such a night as this, Jessica...' Yes, there still was happiness in the world. On the stretcher above him, the bomber was groaning at every jolt. There was no room for thoughts in Mireaux's brain. He was in a high fever [...] *The bomber was thinking about his leg.*

Gardet thinking about his face. Gardet had been a great lover.
Magnin was listening to Vargas on the telephone (*DH* 441, my emphasis)

While the internal focalisation of *Big Money* tends to remain fixed within each fictional sequence – since what is known is principally the result of each specific main character's consciousness –, in *Days of Hope* the mode of internal vision, as the last example demonstrates, is primarily variable, migrating from one character to another, and multiple: each character's point of view contributes to the overall view of the situation.

The discrepancy between the external presentation of a third-person narrative and the importance given to fixed or variable internal focalisation serves a diegetic purpose in the two novels. As far as *Big Money* and Dos Passos' *USA* trilogy are concerned, one can endorse Magny's view of the justification for such a writing strategy:

> The use of the 3rd person is justified. John Dos Passos' heroes think of themselves as others could perceive them; their 'inner life' flows spontaneously in a world of ready-made ideas and expressions […] They do not have any 'inner self', there is nothing personal in them that analysis could reach […] The novelist therefore, in order to restore the specific quality of their consciousness, has no right to employ an inner monologue, or any other mode of direct presentation: it would be to mask their inner nothingness […] Our malaise in front of this ambiguous mode of presentation […] is necessary, it makes us understand fortuitously how adulterated these beings are: we would feel their inconsistency, their absolute void if we were facing them.[14]

The choice of a multiple internal focalisation in a third-person narrative, which also gives the novel a cinematographic feel, testifies to the modernity of *Days of Hope* and to the view, prevalent after World War I, that 'reality' does not have an existence in itself, but only in the relation that each of us may have to it.

Evidence of 'visual writing'

Though, as will be seen, the mode of internal vision is not in itself particularly suited to the film medium, especially in the form in which it appears in the fictional sequences of *Big Money*, direct borrowings from cinema techniques in the novels' treatment of vision can nevertheless be found, particularly with the evidence of what we may metaphorically call 'visual writing'.

The borrowing from cinematic vision and the effect of visual writing is blatant in *Big Money* with the already indicated transposition of Dziga Vertov's technique of 'kino eye', developed from 1918 onwards in the wake of the October revolution in Russia in order to make films politically and to advance the theory and practice of cinematographic montage. Vertov's 'kino eye' technique, elaborated in reaction against a cinema of actors, gave priority to a (then as yet unnamed) 'documentary' approach. Its principles rested on the determination 'to decipher life as it is'[15] and to focus on the economic structure of society. The 'kino eye' technique, aimed at showing life 'as found' ('à l'improviste'), 'is not about using the kino-eye for the sake of it' warned Vertov, 'but is about reaching truth, thanks to the kino-eye, reaching the cine-truth.'[16]

The adaptation of the kino-eye technique and of its mechanical effect of camera vision is especially obvious in the 'Newsreels' sequences of *Big Money*. Not only do the title and the nature of these sequences clearly recall Vertov's influence[17] (as do the 'Camera Eye' titles), but the effect of accelerated montage, produced by the amalgamation of their seemingly diverse and unrelated fragments and the swift passage, as if with a mobile camera, from one item to the next, recalls the accelerated montage effect developed as a basis of Vertov's 'kino-eye' technique. And Vertov himself remarked: 'Between the first series of our kino-eye and the cine-eye of Dos Passos [...] many years went by. And however the construction pattern and even the terminology are the same in both works.'[18]

The expression 'visual writing' appears to be particularly apt for *Days of Hope* – though in a different way – and mostly concerns the descriptive mode of the novel. Malraux's writing in *Days of Hope*, but also in his *Man's Estate* (*La Condition humaine*, 1933) is chiefly the result, as we have seen, of an ordering of scenes elliptically presented through alternating characters' points of view, as if a camera was always inside someone's consciousness. Various characteristics usually linked to cinematographic vision can be detected in the descriptive passages of *Days of Hope*, including for instance effects of close ups and tracking movements.

Developed by D.W. Griffith, the close up in film serves mainly to emphasise a significant detail or motif. In *Days of Hope*, often as a result of the characters' internal focalisation, some angles of vision can be assimilated to close up shots. Such is the case, for instance, with the description of an injured man's face on which falls the first drop of rain as Madrid burns:

> Ramos looked down compassionately at the man's quivering cheek [...] *On the corner of his mouth fell the first drop of rain.* (*DH* 316, my emphasis)

or for the pathetic close up vision of a hand grasping the prison bars:

> Hernandez tried to glimpse the men behind the bars on the far side of the yard, facing the window. They were too far away. All he could make out was the *portion of each hand clutching the bars on which the light fell.* Behind the bars, nothing; only darkness. (*DH* 278, my emphasis)

Close up vision can produce subjective and surreal effects in Malraux's text, such as the shadow of a butterfly flickering in the middle of the battlefield:

> Half his [Barca's] men had fallen, and lay where they fell; the other half had got through. Beside him lay the village grocer, dead, *the shadow of a butterfly flickering on his face.* (*DH* 166, my emphasis)

Tracking movements can also be found. For example when Puig, armed with a machine-gun, throws his car onto enemy cannons in a Barcelona street, it is as if a camera were fixed near him, showing the various elements of the scene as they are caught in movement by his vision:

> *Puig watched the gun crews, unsheltered by their bullet-shields, looming larger and larger,* like close-ups on a screen. *A machine-gun opened fire, enlarged in nearness* [...] Handicapped by the shortness of his legs, Puig leant well forward and stamped with all his might on the accelerator [...] A cramp in his left foot, his fingers knotted on the wheel, rifle barrels jabbing the windscreen, the submachine-gun roaring down his ears – *houses and trees turned a somersault – veering, the pigeons all changed colour* – The Negus shouted something... He recovered consciousness to find the Revolution in full swing, the 18-pounders captured. (*DH* 31, my emphasis)

The intertextual impact of the cinematographic medium thus seems undeniable in both novels and, besides the many allusions to the world of film, is particularly evident in the discontinuous form given to the novels by the fragmented treatment of narrative temporality, cross-cutting and elliptical montage effects, and the descriptive treatments reminiscent of camera vision, as in some sequences of *Big Money* or in some specifically cinematic angle of vision devices in *Days of Hope*.

Paradoxically however, the more blatantly cinematographic of the two novels would appear to be the one less suitable for adaptation as a film. The tetraptych (four-part) composition of *Big Money*, with extra-diegetic sequences framing the main fictional sections, would probably need the recourse to several screens, as in Abel Gance's *Napoleon*, in order to render the complexity of the text. Similarly, the use of the equivalent of a subjective camera, through the internal focalisation of several alternating characters in the novel to express a multiple view of reality, would also be confusing for a potential viewer.

As for *Days of Hope*, Malraux here plays with scenes in the manner of an Eisenstein:[19] the alternation between action and reflective scenes and the parallelism between them recall the montage of some of Eisenstein's film sequences. Though the narrative of *Days of Hope* may appear the more easily adaptable to cinema because of its overall chronological continuity, it is nevertheless interesting to note that when Malraux, who remained a keen film enthusiast all his life, tried to make a film of *Days of Hope* in 1938-39 entitled *Sierra de Teruel*, he only adapted the third part of the novel (entitled 'Hope'), and one can imagine that the use of multiple subjective points of view would indeed be rather difficult to sustain in a film. Such difficulties for filmic adaptation would seem to confirm Zéraffa's view, according to which the borrowings of film techniques would serve primarily to reinforce the specificity of novelistic writing,[10] and as such would signal the advent of a *new* way of writing.

One would however argue that with this kind of 'cinematographic writing', one is not only dealing with the convergence of two arts, as Magny[21] preferred to see it, but primarily with the interrelation and cross-fertilisation between two art forms. Rather than using cinema to enhance literature, as Zéraffa suggests or as avant-garde French novelists and film-makers of the Nouveau Roman / New Novel of the

'50s (such as Alain Robbe-Grillet and Marguerite Duras) went on to do,[22] the choice of 'cinematographic writing' in Dos Passos' and Malraux's novels reveals rather the avant-garde spirit of the modernist period of the 1930s, characterised by a sense of total relatedness of things and translated by the creative impulse of cross-fertilisation among all the arts. These novels forcefully exemplify, as far as is textually possible, Raymond Williams' observation according to which '[a] key element in both Modernism and the avant-garde was a deliberate running-together, cross-fertilisation, even integration of what had been seen hitherto as different arts'.[23]

ND_NOTES TO CHAPTER XI

1. All references to *Big Money* (New York: Queens House Larchmont (limited edition)) and to *Days of Hope* (London: Penguin, 1968) will use this format. Hereafter respectively referred to in the study as *BM* and *DH*.

2. Michel Zéraffa, *Personne et personnage: l'évolution esthétique du réalisme romanesque en Occident de 1920 à 1950* (Paris: Klinksieck, coll. esthétique, 1969), p.96 (my translation).

3. Christian Metz, *Langage et cinéma* (Paris: Larousse, 1971).

4. Gérard Genette, *Narrative Discourse* (Oxford: Blackwell, 1980).

5. By narrative, we understand here the signified or narrative content which Genette refers to as story, as opposed to the term 'narrative' as used for 'the signifier, statement, discourse or narrative text itself.' (ibid., p.27).

6. Claude-Edmonde Magny, *L'Age du roman américain* (Paris: Seuil, 1948), p.68 (my translation).

7. ibid., pp.140-41 (my translation).

8. Christiane Moatti, *L'Espoir de Malraux* (Paris: Hatier, Profil d'une œuvre, 1996), p.51 (my translation).

9. ibid., p.53 (my translation).

10. Magny, op.cit. p.62 (my translation).

11. Susan Hayward, *Key Concepts in Cinema Studies* (London: Routledge, 1996), p.81.

12. Magny, op.cit. p.136 (my translation).

13. Genette, op.cit. p.191.

14. Magny, op.cit. pp.72-73 (my translation).

15. Dziga Vertov, *Articles, journaux, projets* (Paris: 10/18, 1972), p.95 (my translation).

16. ibid., p.180 (my translation).

17. Vertov was in charge of the first cinematographic newsreels of the Soviet government and strove to use the camera to develop what he called 'cine-writing'.

18. Vertov, op.cit. p.228 (my translation). Vertov continues: 'They accuse me of having corrupted Dos Passos in contaminating him with the 'kino eye', whereas he could, so they say, have been a good writer. Others reply that without the 'kino eye' we would not even know who Dos Passos is.' (p.229) (my translation).

19. Malraux collaborated with Eisenstein in 1934 in an attempt to adapt *Man's Estate* (*La Condition humaine*) for the screen. He was later to freely adapt the novel under the title *Sierra de Teruel* (1938).

20. Michel Zéraffa: 'Dos Passos interprets filmic techniques in order to reinforce and to emphasise the specificity of the novel.' (op.cit. p.95) (my translation).

21. Magny, op.cit. p.109 (my translation).

22. As Marie-Claire Ropars-Wuilleumier stresses: 'Impulsés tous deux par la provocation

de Resnais, Duras et Robbe-Grillet ont tous deux obéis à cette loi de l'alternance: passer par le cinéma pour en revenir à la littérature; et se tenir, en littérature, dans la mémoire ou le projet de son détour cinématographique.' ('Both influenced by Resnais' provocation, Duras and Robbe-Grillet both responded to the same law of alternation: to work with cinema in order to come back to literature; and to live, in literature, with the memory or the project of its cinematic *detour*') (my translation). See 'Note sur l'intervalle du cinéma et de la littérature chez Alain Robbe-Grillet', *L'Esprit créateur*, Summer 1990, vol.xxx, no.2, p.38.

23. Raymond Williams, *The Politics of Modernism* (London: Verso, 1999), p.70.

CHAPTER XII

Contact and the Deweyan Local:
The Evolution of William Carlos Williams'
'American Critical Attitude'

Eric White

Eric White's doctoral research at the University of Cambridge (UK) focuses on the 'little' magazine's contribution to the development of American Modernist literature. Previous research includes the impact of degenerationist discourse on the prose and poetry of William Carlos Williams, and the continuity between George Oppen's 1930s and 1960s poetry.

> We do not seek to 'transfer the centre of the universe' here. We seek only contact with the local conditions which confront us. We believe that in the perfection of that contact is the beginning not only of the concept of art among us but the key to the technique also.
>
> William Carlos Williams[1]

William Carlos Williams concluded the first issue of *Contact* magazine with these words. Thus, in December 1920, *Contact* added its voice to the host of little magazines that served as the principal forum for public debate in the early twentieth-century American literary scene. In addition to the submissions that *Contact* attracted from figures who were to play a prominent role in the development of Modernist poetry – Marianne Moore, Ezra Pound and Wallace Stevens among them – the journal provides an indispensable record of Williams' critical maturation. Unfortunately, the magazine has remained little more than a footnote in studies of American Modernism and biographical accounts of Williams. This essay is a component of my ongoing research on *Contact*, its network of related little magazines, and American Modernism; its purpose is to raise *Contact* to the level of a major Modernist work, on a par with *Spring and All* as a statement of Williams' poetics.

My project has enabled me to trace the remarkable confluence of interests that led to Williams', co-editor Robert McAlmon's, and painter Marsden Hartley's prefatory discussions in *The Little Review* and *The Dial*. In their letters and articles, *Contact*'s editors and Hartley found themselves formulating a unique approach to contemporary American art and criticism that would require a new print forum for development. *Contact*'s editorial policy included criticism and content that concerned both the literary and the visual arts, which set it apart from the popular Chicago journal *Poetry* and broadened the scope of *Others*' format.[2] This prospect was not unique in itself: *The Dial, The Little Review, Broom*, and *transition* offered similar range of work and criticism in a more professional package. What *Contact* would offer the public was a mode of thought, a '*Contact* context' if you will, in which the proliferation of modern art and writing might be viewed.

Directed by the much-reiterated avant-garde injunction to 'make it new', Williams' and McAlmon's little magazine advocates the realisation of a highly individualised relationship with the artist's immediate environs. This chapter will focus on Williams' attempt to awaken a sense of local critical awareness in American artists; in particular, the importance of American philosopher John Dewey's article 'Americanism and Localism' to Williams' (and *Contact*'s) evolving literary model will be discussed. Williams' intertextual exploration of Deweyan localism and its implications for the American avant-garde will be examined through a discussion of his essay 'A Matisse', which investigates the possibility of applying localist criticism to 'imported' art. This dialogue between American and 'foreign' locales is elaborated through Williams' study of Rex Slinkard and Kenneth Burke, culminating in his pivotal 1921 essay 'Yours, O Youth'. In this piece, Williams articulates *Contact*'s desire to foster an 'American critical attitude'.

By tracing the growth of this critical vector from Williams' first interaction with Dewey's work, I hope to reveal the complexities and nuances of the magazine's directive. Primarily, I will establish that *Contact*'s localist paradigm does not, as has often been assumed, imply a rejection of or hostility to international artistic advances. By incorporating Deweyan doctrine, Williams and his magazine did not seek to 'transfer the centre of the universe' to the New York scene; rather, *Contact* advocates the foundation of a cognisant centre from which 'the universal' might be understood.

When *Contact* first appeared, its editors hoped to present a third option to the American artist: the maudlin sentiment characteristic of the regionalist movements that *Poetry* fostered seemed technically inert to Williams and McAlmon; yet the technical prowess exhibited by the American exiles (Ezra Pound and T.S. Eliot in particular) seemed overly dependent on a 'modern traditionalism' that 'relates literature to literature, and largely overlooks the relation of literature to reality – age, age-qualities, and environment'.[3] *Contact*'s editors proposed that it was possible to apply a technical vigour to the American artist's own localities and achieve a more authentic work of art than that of the expatriate who rejected (or ignored) his or her place of origin. Their assumptions about authentic artistic expression are founded on the supposition that an apprehension of one's locality, creatively expressed, could assume universal standards of achievement without relying on 'smearing a lick of borrowed culture over so many pages'.[4]

Contact began with a reckless flurry of assertions made in this spirit. McAlmon's inaugural editorial is a frenzied piece that indirectly attacks T.S. Eliot's 'Tradition and the Individual Talent'.[5] However, McAlmon's careless rhetoric and unsupported conclusions render the article more confusing than constructive.

Williams' 'Further Announcement' seems similarly hurried, but his editorial attains a focus that is absent in McAlmon's piece and provides a more coherent introduction to the magazine's editorial policies. Wisely, Williams' first 'announcement' is to state the evolutionary nature of *Contact*'s goals. The section carries a slightly apologetic tone, which is probably in reference to the magazine's opening editorial and cheap production values.[6] Thus, in a phrase that foreshadows the reiterated 'beginnings' of *Spring and All*, Williams acknowledges that 'we have nothing to show but a beginning'.[7]

McAlmon's insistence that *Contact*'s editors and contributors would 'be American because we are of America' is also subjected to a qualification: Williams warns that 'no one need expect [*Contact*] to publish his things simply because they happen to have been written in the United States.' Rather, he maintains, *Contact*'s first priority is to provide a place 'for native work in verse, fiction, criticism, or whatever is written', provided that it demonstrates 'the essential contact between words and the locality that breeds them, *in this case* America' (my emphasis). By implementing this selective editorial policy, Williams proposed that *Contact* 'would limit [its] effort not only to give it force but to give it universality'.[9]

The limitation of effort that Williams describes might be more accurately expressed as a localisation of effort. Throughout *Contact*'s publishing run, Williams and McAlmon continually stress the importance of a critical and artistic focus that demonstrates a 'contact with local conditions', a focus that they feel is necessary to communicate 'extraordinary experience'.[10] This localist emphasis figures prominently in *Contact*'s critical development, and the editors' apprehension of the concept owes a great deal to an article by John Dewey, which appeared in *The Dial* in June 1920, six months before the first issue of *Contact*.[11] In 'Americanism and Localism', Dewey brought to coherent form a number of issues concerning American identity and art that Williams, McAlmon and Hartley had been developing over the past few years. Dewey thus provided an excellent base point from which Williams could expand the critical views that he had begun to address in his earlier *Little Review* articles.

Dewey begins his piece by differentiating between America as a national entity and the United States as a 'loose collection of houses, of streets, of neighbourhoods, villages, farms, towns' – in other words, as a collection of localities.[12] Localism, then, is quite distinct from Americanism; but, he argues, perhaps it shouldn't be. For Dewey, the negotiation of these two American identities is best examined in the pages of local newspapers. As an example, he notices that newspapers which mirror their community's 'intense consciousness' of internal activities often make an earnest effort to foreground the national news they carry. Dewey maintains, however, that 'somehow all this wears a thin and apologetic air. The very style of the national news reminds one of his childhood text-book in history'. By comparison, the local news is treated 'with chuckle and relish'.[13]

The newspaper medium, then, is viewed as most successful (and useful) when it absorbs itself in the forces of its locality. The same can be said, Dewey argues, for verse and prose fiction. He acknowledges that regional short story writers had made some advances in this regard, but had 'hardly got beyond what is termed local colour'.[14] This argument parallels Williams' complaint about the 'prairie muses' and regionalist poets who 'do conventional ditties [...] taking in the ready scene of the place, and whose poetry is judged excellent by the 'connoisseurs' because it is so charming'.[15] Hence, when Williams joins Dewey in advocating the value of American artists' own localities, he rejects any association that localism might have with quaintness, regionalism, or 'local colour'. Dewey notes the shortcomings of exploiting such tropes when he asserts that 'a locality exists in three dimensions. It has a background and also extensions'.[16]

Williams and McAlmon sought modern art and criticism that paid attention to these three-dimensional backgrounds and extensions. Their model is strongly influenced by Dewey's notion that 'we are discovering that the locality is the only universal [...] when the discovery sinks a little deeper, the novelist and dramatist [and painter/poet, as Williams would add] will discover the localities of America as they are, and no one will need to worry about the future of American art'.[17] By extending this line of thought, Dewey implies that the American *identity* could be enhanced if it acknowledged the diversity of the collection of localities that comprise the USA, rather than concentrating on a forced sense of unity. Dewey's article is unclear about exactly how such awareness could be attained, or promoted, on a national scale; his interest in the periodical, however, suggests that the answer is somehow connected to the medium. Were enough editors to acknowledge the forces behind their locality and promote the sort of work that represented those strengths, perhaps a revolution in the 'national' conception of American identity could be effected, starting at the community level. Possibly inspired by Dewey's estimation of the periodical as an instrument, Williams and McAlmon would try to bring these ideas into contact with their own locality by beginning their magazine modestly at a grassroots level.

The *Contact* model, then, relies to a large extent on the development of an artistic apprehension of the Deweyan local. Williams attempts a practical application of this interpretative framework in his prose exercise 'A Matisse', a study of Henri Matisse's painting 'The Blue Nude' that appeared in the second issue of *Contact*.[18] The essay is difficult because of its elliptical reflexivity. It is best appreciated as an aesthetic exercise that explores the possibilities offered by sensual and cerebral contact with the artist's locality. Williams crafts a mobile of localities in transit, from Matisse, his location, and his subject, to Williams, Williams' country, and Williams' subject. He begins by reconstructing the moment of Matisse's creative act in an American gallery: 'On the french grass, in that room of Fifth Ave., lay that woman who had never seen my own poor land'.[19] Throughout the essay, Williams consistently capitalises 'Fifth Ave' but leaves 'french' uncapitalised, so indicating the primacy that he ascribes to his own location and perspective. In this manner, Williams reconfigures Matisse's work to represent a renewed perception of the painter's subject in America.

Williams is careful to designate the location of each participant involved in the production of 'The Blue Nude'. Matisse, the creator, is linked with the sun that permeates the place of creation. The artist's gaze is compared with the sun's rays as his subject 'lay in the sunlight of the man's easy attention', while 'his eye and the sun [...] made day over her'.[20] The activity of the sun and the artist are depicted comparatively, but separately. As the piece develops, the sun that had 'entered his head in the colour of sprays of flaming palm leaves' is finally made indistinguishable from the artist. The union is suggested as Williams imagines the subject entering the 'fullness of [Matisse's] knowledge… as into the eye of the sun himself', and as the essay concludes, the subject 'smiles at the sun', completing the union.[21]

Williams engages in a kind of doubling in 'A Matisse', which depends upon the participants who constitute the scene functioning as a collective aware of its various physical and aesthetic spaces. The sun is invested with artistic ability while the painter is joined to the source of life and sight; as the sun illuminates his scene, so the artist illuminates his canvas – the two function as one in their portrayal of the subject. And it is the painted subject through whom Williams apprehends the locality of the scene: 'She had chosen the place to rest and he painted her resting, with interest in the place she had chosen'. Under these conditions, the woman 'lay in this spot [...] not like Diana or Aphrodite but with better proof than they of regard for the place she was in'.[22] In this reconstruction, Williams affords the nude primacy over classical models by virtue of *her* awareness of her locality: she is *made* more beautiful because she completes the scene with that awareness. For the writer, the artist, the subject, and their place are united with the synthesising capability of their local imaginations.

Williams thus parallels the creative representation of a specific aesthetic domain in painting with the same process in literature through his use of a shared subject. However, Williams must access and invoke his apprehension of the local through the work of a foreign artist – it is almost as though the writer has come full circle. Williams acknowledges this problem by ending 'A Matisse' much as it began, but with one significant change: 'In the french sun, on the french grass in a room on Fifth Ave., a french girl lies and smiles at the sun *without seeing us*' (my emphasis). The scene is unmistakably French; and yet 'she came to America', to a room on Fifth Avenue where Williams could view Matisse's picture of her and be infused with the painting's evocation of its locality. Williams' experience teaches him that 'no man in my country has seen a woman naked and painted her as if he knew anything except that she was naked'; furthermore, he adds that 'no woman in my country is naked except at night.' In this manner, 'A Matisse' laments America's residual puritan streak while suggesting that the painter's vision of and the subject's ease in their shared locality is unrepeatable in America. However, Williams does not conclude the piece there; at the end of the essay proper, under a succession of dashes, appear two slogans:

> John Dewey:-
> We are discovering that the local is the only universal.
>
> Maurice Vlaminck:-
> Intelligence is international, stupidity is national, art is local.[23]

Williams' selection of these quotations is perhaps the best indication of his motivation for writing 'A Matisse', and moreover, of the motivations that laid the foundations for *Contact*. The Dewey quotation emphasises the *discovery* of the local, and Williams had certainly accessed this theme from the closing paragraph of 'Americanism and Localism'. Dewey concludes his article with the assertion that 'the beginning of the exploring spirit is in the awakening of criticism and of sympathy'.[24] The present participles here are highlighted in 'discovering', the word picked out in the citation that Williams chose.

Both Dewey and Williams call for their readers' *active* involvement in their own locality to awaken their sense of identity, be it artistic or critical, visual or literary. In fact, Williams hints that a developed identity requires a multidisciplinary appreciation of the local. Williams, then, views intertextuality as a tool with which to apprehend the inherent diversity of a given locality, and thus as an important dimension of accomplished 'local art'. Perhaps the reader could strengthen his or her identity by making critical connections between representative works of art in different media. Following this line of thought, the preoccupation with 'national stupidity' could be challenged, local art could become internationally intelligent, 'and no one would need to worry about the future of American art'.[25] This, of course, is taking the argument to an extreme. But the reader does get the sense that Williams is attempting to stir something within his audience, to find ways to infuse them with the workings of a mind at one with its locality.

Aware of *Contact*'s localist model, Hartley had brought the artwork and letters of a recently deceased Western American artist named Rex Slinkard to the editors' attention. McAlmon and Williams included reprintings of Slinkard's letters in *Contact*, to which (along with his photograph and four of his paintings) almost half of the third issue was devoted. In 'Yours, O Youth', Williams remarks that Slinkard's letters provide 'evidence of the man's critical attitude toward his art of painting; for this reason [the letters] have a distinct literary value.'[26] Furthermore, they present 'the unironic, unbent vision of youth' that achieves 'a full release without sacrifice of intelligence'.[27] Williams imagines Slinkard as a young man at the peak of his receptive abilities, but who possesses the training to express himself credibly and with full apprehension of his locality. This capacity, Williams asserts, makes Slinkard 'singularly American'; or, more accurately, what Williams hoped would become identified as 'American'.[28]

Williams uses his discussion of Rex Slinkard as a springboard to begin a clarification of *Contact*'s goals, which had been rehearsed in his 1919 *Little Review* articles. Finally, he declares, it is 'the American critical attitude' that *Contact* seeks to establish, and Williams recognises Kenneth Burke, not Slinkard, as the American writer whose work best represents this 'attitude'.[29] While Williams prizes the localist qualities that Slinkard's letters possess, they are 'very young', and though governed by an aesthetic sensibility and obvious intelligence, the letters lack the craftsmanship of his paintings. Slinkard is, however, established as an ideal base point from which to develop the localist perspective that, for Williams, 'illustrates [...] what we mean by contact'.[30] Employing a structure similar to a *Bildung* narrative, 'Yours, O Youth' traces the advancement of this critical attitude from the perceptions of the deceased youth Slinkard to the rationalised critical acumen of Burke.

Using a Native American dancer as an analogy, Williams implies that Burke's article 'The Armour of Jules Laforgue' represents a critical genius that is able to 'reach a distinguished perfection' without losing its 'environmental individuality'. The attainment of such a talent is only possible, he contends, when the 'detail of [...] local contacts [is] consciously noted' and used to the artist's and/or critic's advantage.[31] Williams' emphasis on the *conscious* exploitation of a localist critical awareness is a significant component of his praise for Burke, and it is this reflexive awareness that Williams finds lacking in Slinkard. Williams is satisfied that Burke's article has made an intellectual progression that retains the vitality of Slinkard's localist interaction. Thus, Williams has found in (or projected on) Burke the American critical attitude that had inspired his essay on 'The Blue Nude': an evaluative intelligence that can recreate international genius 'for our special world'.[32] Williams also implies that Burke has apprehended the principles of the critical *locus*, a concept that he had been developing since 'A Matisse' and which would be tentatively resolved in the fourth issue of *Contact*.

'Yours, O Youth' had reiterated Williams' position that *Contact*'s localist critical model did not constitute a rejection of imported art or advocate the transference of 'the centre of the universe' to America. Williams' article 'Comment' in *Contact*'s 'Advertising Number' continues to clarify the magazine's position on the relationship between the American artist and the international avant-garde. In this essay, he supports the position originally formulated by McAlmon's introductory article, which claims that *Contact* 'will adopt no aggressive or inferior attitude toward 'imported thought' or art'.[33] McAlmon's editorial vector remained consistent through subsequent reiterations by himself and Williams, and yet surprisingly, *Contact*'s localist model for American art was repeatedly misinterpreted by its readership.

Even critics cannot resist emphasising the polemics of *Contact*'s localism. For example, while Dickran Tashjian offers a well-balanced and insightful (if brief) treatment of the *Contact* project in *William Carlos Williams and the American Scene 1920 - 1940*, he asserts that because Williams (and *Contact*) 'consistently gave the local a geographic designation', the magazine's ambition 'implied contrast, if not outright opposition, to Europe'.[34] Although it is clear that Williams and McAlmon wanted to challenge the American *subservience* to European schools of thought, Williams' article 'Comment' reaffirms his magazine's position that the American artist 'should acquaint himself with everything pertaining to his wish that he can gather from European sources'.[35] As a final clarification of Williams' stance on this issue, 'Comment' openly applauds the European avant-garde's achievement of a critical '*locus*', which is represented in works such as 'The Blue Nude' and James Joyce's *Ulysses*. If American artists are to achieve works of equal importance, Williams insists, an intellectual exchange predicated upon the equality and validity of each participant's locus must be established. As he explains at the close of 'Comment',

> [t]o bring to America the work of Picasso or de Gourmont, the first thing to do is to establish our own position by thorough knowledge of our own locality, thus giving the foreign work a place in which to arrive. This is the opportunity of the creative artist.[36]

This statement encapsulates Williams' long-standing desire for a renewed dialogue between the critical and artistic modes of expression. Note, though, how the focus of his discussion has shifted from the critic that he exemplifies in 'Yours, O Youth' to the creative artist in 'Comment'. The essay continues Williams' practice of compressing and refining the arguments presented in previous issues of *Contact*, and this time, he emphasises the artist's importance in establishing an authentic American locus. 'Comment' continues to stress the exchange of ideas across the arts, across the continents, and across the barrier between artist and critic. In 'Comment', Williams explicitly challenges the American arts community to cultivate a fertile interaction between artist and critic through a shared adoration of the 'gods of [their own] locality'; for the purposes of 'Comment', the primary responsibility is located with the artist, whereas 'Yours, O Youth' had assigned that responsibility to the critic.[37]

In 'Comment', however, Williams does not examine any artist in particular, and there is a sense of fatigue that pervades the article. 'Comment' seems burdened with Williams' continued defence of his magazine's editorial position, discouragement with its unpopularity, and possibly, the crumbling of the *Contact* scene that he hoped would replace his association with *Others*.[38] Williams' sharp reproach of American periodical literature in the penultimate paragraph hangs over the article's optimistic conclusion, as does the lack of any one writer who exemplifies *Contact*'s aesthetic. In short, 'Comment' lacks the fire of Williams' previous articles. At the close of its fourth issue, it appeared that *Contact*'s localism had ceased to be a challenge – so Williams bequeathed the challenge to new talent.

Although there would be a fifth issue in June 1923, the fourth issue of *Contact* was the last instalment of its editorial discussions of Deweyan localism. The reasons for this, and for the downcast tone of Williams' 'Comment', can be traced to the departure of Robert McAlmon following his marriage to the British heiress Annie Winifred Ellerman, who is better known by her pen name Bryher. McAlmon's expatriation to Paris must have been a painfully ironic conclusion to *Contact*'s localist phase. With the help of the Ellerman family fortune, McAlmon's Paris-based Contact Editions would launch the career of Ernest Hemingway and publish Williams' most influential and 'American' modernist work *Spring and All* in 1923. So the *Contact* project had not only provided Williams with the localist infrastructure that is imbricated in *Spring and All*, it also provided him with the means with which to publish it. It is therefore a compound irony that Modernist research has largely ignored the contribution of Williams' 'home-made' magazine, while *Spring and All* (which was published in France and had similarly low circulation at the time of publication) is generally regarded as the turning point in Williams' critical and artistic development.

I would argue that the time has come for a re-examination of *Contact*'s importance to the American incarnation of Modernist poetics. By examining the evolution of Williams' American critical attitude and its Deweyan localist foundations, I have attempted to demonstrate an aspect of the contribution that Williams' work in *Contact* made not only to his aesthetic maturation, but to a distinctively American embodiment of Modernism. I have also sought to draw attention to *Contact*'s role as an interdisciplinary forum, whose editorial policy fostered an appreciation for, and acknowledged a debt to, art forms other than literature. Using *Contact*'s comparative approach, Williams demonstrates that international artistic advances had immediate relevance to his magazine's intended audience, and crucially, that American artists, working in and with their own localities, had an equally important contribution to make to the international avant-garde movement: 'intelligence is international', but art, after all, 'is local'.

To conclude, it should be noted that there has not been a complete reprinting of *Contact* since 1967. Until this situation is remedied, it will continue to prove challenging to appreciate the work as a whole; however, the effort is well rewarded. While *Spring and All* is rightly acknowledged as the fullest flowering of Williams' American modernist model, one must look to its rough beginnings if one is to appreciate the deep-rooted *locus* from which the work has grown.

NOTES TO CHAPTER XII

Notes to Chapter XII

1. William Carlos Williams, 'Further Announcement', *Contact* 1 (Dec. 1920), p.10.
2. Williams edited *Others*, a little magazine founded by Alfred Kreymborg in 1915, in July 1916 and July 1919.
3. Robert McAlmon, 'Modern Antiques', *Contact* 2 (Jan. 1921), 9-10, p.10.
4. Williams, op.cit. (1920), p.10.
5. Robert McAlmon, 'Contact', *Contact* 1 (Dec. 1920), p.1. Numerous reprintings of this article and the 'Further Announcement' on page 10 attribute the authorship of both works to Williams. However, given the stylistic differences of the two articles, it is more likely that Paul Mariani's assertion in *William Carlos Williams: A New World Naked* (New York: McGraw-Hill, 1981: p.175) is correct, and Williams only wrote the second article.
6. The first two issues of *Contact* were mimeographed on low-grade foolscap paper provided by Williams' father-in-law, and were collated and stapled by one of McAlmon's associates.
7. Williams, op.cit. (1920), p.10.
8. McAlmon, op.cit. (1920), p.1.
9. Williams, op.cit. (1920), p.10.
10. ibid.
11. John Dewey, 'Americanism and Localism', *The Dial*, Vol. LXVII (June 1920), pp.684-88.
12. ibid., p.684.
13. ibid., p.685.
14. ibid., p.687.
15. William Carlos Williams, 'A Maker', *The Little Review*, Vol. VI. No. 4 (Aug. 1919), 37-38, p.37.
16. Dewey, op.cit. p.687.
17. ibid., pp.687-88.
18. William Carlos Williams, 'A Matisse', *Contact* 2 (Jan. 1921), p.7.
19. ibid.
20. ibid.
21. ibid.
22. ibid.
23. ibid.
24. Dewey, op.cit. p.688.
25. ibid., p.688.
26. William Carlos Williams, 'Yours, O Youth', *Contact* 3 (Spring 1921), 14-16, p.15.
27. ibid.

28. ibid.
29. ibid.
30. ibid., p.16.
31. ibid., p.15.
32. ibid.
33. McAlmon, op.cit. (1920), p.1.
34. Dickran Tashjian, *William Carlos Williams and the American Scene 1920 - 1940* (Whitney Museum of Art, 1978), p.53.
35. William Carlos Williams, 'Comment', *Contact* 4 (Fall 1921), 18-19, p.18.
36. ibid., p.19.
37. ibid., p.18.
38. For a biographical account of Williams' experience with *Contact*, see Chapter Four in Mariani. Mariani's study emphasises the difficulty that Williams had in producing the periodical, and cites the editor's reaction to *Contact*'s poor sales: 'I am nearly crazy with paying attention to halves and quarters (not dollars!) – broken pieces of men that have me sick trying to patch up something out of the mess' (p.175).

CHAPTER XIII

'Connect-I-Cut': Hanging on the Telephone with Kafka, Woolf, Proust and Joyce

Garin V. Dowd

Garin V. Dowd is Lecturer in English at Thames Valley University in London. His areas of interest include the work of Samuel Beckett, contemporary French philosophy (especially Deleuze and Guattari), Literary Modernism and aspects of French cinema. His publications include articles on the work of James Joyce, Samuel Beckett, Maurice Blanchot and George Oppen in *Angelaki: Journal of the Theoretical Humanities*, *The Journal of Beckett Studies*, *Samuel Beckett Today/Aujourd'hui* and *Forum for Modern Language Studies*.

> In the beginning the telephone, yes, at the beginning of the telephone call, in the beginning, some telephone call.
>
> Jacques Derrida[1]
>
> Well yes, here I am in 'connect, I cut,' as the little one said from the empty fortress.
>
> Jacques Derrida[2]

Intertextuality as telephonics? Hearsay? Or *ouï-dire* according to Jacques Derrida.[3] For the latter, to speak is already to have said *yes* in response to the injunction to speak; it is to have acceded to an imperative, and specifically, to a *telephonic* imperative. Before exploring the intertextual cluster – formed by the four modernist authors named in my title – centred on moments of telephony, I wish to attest to something of the intertextual matrix of this article and the way in which it itself is a response to a call, and not only to a call for papers.

Writing in 1979 Jacques Derrida refers to a conversation between him (or his epistolary surrogate in 'Envois') and a graduate student named 'Metaphysics'.

> Refound here the American student ... the one who was looking for a thesis subject (comparative literature), I suggested to her something on the telephone in the literature of the 20th century (and beyond), starting with, for example, the telephone lady in Proust or the figure of the American operator, and then asking the question of the effects of the most advanced telematics on whatever would still remain of literature.[4]

In effect Derrida's aside is typically prescient, given the proliferation of responses which recent years have witnessed to precisely the question of 'the effects of the most advanced telematics on whatever would still remain of literature'. It is not my purpose here to pursue this latter question as such. Rather, I wish to allow to take place in this piece, *on this paper*, the noisy exchange between several Modernist texts *on the telephone*. This exchange should occur within, and it was in fact Derrida's suggestion to the student known in 'Envois' as 'Metaphysics', the field known (and named, parenthetically, by Derrida) as comparative literature.

Telephony, as Derrida suggests, predates the invention of the telephone itself. Literary evidence is easy to come by, but none seems, to my mind, more explicitly demonstrative of the 'precession' of telephony than the following quotation from Sheridan Le Fanu's story 'Green Tea' (published in serialised form in 1869 and later in the collection *In a Glass Darkly*):

> Dear Dr. Hesselius. It is here. You had not been an hour gone when it returned. It is speaking. It knows all that has happened. It knows everything – it knows you and is frantic and atrocious. It reviles. I send you this. It knows every word I have written – I write. This I promised, and therefore write, but I fear very confused, very incoherently. I am so interrupted, disturbed.[5]

What disturbs the distraught Rev. Jennings is, it transpires, a small, malevolent, and eloquent monkey, an aberration or visitation which may or may not be brought on by overindulgence in green tea. The monkey not only disturbs the Reverend in his prayers but also interrupts and disrupts his writing, his act of inscription. Which would make Le Fanu's tale especially receptive to Derrida's explanation of the modality of telephony:

> So, a telephonic interiority: for before any appliance bearing the name 'telephone' in modern times, the telephonic *techne* is at work within the voice, multiplying the writing of voices without any instruments, as Mallarmé would say, a mental telephony, which, inscribing remoteness, distance, *différance*, and spacing [*espacement*] in the *phone*, *at the same time* institutes, forbids, *and* interferes with the so-called monologue [Derrida's emphasis].[6]

However I am concerned here less with the alleged precession of telephony, than with its presentation in Modernist literature. (That having been said, it will not be so easy to dispel the question of precession and the issue of spectrality which it inaugurates.)

At the time of each the texts – by Kafka, Woolf, Proust and Joyce – to which the pages following will turn, the telephone, and the possibilities of communication that it afforded, were not identified in the way they are today. Today, telephone communication is not simply a technological aid in the cheating of geographical distance; rather it must be conceived of as part of a generalised prosthetics (a technosphere imbricated in the biosphere), such that it generates its own virtual space, an *extension*, so to speak, of physical spatio-temporal co-ordinates. This new space is signified for example in the manner in which – in a myriad of types of call – one joins a queue with other callers, a queue which may be controlled by a virtual call service operating in the name of one's bank or other institution.

The generalised prosthetics, of which the telephone is but one emblem, is of course even more emphatically suggested by the mobile phone which itself, despite its alleged mobility, can be thought of as contributing to what Paul Virilio has called the generalised stasis and inertia of our contemporary moment.[7] What better way, after all, of fixing oneself to the spot than by announcing, or broadcasting via one's cellular phone that *I am here*, on the bus, walking down the street, in a queue at the supermarket check-out … stationary?

The spectral intrusion of the *telephoned* voice into the literary is however more complicated than it may first appear. Proust's narrator displays a singular horror before its 'angels'. Kafka is simultaneously intrigued and troubled by this spectrality. Joyce, in *Ulysses*, as Derrida has pointed out, can be said to have written an entirely *telephonic* novel. Woolf, for her part, stages in *To The Lighthouse* a telephonic moment within parentheses which very graphically illustrates certain of the consequences for the remains of literature in the light of telematics, advanced or otherwise.

This article construes itself as a 'switchboard' within Modernism and charges itself with the task of crossing the lines carrying the distinct voices of Kafka, Proust, Woolf and Joyce. It explores what it takes to be the generalised spectrality associated with the telephone in Modernism. In *calling themselves*, in placing the telephonic within the inscribed, these texts, in distinct ways and to varying degrees, are involved in an act of de-scription, a constitutive, purgative and emptying abeyance.

The telephone in the Modernist novel operates as a prosthesis. The written word has appended to it a *techne* which at once *mimes* it, through internal *mise en abîme*, and *mines* it, empties it through its very (constitutive) alterity. That will be the thesis advanced in what remains of this chapter.

Please hold the line.

EX-DIRECTORY: KAFKA

Nowhere is the distance and *différance* of telephonic communication more emphatically staged than in the opening pages of Kafka's *The Castle*. There, in the grand tradition of the Gothic, the protagonist K. finds himself at a remove, in the village which is outside but connected to the eponymous castle, under the shadow of its elevated fortifications, struggling to get *through*.[8] The general opinion of the villagers, we learn, after an inquiry is made via telephone on K.'s behalf and his proposed visit rejected, 'was that K. would get no answer at all' in attempting to make the call himself.[9] K. does however get some response: 'The receiver gave out a buzz of a kind that K. had never before heard on the telephone'. Instead of clear communicative exchange, what K. receives is feedback, the entropic noise of dissonant graftings. The improper:[10]

> It was like the hum of countless children's voices – but not yet a hum, the echo rather of voices singing at an infinite distance – blended by sheer impossibility into one high but resonant sound which vibrated on the ear as if it were trying to penetrate beyond mere hearing.[11]

The problem, quite frequently, and perhaps always, in Kafka, is one of belonging and belongings, of propriety and property, of belonging within the context of a system of bureaucracy and power. The castle is described in terms of an internal connectivity and contiguity (the contiguous offices), from which the protagonist is cut off (more of this connect and cut later).

K. cannot, as it were, get on-line. This fact is a reminder that the task of hooking into a series from which one is blocked is always what falls to Kafka's protagonists. However, more generally, connection with and prolongation of a series, and negotiation or promotion of ellipsis and blockage are, together, another way of approaching the modernist text in comparative literature.

CALL ON LINE 1: WOOLF

The moment of telephony in the modernist novel is also, in a sense other than that exemplified in *The Castle*, one of interference, the implosion of a moment of teletechnology into inscription. The author

Chapter XIII

breaks off from one mode of communication and branches into another. What is most interesting about the moment of telephony in *To the Lighthouse* is that it is deliberately placed in parentheses as if to underline the fact that there is interference. Derrida has alerted us to the link between telephony and brackets. In an interview from 1975 collected in *Points* he asks:

> But how is one to efface or lift the brackets once one begins writing [here and now] anything whatsoever? Writing – already in the tongue – would operate, with regard to immediate adherence… written hooks – dashes, 'parentheses', (quotation marks) – also hook up, by the same redoubled token, with the mother.[12]

It is also, in its way, a very tangible mark of an awareness of the multiplicity of Bergsonian *duration*. In this instance the parenthesis encloses an aside from the point of view of William Bankes:

> ('Nature has but little clay', said Mr. Bankes once, hearing her voice on the telephone … He saw her at the end of the line, Greek, blue-eyed, straight-nosed. How incongruous it seemed to be telephoning to a woman like that […]
> […] what progress … with an hotel which they were building at the back of his house. And he thought of Mrs. Ramsay as he looked at that stir among the unfinished walls […] if it was her beauty merely that one thought of, one must remember the quivering thing, the living thing (they were carrying bricks up a little plank as he watched them), and work it into the picture […] He must go to his work.)
> Knitting the reddish-brown hairy stocking […] Mrs. Ramsay smoothed out what had been harsh in her manner a moment before, raised his head, and kissed her little boy on the forehead. 'Let's find another picture to cut out,' she said.[13]

This passage is an example of the switch – typical of Woolf – from the outward directed thought of Mrs Ramsay to the reverse gaze, from someone else, examining or reflecting upon her (in short *telephoning* her).

Bracketing Mrs Ramsay and playing back the words of William Bankes to her via a kind of internal answering machine, Woolf has Bankes reflect that it is incongruous to be telephoning *to* a woman like this. The very oddity of the preposition here, to our contemporary idiom, highlights the *différance* of the telephone which is contrasted explicitly here with the self-presence and voluminous identity of Mrs Ramsay, whose quivering is contrasted both with the spectrality of the telephonic and the inanimate bricks carried by the builders working on the hotel outside Bankes' window.

This passage is also interesting because it introduces the novel's third image of creation or construction to take the form of a line – the first being the wool with which Mrs Ramsay is knitting a stocking for the lighthouse-keeper's child, the second being the painting awaiting its line which Lily Briscoe is in the process of attempting, while the third, we now discover, is the hotel which Bankes observes in the process of construction outside his window wherein bricks are carried up the vector of a little plank. 'He thought of Mrs Ramsay as he looked at that stir among the unfinished walls'. Within parentheses Mrs Ramsay is conjured and bracketed within the unfinished walls.

This entire section demands attention from the point of view of how time is represented. Outside, before the parenthetical telephone call between Ramsay and Bankes, outside the playback within parentheses on the novel's answering machine, Mrs Ramsay wants to measure the stocking against James' leg. He resists, not wishing to assist his mother in displaying affection for a child other than himself. Then she looks up and in a remarkable reverie contemplates the house, its furniture and the importance in her view of keeping doors closed and windows open – a failure to do this has led she feels to the disintegration of the house and its contents. There is a need to maintain parenthesis, for what, after all, would a closure which allows for opening be, other than a *parenthetical* closure? (I wonder, parenthetically, if I hear in this word a thesis on parenthood, or at the very least, maternity.) Having been distracted by a memory of her Swiss maid, this series of associations is brought to a halt by Ramsay's expression of annoyance at the fact that James will not stand still: 'Stand still. Don't be so tiresome!'[14]

Now between these references to two events – she tries to measure the stocking and James squirms – one would presume little more than a few seconds should have passed. And yet it takes the reader several minutes to get from event one to event two. However it is not just in the interplay of story and discourse that unsettling temporal distortions and aberrations are at work. Within the parenthesis a conversation on the telephone is held, that is to say at once *spoken, reported* and *maintained*.¹⁵ However, what is singularly unclear about this is when the conversation took place. It is possible but by no means certain that it took place some years ago. Thus, while between event one and event two as described above a longer time elapses as we read than elapses in the room itself, in this second example we are propelled to a significantly more radical degree from one time to another, or to the other of time, a sense of oscillation captured well in the French *autrefois*. In the case of the second example there are no signposts which tell us: 'This is Mr Bankes *remembering* a telephone conversation'. The event is simply put within brackets, and the reader left uncertain, having entered the parenthetical enclosure, as to how to locate it in relation to the events in the room, in the space and espacement of Bergson's multiple duration.

Parentheses, then, operate according to a logic of *connect-I-cut*, as the text indicates: 'Let's find another picture to cut out' says Mrs Ramsay to James outside the parenthesis which has just come to a close.

CALL ON LINE 2: PROUST

The spectral recollection of the other which inhabits one and the *incompossible* and divergent temporality (the *autre(s)fois*) which one, by virtue of this fact, inhabits, conspire to render the space and time (container and contained as it were), respectively, incommensurable, the one with the other.¹⁶ Nowhere is this more evident than when Proust's narrator is – albeit reluctantly – on the telephone (that great demon of the *Recherche*).

For Proust's narrator the telephonic network is populated by decidedly demonic deities. The telephone operators are described as 'the Daughters of the Night, the Messengers of the Word, the Deities without form or feature'.¹⁷ The vampiric connotations of 'Daughters of the Night' are far from incidental. Despite the immediacy of telephonic communication – and Kafka was also sensitive to this issue – the exchange is subject to a parasitism (at least as far as the narrator is concerned), a quality which facilitates the emptying of the present, the mutation of 'passing state' into *passage*:

> it seemed to me as though it was already a beloved ghost that I had allowed to lose herself in the ghostly world, and, standing alone before

the instrument, I went on vainly repeating: 'Granny, Granny!', as Orpheus, left alone, repeats the name of his wife.[18]

The narrator's anamnesis is also more generally that which characterises Proust's writing, and clearly it registers what Lyotard has called a 'resistance to the procedures for controlling time'. The *dispositifs* by means of which the *Recherche* explores the status of the subject within the context of a system of communication (amongst which one can identify, for example, the train, the theatre and the telephone) can be said to fall into two categories. They tend to emphasise either a programmatic or a telegraphic element. For instance the letter which the narrator sends to his mother early in the novel ('an exquisite thread was binding us')[19] is programmatic in so far as it projects and manipulates. The theatre in which Berma performs is also a space in which individual perception is arranged, or programmed, by means of architecture. Telegraphic communication, by contrast, is communication from afar, and lacks, in a sense, the intimacy which grounds programming.[20]

In general it is true of the *Recherche* that Proust rarely allows the two to fuse to form what would be a neutralising *teleprogramophony*. Instead, Proust's writing knows how to leave to the event that part which is not reducible to a 'what happened'. This is certainly true when his narrator, and hence his novel, is *on the phone*.

CALL ON LINE 3: JOYCE

Here I do not wish to repeat or simply gloss Derrida's fine reading of Bloom-at-the-telephone in 'Ulysses Gramophone'. However I do wish to tap into that reading to a degree, and to connect it to what has been identified in this paper as the strange spectrality of the telephonic within the modernist text.

Bloom's monologue (problematic though that term be) manifests throughout *Ulysses* a divergent series creating not harmony but dissonance and atonality. This leads Derrida to find in Bloom's interior monologue what he calls 'a telephonic interiority ... the telephonic techne is at work in the voice ... inscribing distance, *différance* and spacing in the *phoné* ... (this) at once institutes, forbids and jams (*brouille*) the so-called monologue'.[21] Branched as it is onto several 'lines' simultaneously, in the interior of Bloom's monologue there is *noise*. The thoughts that a reader might attribute to him are already and in advance worked by this constitutive multiplicity. The multiplicity to which Bloom is host however must be distinguished from that to which the barmaids in the Ormond Bar (scene of Bloom's activity) are receptive. Bloom's multiplicity is *necessary* by contrast to that of the barmaids which is merely *contingent*.[22] Miss Douce's bronzeness, for example, only switches into a multiplicative mode when it enters into contrapuntal relation with that with which it is programmed to converge (harmonise): the bronzeness of Douce fuses with the goldness of Kennedy to form the harmonic 'bronzegold'.

By contrast, Bloom's monologue, owing to the density of connections for which it acts as the 'switchboard', is subject to 'jamming'. Unlike the other ears in the Ormond which act as unproblematic receptors, since they are branched only onto those emitters which will allow the ultimate convergence of the series they each in turn prolong, Bloom is prone to listen with his 'your other ear'. Bloom operates on the basis of intensive *ordinates* which lack self-identity, rather than spatio-temporal co-ordinates which would retain that identity.

One of the many calls heard within the Ormond Bar is that of the sea, a call which can be heard through the sea-shell (which, when held to the ear is after all nothing more, nothing less than a telephone) wielded by Douce, Kennedy and Lidwell:

> And look at the lovely shell she brought.
> To the end of the bar to him she bore lightly the spiked and winding seahorn that he, George Lidwell, solicitor, might hear.
> – Listen! she bade him.
> [...]
> Ah, now he heard, she holding it to his ear. Hear! He heard. Wonderful. She held it to her own and through the sifted light pale gold in contrast glided. To hear.
> Tap.
> Bloom through the bardoor saw a shell held at their ears. He heard more faintly that that they heard, each for herself alone, then each for other, hearing the plash of waves, loudly, a silent roar.
> Bronze by a weary gold, anear, afar, they listened.
> Her ear too is a shell [...]
> The sea they think they hear. Singing. A roar. The blood is it. Souse in the ear sometimes. Well, it's a sea. Corpuscle islands.[23]

While the tympana of 'Sirens' have varying degrees of porosity and sealedness, the ear is only one among many organs of perception and communication encountered. It takes its place among an array of other devices which double, mimic, represent, convey, transfer, repeat or establish a system of *correspondence*. Among these devices are the seashell, the garter, Bloom's writing paper, his blotting pad, the catgut which he winds around his fingers, the mirror in the bar, the tuning fork and the piano. Each of these devices communicates either harmonically or discordantly with the character it annexes, hooks up with or connects to. Each is either part of a harmonic series and therefore converges, or part of a discordant series and diverges from the chapter's fugue.

For both the barmaids and the singers, in the passage quoted above, the sea-shell together with its 'other' voice, 'the plash of waves', function as the site of a pure and unproblematic repetition: 'What are the wild waves saying?' asks Lidwell. For Bloom, however, the relation between Being and representation is more problematic. According to the harmonic model adhered to by Douce, Kennedy and the majority of the others present in the bar, Being and representation ultimately occupy the same place: the sea coincides with its sonic representation. However, according to Bloom's model, 'the ear too is a shell'. The vehicle of representation is confused with the organ of reception. Via this imbrication, a multiplicative modality is introduced to the relation between Being and representation:

> The sea they think they hear. Singing. A roar. The blood is it. Souse in the ear sometimes. Well, it's a sea. Corpuscle islands.[24]

The façade which would retain for the sea and for the listener their respective spatio-temporal co-ordinates is dissolved in Bloom's perspective, and instead the one permeates the other. For Bloom it is not the case of repetition *qua* repetition, but of repetition as other. Interiority is shattered to the profit of an exteriority which undermines the distinction interior-exterior (which distinction is necessary to the prolongation of harmonic accords through the barmaid-singer series).

Unlike the other elastic and vibrating façades/tympana in 'Sirens', Bloom's elastic does not remain intact. While it can 'buzz' and 'twang' like the tuning fork in response to being 'plucked', it emerges from the encounter no longer itself, but fragmented.[25] Clearly, then, the elastic band wielded by Bloom is part of the dissonant series of half-open devices which in annexing or being annexed upset spatio-temporal co-ordinates and self-identity.

But of all the façades-tympana associated with Bloom none perhaps is more crucial than that established by the sheet of writing paper upon which he composes his letter to Martha Clifford. It is here that the crux of 'Sirens' complex system of accords and discords finds its clearest exposition.

Bloom's 'troubled double', his 'your other eye' is annexed via the tympanum of the writing paper to 'that other world' represented by Martha. Via what in effect becomes a porous façade the murmuring Bloom ('Bloom mur: best references') becomes Henry Flower.[26] Thus, folded or *complicated* in the site-of-enunciation-Bloom is the site-of-enunciation-Martha.[27] An actual dissonance is operative. Bloom-as-site-of-enunciation differs from itself: it is an aggregate of folds and intervals, the actual dissonance of which cannot be resolved. Henry cannot be returned unproblematically to Bloom. Bloom's otherness cannot be neutralised (or overridden by being a mere detour to identity and self-presence), which fact is attested to by Bloom blotting his letter in such a way as to prevent it being read, detective-like, from the blotting pad: 'Blot over the other so he can't read. Right Idea prize titbit. Something detective read off blottingpad'.[28]

Which would leave one in the situation of not being able to re-call oneself, of being kept at the other end of the line, in abeyance, and back where we started, with the precession of telephony.

INTERFERENCE: DERRIDA

In one of the many readings of the postcard at the generative centre (the 'Central') of *La Carte postale* depicting Socrates and Plato, Derrida ponders the possibility that Socrates is telephoning and Plato whispering in his ear. What is then posited is a relation, a communication, whereby Freud plugs in to a Platonic 'answering machine' (for what, after all are the *Philebus* or the *Symposium*, if not machines for generating the right Socratic *answers*?).[29] The communication, the text continues, is subject to scrambling and interference (Freud doesn't have enough *credit*). Thus the spectral is released into the communication, and into conversation with Freud: 'the demon speaks to Freud, directly, from the beyond, like his ghost which says to him 'wait', hold on, come back with your spool, don't hang up'.³⁰ Freud is not in this respect unlike the Reverend Jennings of Le Fanu's tale: he is 'terribly interrupted'. However, as Derrida convincingly shows in the section on 'Beyond the Pleasure Principle', through the complex detour of the PRs (both *principe de réalité* and *poste restante*³¹), Freud 're-calls' himself and attempts to stave off the troubling consequences of his own theory. One could argue that Freud locks himself in the hermetic cycle of what Gilles Deleuze and Félix Guattari call the 'paranoid machine'.³²

HANGING UP: GEORGE OPPEN'S '(telephone)'

It is hardly surprising that the modernist text should set itself the task of re-calling itself, of hooking-up with teletechnology, and of countermanding the inscribed by means of parenthetical telephony. That the great modernist authors should take writing into a detour of telephony is to be expected, since their work in different ways is concerned with reflecting upon the nature and the limits of mediation via writing. The staging of the moment of telephony is at once a *mise en abîme* and a way into the articulation of the very problem of spacing, distance and *différance* which characterises the modernist text.

The moment of telephony, the parenthetical moment which puts writing in abeyance, behind the spectre, is at once a moment wherein the text hooks up with an other voice (an *autrefois*, a yesterday and *an other time*) and is un-hooked from itself ('connect, I cut'). The text waits, we wait, interminably. This might begin to describe the effects of the most advanced telephony on what remains of literature, or at least on what remains of the modernist text on the telephone in comparative literature. The poet George Oppen, writing in 1934, is uncannily close to illustrating, microcosmically, the concerns articulated in this paper. In the third of poems grouped under the sequence title 'Drawing', from the collection *Discrete Series* we read:

Written structure,
Shape of art,
More formal
Than a field would be
(existing in it)——
Her pleasure's
Looser;

348

'O———'

'Tomorrow?'———

Successive

Happenings

(the telephone)[33]

Oppen's poem stages the tension between writing as inscription and the inscription of the *telephoned*. The opening line gives 'written structure', while the closing line of the first stanza yields the spacing and opening of "O———". Immediately following, succeeding this, the word 'tomorrow' is hung in the centre of the poem by the hook of its question mark and the further hooks of inverted commas. Below this apparatus (*appareil*) we find seriality in 'Successive' and the event in 'Happenings'. Outside the poem (outside the written structure, but *written* nonetheless) but also plugged into it, its very own technical supplement and prosthetic, we find, open bracket, the telephone, close bracket. *Hang up.*

At the outset I suggested that hooking into a series, achieving adherence, and negotiating or modulating this with regard to discontinuity and blockage were concerns in Modernist literature. Kafka's protagonist is cut off from the series while his letter-writer (in the letters addressed to Milena and Felice) is, as Deleuze and Guattari have shown, caught up in a feedback loop of vampiric 'connect-I-cut', the subject existing only in the spatio-temporal aberration of this distant relation, this distanciating form of relation.

Woolf in *To the Lighthouse* orchestrates a profound meditation on seriality and succession, the blocked line of Lily Briscoe's painting finally released in a moment coterminous with the interruption of the spectral Mrs Ramsay. Proust's narrator is always there, at the telephone, in the sense that his entire being is at the service of involuntary memory to which he can do nothing but accede, and to the call of which he always, in advance, will respond. Finally Bloom, for Derrida the embodiment of a mutant Heideggerian teletechnological *Dasein*, is there in spacing, in telephony, in the intertext. To 'hear' all of this is to proclaim yes, unprepared, automatic, as if ventriloquised by the Other at the end of the line. It is to subscribe to what Derrida, in translation, calls 'hearsay'.

As far as it appears in Modernist literature, then, the telephone is not merely metaphorical, and not always merely a decorative index of modernity. The telephonic, as this article has tried to show, is constitutive. Programming and being programmed from afar, by another voice or site of enunciation and by other texts, by the great skein of voices that is the intertext. It has not been the contention of this paper that the four authors draw upon a common intertextual network; rather it has been my aim to argue that in telephoning themselves each author sets up a kind of feedback loop to a common matrix. That matrix, generative and central, but by the same token always outside, is the telephonic, the great switchboard, the skein of voices.

Concluding, then, in a comparative mode, it would seem that Kafka's fascination with the telephone is part of a larger concern with inscription and in particular with parasitic inscription at a distance and multiplicative interactions of networks of communication. Woolf's *To the Lighthouse* is a remarkable concatenation of lines forming a dense network. At the still centre of the novel lies her bizarre and mesmeric parenthetical telephony, the answering machine which cannot answer back, a little bit of dead in the living. The revenant also comes to haunt Proust's *Recherche*, and once more in the form of a telephoned voice emptying the present, injecting, interrupting with alterity. In a chapter of *Ulysses* which explicitly gestures us towards some (telephone) call, namely that which would lure the sailors to their death, the voice is ultimately that which must be graphed (as in Bloom's letter), the written word 'phoned'.[34]

Hang up.

NOTES TO CHAPTER XIII

Notes to Chapter XIII

1. Jacques Derrida, 'Ulysses Gramophone: Hear Say Yes in Joyce', in Derek Attridge (ed.), *Acts of Literature* (New York and London: Routledge, 1992), p.270.
2. Jacques Derrida, 'Envois', in *The Post Card: From Socrates to Freud and Beyond*, trans. Alan Bass (Chicago: University of Chicago Press, 1987), p.113.
3. The French title of Derrida's paper on Joyce, a contribution to a Joyce Symposium, plays on the homonym oui-dire ('yes-saying') and ouï-dire (hearsay). See Derrida, op.cit. (1992).
4. Derrida, op.cit. (1987), p.204.
5. Sheridan Le Fanu, 'Green Tea', in *In a Glass Darkly* (Oxford: Oxford Worlds Classics), p.34.
6. Derrida, op.cit. (1987), pp.271-72.
7. See for instance Paul Virilio, *Open Sky*, trans. Julie Rose (London: Verso, 1997). Here, taking forward a thesis introduced in previous works, Virilio argues that the 'wired neighbourhood' promotes a generalised stasis, a reluctance to move, a disavowal of displacement. We are witness, Virilio proclaims, to the 'loss of the locomotive body' (p.34), which may result in what he comically describes as an escalation in 'parking accidents' (p.25). One of the most striking visual representations of these phenomena occurs in the opening sequence of Wim Wenders' film *The End of Violence*.
8. Franz Kafka, *The Castle*, trans. Willa and Edwin Muir (London: Vintage, 1999). This is true not only of such novels as *Dracula* but also of postmodern Gothic novels such as Witold Gombrowicz's *Possessed*.
9. Kafka, op.cit. p.26.
10. Gilles Deleuze and Félix Guattari in their study of Kafka:
    'Kafka distinguishes two series of technical inventions: those that tend to restore natural communication by bringing people together (the train, the car, the airplane), and those that represent the vampirish revenge of the phantom, where there is reintroduced 'the ghostly element between people' (the post, the telegraph, the telephone, wireless telegraphy)', in *Kafka: Toward a Minor Literature*, trans. Dana Polan (Minneapolis: University of Minnesota Press, 1986), p.30.
11. Kafka, op.cit. p.26.
12. Jacques Derrida, 'Between Brackets I', in *Points*, ed. Elizabeth Weber (Stanford: Stanford University Press, 1995), p.9.
13. Virginia Woolf, *To the Lighthouse* (Harmondsworth: Penguin, 1992), pp.34-35.
14. ibid., p.33.
15. The dual sense, of being held, i.e. conducted and held in the now (*maintenant*), is what I wish to suggest here.

16. The concept of incompossibility as utilised by the rationalist philosopher Gottfried Wilhelm Leibnitz allows him to argue that although all things are possible, only things *compossible* with the world willed by God have a *necessary* existence. Things are *incompossible* (and have merely a *contingent* existence) if they do not harmonise with that world. Gilles Deleuze has shown how Proust's work actually affirms rather than rejects that which is incompossible (with a given world). See Gilles Deleuze, *Proust et les signes* (1964) expanded edition (Paris: Presses Universitaires de France, 1986), p.154.

17. Marcel Proust, *Remembrance of Things Past*, 3 Vols., trans. C.K. Scott Moncrieff and Terence Killmartin (Harmondsworth: Penguin, 1983) Vol II, p.137.

18. ibid., Samuel Beckett's verdict is as follows: 'he is not there because she does not know that he is there. He is present at his own absence' (Samuel Beckett, *Proust and Three Dialogues* (London: Calder, 1987), p.27). I take the term 'passing state' from Leibnitz. In works such as *The Monadology* Leibnitz sets out his philosophical system whereby 'monads' (for the purposes of argument let us think of them here as equivalent to 'subjects') retain a core of identity throughout and during the *états passagers* to which they are host over time. Passing states, moreover, have already been programmed by a Divine artificer; thus alteration, strictly speaking, is an illusion, the incursion upon the monad of alterity likewise. This conception of change, alteration and alterity is to be contrasted with what I here call passage, which would be a kind of radical expenditure, a becoming and alteration beyond recuperation and recompense. A passing which passes. For an account of passage to which this article is indebted, see Jean-François Lyotard, *The Inhuman: Reflections on Time*, trans. Geoffrey Bennington and Rachel Bowlby (Oxford: Polity Press, 1993), pp.47-48. The role of passing states in the constitution of the monad is explained in *The Monadology*, section 14, in *Gottfried Wilhelm Leibnitz - Philosophical Writings*, ed. G.H.R. Parkinson (London: Everyman, 1979).

19. Proust, op.cit. Vol. 1, p.38.

20. Philippe Lacoue-Labarthe has provided, for my purposes, a very useful concept of intimacy. In *Poetry as Experience* intimacy is the presence of the other in oneself and thus, an interruption. See *Poetry as Experience*, trans. Andrea Tarnowski (Stanford, Cal.: Stanford University Press, 1999), pp.61-64.

21. Derrida, op.cit. (1987) p.271.

22. Here I draw on findings presented elsewhere in an article entitled 'Disconcerting the Fugue: Dissonance in the 'Sirens' episode of Joyce's *Ulysses*', in *Angelaki: Journal of the Theoretical Humanities* 3.2, 1998.

23. James Joyce, *Ulysses* (Harmondsworth: Penguin, 1969), pp.279-80.

24. ibid., p.260.

25. ibid., p.276.

26. ibid., p.278.

27. 'Complicated' in the sense of the Neoplatonic philosophical concept *complicatio* or co-implicated, by means of which two elements in a relation are folded one into the other.

28. Joyce, op.cit. p.279.

29. Obviously it is from Derrida that I adapt the idea of the answering machine in my reading of *To the Lighthouse* above.

30. Derrida, op.cit. (1987) p.31.

31. See 'Envois' in general for Derrida's sinuous working-through of the complex traffic of Freud's own postal system. For a more precise formulation of the problematic, 'Freud's Legacy' and 'Paralysis' should be consulted. The latter best serves our purposes here when Derrida shows how the PR (reality principle/*poste restante*) is at the service of the PP (pleasure principle/postal principle) in the latter's pursuit of mastery of the pp (unbound primary processes). See especially Derrida, op.cit. (1987) pp.350-51.

32. 'Connect-I-Cut' is the phrase attributed to a patient, Little Joey, by Bruno Bettelheim in his study *The Empty Fortress*. The child turns himself into a kind of machine, locked into a hermetically sealed universe (which Bettelheim concludes is autistic). For Deleuze and Guattari the verdict of autism is incorrect. Of even less utility is an Oedipal interpretation – that Joey makes himself into a machine because of his mother's failure to provide for him in some fashion. All machines are hooked into other machines. Each machine cuts the *hyle*, the flow, but its cut, that which makes of it a machine, is also its connection. Hence *connect-I-cut*. What has happened in the case of Joey is that this machinic assemblage has turned around upon itself. The machine has stalled as it were. It is all connection and all detachment: a paranoid machine. See Deleuze and Guattari, *Anti-Oedipus*, trans. Helen R. Lane, Robert Hurley and Mark Seem (London: Athlone Press, 1984), p.37 ff.

33. George Oppen, *Collected Poems* (New York: New Directions, 1975), p.14. I am indebted to Eric White for pointing me in the direction of this poem and especially its parenthetical telephone.

34. I have in mind Derrida's assertion that the final Yes (yes being quintessentially telephonic) in Molly's monologue 'can only be vocalised as a grapheme and written as a phoneme', in Derrida, op.cit. (1992) p.267.

Typesetting by **Elefthæria Machæras**
ARTELIER, 3 Efthidimou St., 104 42, Athens, Greece
Tel./Fax: ++30 210 515 46 43

for **Philomel Productions Ltd**, Dublin, Republic of Ireland
UK contact address :   1 Queen's Gate Place Mews
London SW7 5BG, England, UK
Tel : ++44 (0) 20 7581 2303
Fax : ++44 (0) 20 7589 2264
e-mail: philomelbooks@hotmail.com

Book cover: Christos Georgiou
Artwork: Paul S. Vlachos
Book design: Sophia Kakkavas
Printed and bound in Greece

ISBN 1 898685 42 8
     2002

Woolf Nietzsche Wilde
                    Butor   André Gide   Marinetti   Woolf
E. M. Forster   Derek Walcott   Augustine
          Kavafy   Charles Baudelaire   Michael Afflaq
       Aragon   Edgar Allen Poe
Mc Almon   Malraux   Baroja
netti   Butor   Kafka   Woolf
                John Dewey   T. S. Eliot   Joyce
       Lorca   Nietzsche   Beckett
Hofner Benjamin   Kavafy   Proust
   Malraux   John Dos Passos   Woolf
William Carlos Williams   E. M. Forster   Koeppen   Thomas Mann
yce   Benjamin   Baroja   John Dos Passos   Kafka
  Ezra Pound   Michael Afflaq   Becke
                    Koeppen
cott   Butor
         Nietzsche   Robert Mc Almon   Marinetti   Aragon
tt   Proust
rinetti   Joh

Baroja

Joyce

Marinetti

T. S. Eliot

Proust

Kavafy

Ezra Pound

Edgar Allan Poe

Beckett

E. M. Forster

Charles Baudelaire

Robert Mc. Almon

Mann

Koeppen

William Carlos William

Proust

Woolf

Joyce

Baroja

Nietzshe

Derek Walcott

Marinetti

Gide

Charles Baudelaire

Koepp

Marinetti

John Dos Passos

Joyce

Michael Aflaq

Walcott

Nietzsche

Wilde

Edgar Allan Poe

Benjamin

Aragon

Koeppen

Proust

Kavafy

Marinetti

Augustine

Charles Baudelaire

Kafka

Augustine

John Dos Passos

Derek Walcott

Malraux

Beckett

Woolf

John Dewey

William Carlos William

Robert Mc. Almo

Kavafy

Butor

Lorca

André Gide

Mc. Almon

T. S. Eliot

Butor

Woolf

Kafka

Thomas Mann

Derek Walcott

Joyce

Augustine

inetti

Woolf Nietzsche Wilde
                    Butor
          Derek Walcott   André Gide   Marinetti   Woolf
E. M. Forster   Kavafy   Augustine
                Charles Baudelaire   Michael Aflaq   Jo
        Aragon   Edgar Allen Poe   Malraux
Mc-Almon   Baroja
netti   Butor   Kafka   Woolf   Joyce
            John Dewey   J. S. Eliot
        Lorca   Nietzsche   Beckett
Kafka Benjamin   Kavafy   Woolf   Proust
    Malraux   John Dos Passos   Proust   E
William Carlos William   E. M. Forster   Koeppen   Thomas Mann
yce Benjamin   Baroja   John Dos Passos   Kafka
    Ezra Pound   Michael Aflaq   Becke
cott   Koeppen   Butor
          Nietzsche Robert Mc Almon   Marinetti   Aragon
tt   J
            Proust
arinetti   Joh